Modern Anti-Realism and Manufactured Truth

International Library of Philosophy

Editor: Ted Honderich
Professor of Philosophy, University College London

Modern Anti-Realism and Manufactured Truth

Gerald Vision

R
ROUTLEDGE
London and New York

First published in 1988 by
Routledge
11 New Fetter Lane, London EC4P 4EE

Published in the USA by
Routledge
in association with Routledge, Chapman and Hall, Inc.
29 West 35th Street, New York NY 10001

Phototypeset in Linotron Times by
Input Typesetting Ltd, London
Printed in Great Britain by
T. J. Press (Padstow) Ltd, Padstow, Cornwall

British Library Cataloguing in Publication Data
Vision, Gerald
Modern anti-realism and manufactured
truth. (International library of
philosophy).
1. Philosophy. Realism
I. Title   II. Series
149'.2

Library of Congress Cataloguing in Publication Data
Vision, Gerald.
Modern anti-realism and manufactured truth/Gerald Vision.
p.   cm.—(International library of philosophy)
Bibliography: p.
Includes index
1. Realism.   2. Truth.   3. Values.   I. Title.   II. Series.
B835.V57   1988
149'.2—dc19   88–9701

ISBN 0–415–00097–1

For Pamela and Todd,
acute critics of my philosophy and my life

CONTENTS

Contents

Part II

Contents

PREFACE

We are witnesses to an age in which the comfortable assumption that reality is 'out there' to be discovered is being, or has been, replaced in philosophy by the adage that all conceptions of reality are saturated with our mental projections, if not wholly products of cognition. According to the new creed, our notions of reality are the upshots of conceptual contributions, indigenous purposes, 'ways of worldmaking', social and economic milieux, semantic practices, the assumptions of prevalent scientific theories, or even our fertile imaginations. Truth is not, so the story continues, a reflection of 'the mirror of nature'; we do not gain it by matching our thoughts or words to a preformed world, but we manufacture the constituters of truth in the process of cognition. What began as a murmur of discontent with Berkeley and Kant in the eighteenth century is now not only an orthodox chorus, but is regarded in some quarters as the merest truism. This is not without historical excuse. The metaphysical dustbin is crammed full of theories about reality and our relation to it, in which cognition plays a modest role. Even theories which preserve the errors of the past as necessary steps towards a (then) current final truth have run their course. It is no wonder that thinkers reflecting upon the obsolete theories of their forebears, and mindful of our continuing fallibility, are reluctant to offer more of the same. The very possibility of successfully delineating our relation to a mind-independent reality is now widely doubted. A strong anti-realist tendency has flourished in this intellectual climate – not only among

Anglo–American and Continental philosophers, but also among writers in various related disciplines.

In the following pages I espouse a view very much out of sympathy with this strain of contemporary anti-realism (occasionally called 'neo-anti-realism'.) There is nothing remarkable in that, ritual slayings of one's philosophical ancestors having become tediously commonplace. But in spite of my dissent from some of their most important conclusions, I would like put in a good word for certain individual proponents of the view. The (occasionally corporate) anti-realists treated in the final three chapters have views composed of many elements, some of which mark significant insights. In particular, they have located genuine problems for the varieties of realism which they criticise. My complaint against them is that they go too far by repudiating the very world which those realist views sought to capture. Consequently, while I counter-attack, say, the fideist views in Chapter 8 and the incommensurability thesis in Chapter 9, I have no desire to revive the atomistic picture theory or the positivist philosophy of science which they, respectively, attack. The task is rather to disentangle realism's legitimate claims from the trappings it has acquired in more ambitious metaphysical schemes.

No attempt is made in these pages to demonstrate the existence of a mind-independent world. That would seem to require a full-dress inquiry into the proper objects of knowledge and perception, or into the inferences we are entitled to draw from such objects. Though we shall be evaluating a number of proposals which incorporate epistemic concepts and assumptions, we shall not be engaged in this more basic sort of epistemological enterprise. Instead it is argued that our conception of truth, together with the kinds of truths we generally believe in, implies such a world; and that, the sceptic aside, anti-realism hasn't made out a satisfactory case against either the conception or the belief. Put otherwise, I shall collect what I take to be the valid reasons for believing that our everyday truths earn that status by disclosing things about a world which is at least in some respects non-mental and cognition-independent. I maintain that this view is not merely a vestige of a superannuated metaphysics, but something for which we still have compelling reasons. To see this we must not only explore the view without its usual adornments but, as mentioned above, we must extricate its core from other concerns with which the tradition has burdened it.

My impression is that what philosophers commonly call metaphysical anti-realism is now a widely accepted paradigm. In some areas which intersect very haphazardly with the concerns of professional philosophers – say literary, anthropological and sociological theory – the notion that reality is constructed by cognizers is by now an uncontroversial supposition; an article of group initiation or a prerequisite for getting a serious hearing. Such anti-realism has succeeded in becoming identified with up-to-date and progressive thinking, while realism has been relegated to the stodgy, cobwebbed tradition of less enlightened times. Indeed, like the term 'bourgeoisie', 'realism' is in some circles an expression of mild opprobrium, suggesting – as does 'bourgeoisie' – an identification with the wrong set of values. One manifestation of this sort of anti-realism is relativism about truth and conceptual schemes. In certain disciplines such relativism has become virtually synonymous with tolerance.

While my central topic concerns only the forms of anti-realism which have sprouted in analytic philosophy, I had also wanted to address more directly this grander culture of anti-realism. For while the latter may be diffuse and elusive, its present impact is unquestionably tremendous. However, as my writing progressed, it became evident that it would make the present work unmanageable, both in bulk and readability, to integrate a discussion of those larger themes into the main narrative. Among other things, some of the anti-realisms alluded to here are motivated by specialist methodologies and distinctive lores. To handle them would have required broad surveys of their literatures and the principles upon which they operate. If I might be allowed a sweeping and dogmatic assessment of their specialist reasons for anti-realism, I'd venture that they rest on a combination of doubtful interpretations of concrete cases and fallacious inferences. But this is certainly no substitute for a careful examination of the anti-realist evidence. However, although we haven't directly identified the larger anti-realist culture in the body of this study, our work has a vital bearing on its claims. No form of anti-realism can be plausible without philosophical support. Our defence of a realist conception of truth is designed not only to undermine all support of that kind, but more specifically to preclude any view requiring truth to be essentially invented by cultural or cognitive means.

Metaphysical anti-realism is also ascendant in professional philosophy. This is not because anti-realists outnumber realists among professional philosophers, but because anti-realists have been more successful in getting across their message to the relevant audience. Movements gain the day not primarily by converting their greybeard opponents, but by capturing the imagination of the next generation: in this case the younger philosophers and students. Anti-realism has succeeded in this for reasons which are not difficult to fathom. While scores of philosophers, perhaps even a majority of those interested in the question, may operate upon realist assumptions, anti-realists (at least in the English-speaking tradition with which I am most familiar) have been more energetic in producing a number of striking and widely discussed manifestos having anti-realism as a central theme. Few realist works since the Second World War can challenge for impact the highlighted (apparently) anti-realist lessons in works by the likes of Wittgenstein, Kuhn, Dummett, Putnam, Goodman and Rorty. Their success consists not only, or even mainly, in the fact that they have enlisted a number of converts to their views; but more importantly in the fact that they have managed to define the issues in their own terms. Part of the argument below is that this has moved some realists both to accept disadvantageous ground-rules and to state their own views badly. Moreover, while influential recent thinkers such as Quine and Davidson are extremely dubious allies of anti-realism, their work has been exploited first and most successfully by that camp. Exceptions to my generalization may come readily to mind. Two which occur to me are Bernard Williams and John Mackie, each of whom has written impressively in defence of realism. But as a broad overview, my remarks stand. Nothing of substance depends on the accuracy of this summary, but I offer it, for what it may be worth, as my impression of the current state of the issue in Anglo–American philosophy.

Many issues divide realists and anti-realists, and we shall be ignoring all but one aspect of their differences: namely, their respective views of truth. A pivotal area, neglected by us, is the dispute over the character of values and moral judgments. Realists hold that such judgments are 'objective' or state that such objective states occur. Nothing said in what follows requires the adoption of a realist view here or in a number of similarly crucial areas. Nevertheless, our inquiries have a kind of general relevance which bears on all such issues. For example, the issue about objectivity may be made to turn on whether moral judgments admit truth-values. Certain anti-realists, maintaining that 'p is true' says no more than plain 'p', might allow that moral judgments have truth-values compatibly with their lacking objectivity. Our concern with that view of truth can scarcely avoid having some implication for this dispute.

I am grateful to a number of people for advice and support with this project. David Welker, in particular, read the whole in various stages of draft and made a number of helpful comments. I have also sought, and received, the sage advice of Hughes Leblanc, Jitendra Mohanty, Richard Shusterman and William Wisdom on various parts of the manuscript. Students at Temple University and the University of East Anglia have heard these views in various stages of development, and have contributed to their refinement in more ways than I can now recall in adequate detail. Nadia Kravschenko not only did yeoman work in typing the manuscript but bore with unfailing good cheer my frequent requests for changes and retypings. No one suffered more from my preoccupation than Sue Vision. I am greatly in her debt for subordinating so many of her own plans to my obsession.

ABBREVIATIONS

There will be frequent cross-references to the following items. This list should prove handy for reference.

I *Characterizations of what various theories of truth purport to supply*
  (1) The condition *constituting* a statement's truth (or, *making the statement true*)
  (2) What statements refer to
  (3) Our means of telling if a statement is true
  (4) The criteria of or standards for a statement's being true
  (5) The circumstances (linguistic, conversational, epistemic) in which 'true' may be used
  (6) The purpose (point) of saying that a statement is true
  (7) The meaning of the phrase 'is true' or 'it is true that'
  (8) The definition of 'is true' or of truth
  (9) Necessary and sufficient conditions for a statement's truth
  (10) The explanation of a statement's truth

II *Correlative questions to which the characterization (1)–(10) would be answers*
  (1') What are the conditions *by virtue of which* a statement is true?
  (2') To what do statements refer?
  (3') What are the means by which we can tell if a statement is true?
  (4') What are the criteria of (standards for) a statement's being true?

(5') In what circumstances (linguistic, conversational, epistemic) may 'true' be predicated of a statement?

(6') What is the purpose (point) of saying that a statement is true?

(7') What is the meaning of the phrases 'is true' and 'it is true that'?

(8') What is the definition of 'is true' or of truth?

(9') What are the necessary and sufficient conditions for a statement's truth?

(10') What explains a statement's truth?

These items, and the occasional distinctions between them, are explained more fully in Chapter 2.

PART I

I

INTRODUCTION – THE TOPIC EXPLAINED

1 GENERAL DIFFERENCES

From its inception to the present, philosophy may be viewed as a series of struggles between various realisms and anti-realisms. Like any historical thread, this approach involves a measure of distortion, a fitting of a tangled course of events on to a well-defined pattern. But it is at least as promising as the many other general themes which have been imposed upon and which have illuminated the subject, and herein lies a clue as to just how central the distinctions between realism and anti-realism have been. On virtually all the major issues dividing philosophers there has been at least one realist and one anti-realist antagonist. But what might these various similarly labelled views have in common? To begin with, of the pair 'realism'–'anti-realism', the latter term is the less instructive, serving merely to cover a loose collection of opposition views. For a variety of disputes it has embraced quite a motley, sometimes even incompatible, aggregate of more specific doctrines such as idealism, emotivism, materialism, behaviourism, phenomenalism, constructivism, operationalism, verificationism, instrumentalism, nominalism and pragmatism. Thus, to understand the opposition, we seem better advised to begin with an attempt at comprehending realism. But, here also realist alternatives are often tenuously related at best; precise but unobjectionable description has been notoriously elusive. However, counsels of despair are unhelpful, and realism still seems the best place to start. Thus, let us begin by trying to convey the general

3

idea, while revising and qualifying until we eventually gain an understanding fit to withstand critical scrutiny.

2 A TYPOLOGY OF REALISMS

Intuitively we may wish to distinguish things from truths. Realism can be a view about things *or* truths. Beginning with things, or a narrower class of them, realism is the view that

(a) things (of type X) exist,
(b) their existence is independent of our ability to cognize them.

(b) tells us that the existence of precisely those things does not rely upon peculiarities of our cognizing equipment. Next, the realist about truths holds that beliefs or claims (perhaps of a certain restricted type) accurately reflect and are made true by non-subjective states of the world.

Some readers may have already detected glaring flaws in this first stab. Realism about minds or mental states – say, dualism – surely is about a cognition-dependent class of things. Here it is the anti-realist who denies that the class is mental. Moreover, differences between, say, realists and nominalists about abstract entities need have little to do with what the cognizer projects onto the world. But let us proceed with this flawed characterization for a while. It is still useful in bringing us to appreciate the nature of some of the disputes.

Against this claim the anti-realist may offer a number of rejoinders, ranging from the contention that our grasp of a situation is projected onto the world through our distinctively human style of mentation, to the claim that our modes of cognition, although not entirely projections, are sufficiently infected by own mental contributions to change its objects essentially. Or, an anti-realist might claim that the realist's subject-matter is spurious; there is not even enough in it to be explained away. Perhaps what the realist supposes to exist is in reality entirely delusive, or, less harshly, is ultimately identical with, and thus reducible to, a very different sort of thing. It is no doubt usual for anti-realists to epistemologize or make cognitively dependent a sort of thing that realists had believed (b) to be true of. Realism about minds and their states is, as we have seen, an exception to this. In the case of the mental, the anti-realist, taking advantage of this last kind of rejoinder (reductive analysis), may argue that the mental dissipates into neurological processes or complexes of behaviour and dispositions to them, both of which are publicly observable physical transactions. Indeed, certain realists have pounced upon a possible anti-realist combination of demanding epistemologized subject-matter in one area and non-mental subject-matter in others to argue against the aims of a broadened anti-realism.[1] But setting aside the merits of the view, the point to be emphasized is that in the various areas in which realism is disputed, although epistemologizing the subject-matter is a typical anti-realist tactic, it is not necessary in many cases and not possible in some.

Realism (/anti-realism) may also come in two types: *local* and *global*. These do not bear an exact part–whole relationship. Global realism is realism about a particular subject, truth. Local realism may be realism about any other subject: put in each of our idioms, it may be realism about particular kinds of things or about certain kinds of *truths*. But it is not about truth as such. This may be confusing. Perhaps it seems clearer just to take a sort of realism about a collection of local realisms, or certain especially central local realisms, and call that global realism. (As we shall see later, these are among the things that have been called *metaphysical* realism.) But part of our task is to untangle some serious confusions in previous assaults upon these issues; and to do that we need precisely the set of contrasts just introduced.

Local realisms (/anti-realisms) cover an extraordinarily broad spectrum of topics, including the physical world, scientific laws and theories (theoretical constructs), moral or evaluative judgments and properties, abstract entities (including numbers and geometrical figures), modalities, the mental, secondary qualities, dreams, counterfactuals, the past and the future. Despite the fact that commitments to the cognitively independent existence of any of these sorts of things may be indeed broad, each is entitled 'local' here. As stated above, global realism is not just a commitment to the non-cognitive existence of all or a certain number of these sorts of entities, but concerns the nature of truth. It is not even a view, save indirectly, about classes of truths (namely, the extension of truth). Phrased in the truth idiom, local realisms are doctrines about certain classes of truths or fragments of language.

Although local and global realism are not straightforwardly related as part to whole, local commitments are often taken to bear on global ones. For example, a long series of local commitments, or even a single commitment in a vital area, may be taken to support global anti-realism. (We shall say more about this presently.) Nevertheless, one can combine global realism with various forms of local anti-realism.

We have yet to say just what global realism (/anti-realism) is. We should remedy that omission quickly because the chief aim of this work is to defend global realism: both directly and through an examination of the prospects of various forms of anti-realisms that reject it. We shall also have occasion to mention local realisms (/anti-realisms). But they are not the main topic of this work. Thus, let us say more about global realism and its contrasts.

3 GLOBAL REALISM AND OTHER OPTIONS

Roughly, global realism claims that the truth of a statement or belief is constituted by its relation to a situation in the not-essentially mind-dependent world. It is crucial to this view that though the situation making a statement or belief true *may be* cognition-dependent – as when, say, the statement is about someone's ideas – this does not flow from the theory. It can be cognition-dependent only because of the particular subject-matter, never because of the nature of the truth-relation itself. As with other forms of realism, we can formulate the view either as about a *thing*, truth, or as about truths about that fragment of language whose topic is truth itself.

What is the relation between global and local realism? As we have said, one can be a global realist about truth in general, and still maintain a local anti-realism about, say, the alleged truths of ethics or mathematics. The key to the relation between global and local realism lies in global anti-realism. For it is difficult for a global anti-realist, who holds that truth does not consist in a relation between statements (/beliefs) and non-epistemic reality, to be a realist on many local issues. If truths about, say, the physical world are about what exists mind-dependently, how can the physical world itself exist mind-independently? What global realism does is to remove this particular barrier to local realisms of any sort. Thus, it is a preliminary to most sorts of local realism one may wish to hold.

The global anti-realist may hold that the truth constituter, whatever it may be, cannot be something mind-independent. Or, as we shall see shortly, he may hold that there is nothing, mind-dependent or otherwise, that makes statemental utterances true. They may be called true for some other reason, or for no reason at all.

Although local realism (/anti-realism) is only an incidental topic for us, it does come up from time to time. When it does, how should it be discussed: in terms of things or truths? There is an appealing simplicity in framing these differences as about things. The realist believes that universals, or physical objects, or minds, or superstrings exist, while the anti-realist rejects these beliefs or qualifies them in certain ways. Although these formulations may not be final, this straightforward way of posing the differences has considerable appeal. However, nowadays the issue is nearly always framed in terms of truths for a fragment of language. Instead of asking, say, whether leptons exist, philosophers have queried whether statements about leptons have a truth-value (are true or false); and if so whether they can only be true in virtue of being shorthand for statements of another sort, or whether their truth-values attach without aid of paraphrase. It is this terminology of truths that I shall adopt in subsequent discussion. We shall consider local realism and anti-realism as adopting conflicting views about the presence of truth values in a certain fragment of language. For example, the moral realist holds that moral judgments make objective claims, or claims that can be judged straightforwardly true or false. She need not hold that *all* moral judgments have truth-values; but must hold that many do. Note also that relevant language fragments occasionally overlap. A moral judgment may be claimed to be a necessary truth, thereby engaging both the issue of the objectivity (truth) of moral judgments and that of the truth status of modal statements.

Can every local dispute over types of things be rephrased as one about types of truths? I have not encountered the sort of snare that would lead to a suspicion that the questions were in principle of a different order. But even if there were a basis for the suspicion, there are strong inducements to adopt the truth idiom. The most important is that it allows us to make a direct contact with the global issues. Global realism and anti-realism, phrased in either idiom, are about the nature of truth itself. As we just noted, if the issue is decided in favour of the anti-realist's epistemologized conception of truth, it is difficult to see how local realism about anything other than minds could survive. And this would be because *truths about those things* involved our own conceptual contributions. Another reason favouring the truth idiom even for local doctrines is that it makes clearer sense of a stock reductionist manoeuvre. Reduction plays a leading role in these disputes. The reductionist may maintain that *things* of type A are really just things of type B: desks are just collections of molecules or sense-data, thoughts are just collections of behavioural dispositions, meanings are just complex intentions. Such claims appear to make sense, but in this form they are difficult to evaluate. It may seem an improvement to reformulate them as claims about sentences of type A', mentioning As, being paraphrasable or translatable by sentences of type B', mentioning only Bs instead of As. This is not problem-free. Debate has raged over the standards for adequate paraphrase or translation, or whether standards are even possible. Nevertheless, the change has struck many as an advance in clarification, both for showing us what the first sort of reduction might amount to and where the issues over it lie.

Against this it may be urged that the reduction could allow the realist to hold that because A' sentences abbreviate B' sentences, the former have truth-values after all: namely, the same truth-values their corresponding B' sentences take. Since reduction for sentences does not decisively settle the question whether the source vocabulary admits truth-values, the truth idiom does not capture the division between realism and anti-realism we had wanted. For that reason Michael Devitt has maintained that it is better to phrase physical realism simply as the view that 'common sense physical entities exist independently of the mental'.[2]

There is a valuable point in this line of reasoning. We cannot resolve local realist/anti-realist antagonisms just by having a paraphrase in hand. We must know more about the character of the paraphrase. This is a point to which we shall return shortly. Meanwhile, we may note that this is not so much an objection to the truth idiom as it is to the particular deployment of reductive analysis. Nevertheless, it is certainly not grounds for preferring the thing idiom, since perfectly analogous difficulties arise there. Although I have given reasons for favouring reductions framed in a truth idiom, those in terms of things are certainly sensible, and have an historical prominence. Perhaps the most notorious example of a reductive analysis is John Stuart Mill's phenomenalist slogan, 'Matter . . . may be defined as a Permanent Possibility of Sensation',[3] in which one kind of *thing* is analysed in terms of another. If this allows us to continue saying that matter exists, it supplies a perfectly analogous objection to using the thing idiom to the one just noted against the truth idiom. If we believe that the objection is avoidable here because, as Devitt's formulation discloses, what we want is not the mere existence of matter, but its existence 'independently of the mental', the same option must be extended to the truth idiom. Matter exists if statements about it are *non-epistemically* true *and* true independently of truths about what is mental. This is more complicated than Devitt's formulation, but it is also more pertinent. For even if we could divide entities into mental and non-mental, and matter as a class fell into the latter category, physical realism might be in peril if it also could be shown that truths about matter were all cognitively dependent. This sweeping sort of anti-realism could nullify the customary ends of those who support physical realism (cf. Kantian transcendental idealism).

But epistemologized truth is not the only threat to realism about truths. Consider again a case of local anti-realism for a language-fragment F. An anti-realist may maintain that the statemental utterances of F do not state objective states of affairs or facts, but he may allow that such utterances could be said to have truth-values on the grounds that saying '*p* is true' for this fragment adds nothing to saying '*p*'. I shall call this a *deflationary* view of truth. Its most celebrated embodiment, though not a local application, is the Assertive Redundancy or Logical Superfluidity Thesis, to be examined more thoroughly in Chapters 2 and 4. Later in this chapter I shall explain why we should take an across-the-board deflationary view to be a variety of global *anti*-realism. But for now we need only notice that it is compatible with a denial that the utterances of F objectively state anything. Thus, it can be used in conjunction with anti-realism about F. This means that ascribing non-epistemic truth-values to F is no guarantor of realism about F. In accepting the deflationary view for statemental

9

utterances in F, the anti-realist has cleverly devised a way to concede the realist her truth claim and sever it from its realist consequences. This further bedevils efforts to get a precise characterization of the relevant differences.

Returning to reductive analyses, we see that similar complications stop us from unproblematically identifying instances of local realism. Paraphrase or translation appeals to anti-realists because it affords a means for showing that an apparent ontological commitment of a kind the anti-realist finds troublesome is dispensable. However, paraphrase and so on is not reserved exclusively for anti-realists. For example, realists in moral philosophy are known as cognitivists; and one branch of this group has sought to show *that moral judgments make objective, truth-valued claims about the world*, some of which are true, *by* showing that their distinctively moral predicates, such as 'right' and 'good', are identical with, and thus analysable in terms of, non-moral predicates such as 'promotes the general interest' or 'is commanded by God'. Even professed moral sceptics who maintain, say, that 'right' means no more than (/is analysable in terms of) 'is liked by —————', where the blank is filled by the name of the judger, may end up as moral realists in spite of themselves. Anti-realists, non-cognitivists in this quarter, hold that moral utterances do not, even in purport, make objective claims. They offer a variety of different alternative accounts of the function of moral utterances; and among their proposals are also some reductive analyses. But, in this case the analyses are, say, in terms of replacing the original indicative utterances with at least partly optative or imperative ones.

None of this should be construed as presupposing the acceptability of traditional reductive analysis. This is merely an historical observation. Whatever its virtues or vices, such analysis has found favour, and it has not always been in the service of anti-realism. How then do we tell whether a putative analysis is anti-realist or a defence of realism? One clue is how radically divergent the translation is. If it stays close to the original, it may be merely intended to clarify it or make it more precise. But ultimately there are no reliable methods for deciding the issue just by viewing the products of analysis. These are not realist or anti-realist analyses as such, but only realist or anti-realist uses to which analyses are put. The larger argument in which they are embedded determines how analyses are regarded, and thus whether they are taken by their proposer, or should be taken by us, as disposing of a problematic fragment of language or as clarifying (the logical form of) a perfectly good one.

4 THE CORRESPONDENCE THEORY OF TRUTH

As we have already stated, our main concern is global realism and anti-realism. We say of some utterances that they are true, of others that they are false. What accounts for this difference? (I have intentionally left it vague, for reasons that emerge in the next chapter, whether we are asking about the difference between truth and falsity or between our calling things true and false.) The realist holds that something about the state of the world, independently of our view of it or the concepts with which we grasp it, accounts for the difference. Of course, as we saw, exceptions are made for truths that concern subject-matters which may be in some way mind-dependent. But the element of cognition that enters the account of truth in those cases is not introduced through the nature of truth itself.

This sounds very much like what is usually called the Correspondence Theory of Truth (hereafter 'Correspondence' for the theory, 'correspondence' for the relation). In fact, a minimal description of Correspondence says very little more, if anything at all, than does global realism. I shall use these terms interchangeably throughout this work; for Correspondence – the view that truth-bearers are true by virtue of their relation to a situation in a mind-independent world, save for truths about minds, their states and properties – is virtually the only option for fleshing out the global realist doctrine. If they differ significantly it is in their contrastive sets. Correspondence, whatever else it may be, is a theory of truth. And it contrasts primarily with other traditional theories of truth, such as Coherence and Pragmatism, and with various deflationary theories about truth, such as Redundancy. Global realism contrasts not with other theories of truth – at least, not directly – but with various views that impose adequacy conditions on truth for any theory of it to satisfy, and which rule out Correspondence by virtue of the conditions imposed. In Part I, where we consider primarily alternatives of the first sort, we

11

shall speak mainly of Correspondence. In Part II we shall be dealing above all with attempts to show that truth is epistemologized or cognition-dependent. There we shall speak mainly of global realism. (It should be noted that once global anti-realism has completed its task to its satisfaction, it need not go on to espouse any full-fledged 'theory of truth'. Indeed, nowadays few global anti-realists do so.)

Against global realism the anti-realist may make any of several replies. He might hold that something indelibly linguistic or mental makes our utterances true, such as harmony between sets of potential truth-bearers (Coherence), or the ability of our true beliefs to lead to further satisfactory experiences (Pragmatism). Alternatively, he might hold that our conception of truth for utterances is a construction out of our conception of their assertibility-conditions. From this it is concluded that truth cannot be a matter of a relation to a world that, in principle, has nothing to do with our conceiving it. Forms of what I shall call 'veramental relativism' are also anti-realist in this sense; they maintain that what is true and false is relative to a certain conceptual or social framework, and thus has nothing to do with a supposed world that might exist independently of our conceiving it. Each of these anti-realisms epistemologizes truth. Each issues in advance a guarantee that we shall have epistemic access to particular truths by making truth's conception rely on something within the ambit of our experience or, if we think of groupings as peculiarities of cognizers, the set of concepts under which we view things.

Yet another anti-realist response would be to say that *nothing* makes an utterance true or false. No one is likely to put it so bluntly. But the deflationary view to which we alluded earlier, Assertive Redundancy, seems to affirm this disguisedly in its account of *what it is to say* that something is true. It claims that to say that *p* is true is to say nothing more than that *p*, and thus 'is true' says nothing further about '*p*'. There are a number of subtle variations on the formulaic 'to say . . . is just to say . . .'. For example, Michael Williams writes: 'If we like . . . we can say that our success is explained by the truth of Einstein's theory. But we might just as well say that it is explained by Einstein's theory. Nothing has been done to show that the first explanation is more than a stylistic variant of the second.'[4] Of course, views about what it is to say that something is true may appear very different from views about what it is for something to be true. But it is vital to deflationary theories to hold or assume that the only permissible content for the latter sort of view is what can be culled from the former. There is no independent inquiry into the nature of truth other than one into what it is to say that something is true.

Some, including Williams, protest that Redundancy is not a variety of anti-realism, but a minimal form of realism. The key to their contention is that deflationary views do not epistemologize truth. But this is at best inconclusive. Ultimately the issue is terminological; the positions can be meted out as one wishes. But there are reasons for ranking deflationists (= Redundancy theorists) among the anti-realists. For one thing, if global realism is Correspondence, and it is precisely Correspondence that they seek to deflate, Redundancy is certainly not a form of global realism. For another, it is not true in general that anti-realisms require the cognition-dependence of their subject-matters, as nominalism and behaviourism make clear. This undermines the reason given above by deflationists for their realism. But, most importantly, card-carrying global anti-realists not infrequently appropriate deflationary views of truth as a starting-point for their arguments against global realism.[5] Redundancy could not be a premise in an argument for anti-realism if it incorporated realism. Either anti-realists proceeding in this way are flagrantly inconsistent or (what seems more likely) Redundancy is not a form of realism.

Perhaps deflationists who concede these points will none the less insist upon a trichotomy: realism, anti-realism, or neither. This would avoid the misleading association of those who stop at a deflationary theory with those who proceed to epistemologize truth. This may seem more judicious, since I have admitted that this is a terminological issue, and dichotomies do have a tendency to lump together disparate items. Nevertheless, I still prefer my earlier classification because it is useful to place on one side everyone who would deny a realistic account of what makes a statement true. I propose to defend Correspondence against all such views. Not that my division lacks additional justification. For example, it more accurately tracks the way the issue has developed historically. It seems to have been the original intention of deflationists to reject any account of the sort we have described rather than to supplant it with a better one. Their usual commentary on their accomplishment is that the realist's problem has been shown to be bogus. Moreover, they do this by way of a sort of argument closely fitting the pattern of reductive analysis identified earlier as a prime tactic of local anti-realism. For all these reasons, we shall take Redundancy as a form of global anti-realism.

5 TRUTH AND IDEAL THEORIES

There have been other names for what we have been calling 'global realism', and other characterizations of the view that is supposed to take its place, roughly, in the debate with epistemologized truth concepts. 'Metaphysical realism' is perhaps the most popular of these titles. Although I shall use that term (sparingly) where it is appropriate, by and large I prefer to stick with 'global realism': not out of fondness for neologisms, but to avoid confusion. Occasionally, the view that there is a mind-independent physical world has been called 'metaphysical realism' or 'scientific realism'. Both titles have also been used for the view that our theories, at their best, accurately explain, predict or describe such a world. As such, these are local realisms, but their localities are often deemed central enough to supplant global realism (/ Correspondence) as the contrast to epistemologized truth. When this occurs, Correspondence may be pushed into the background or drop out of the picture altogether. Again, metaphysical or scientific realism has often conflated certain of these tenets (for example, Correspondence and mind-independent reality) with no clear indication of their precedence. It is best to withdraw from currency so battered a coin. Global realism, if not perfectly clear, at least has the advantage of not attracting some of the culpable association of the prior confusions.

However, when explicitly concerned with the nature of truth, there is a common characterization of metaphysical realism that some appear to believe should replace global realism as the focal position: namely, the view that

(C) Our best, ideal, theories might turn out false.[6]

This is the view, it has been claimed, that global anti-realism confronts directly. I shall maintain that (C) has fatal drawbacks in this connection; but before detailing them, let us dwell on a few reasons *for* taking (C) to represent the basic realist outlook.

The view (C) embodies a popular conception of realism as resting on an ontological argument for the existence, or at least the possibility, of a truth greater than which can be recognized – a truth that would be unrecognizable if it obtained. But this raises a further question about the modality: the 'able' in 'recognizable'. Must it be inconceivable that anything, save perhaps – but only *perhaps* – God could recognize it? Or, is it sufficient that the truth be unrecognizable by creatures having, as Dummett puts it, 'our position in space and time and our particular sensory equipment and intellectual capacities'?[7] (And these are only two extremes between which there are other readings.) Anti-realists seem to incline toward Dummett's interpretation. But however the possibility in question is regarded, this way of describing the issue may seem to make the difference between realism and anti-realism more concrete. Realists may be attracted to this characterization because, if there were a way of producing (by indirection) an unrecognizable truth, their view would be immediately vindicated. Of course, demonstrations are never as irresistible as this. Any specimen unrecognizable truth which the realist may believe he can indirectly produce will be subject to the same battery of anti-realist and realist debunking and rejoinders that have marked the controversy all along. No example will be indisputable. Moreover, producing such a case could establish realism only against forms of anti-realism with cognition-dependent truth. It would not settle anything between global realism and Redundancy. But it may appear to antagonists to pinpoint more accurately vital differences between realism and its primary opposition.

Despite this, at best (C) encapsulates one naturally expected consequence of global realism, and not its heart. The central question for us is, of any given truth, what makes it true. And this question applies as much to truths that are recognizable as to any others. To illustrate, suppose that an anti-realist maintained that all truths possessed the property of *being effectively decidable*. And, let us also suppose that each discoverable truth had both this property *and* whatever property Correspondence requires of it, call it G. But even granting further that being effectively decidable and having G are the only candidates for truth-constituters, there is still a question about any given statement as to which of these two properties *accounts for* its truth. That the difference, framed in this way, is difficult to decide, perhaps more difficult than the truth of (C), is no excuse for framing it inadequately, or for confusing it with another issue.

A critical shortcoming of (C) is that someone holding Corre-spondence *could* consistently reject it. If (C) were our canonical description of the relevant brand of realism, this would make the holder of Correspondence quite paradoxically a non-realist at the very least. But how could it happen? It would require that a Correspondence theorist reject the possibility of unrecognizable truths. This might work in the following way. The crucial point is not that the realist should accept the possibility of unrecognizable truths, but that she should not reject them *because of* something in her account of truth itself. For one sort of anti-realist the problem cases are putative truths which are called 'verification-transcendent'.[8] Let us suppose that these kinds of cases could be summarized in a short list. There may then be considerations to show that, contrary to initial appearances, each kind of case is not really unrecognizable or that its statements fail, for reasons unrelated to the present issue, to have truth-values. If this exhausted the problem cases, or could be believed to exhaust them, the Correspondence theorist might hold that there could not be unrecognizable truths.

To this it may be replied that one could never know that the list of problem cases is complete. But this would be to confuse the fallibility, or even the falsity, of the claim with its intelligibility. Even if the position were false, the point is that it is a consistent one, and it shows how the acceptance of Correspondence need not commit one to accepting (C). Since Correspondence is more fundamental to global realism than (C), and (C) does not follow from Correspondence, the question of unrecognizable truths cannot be the basis of the difference between global realism and anti-realism.

We may note in passing that some critics of Correspondence and metaphysical realism (when used as we have been using the term 'global realism') have imagined that on those views the gap between utterances and reality must be unbridgeable. It has been claimed that realism is prevented from attributing to anyone a grasp of its notion of truth,[9] or that it puts the truth-constituting world out of reach.[10] More will be said about this in Chapter 2 (see especially the discussion of characterization (3)). For now we may simply remark that from the differences we have outlined these assessments sound more alarmist than judicious. Correspondence may not explain, or seek to explain, how we grasp any particular truths; but we cannot infer from this that it is inconsistent with any such explanations or that, just because the world which it claims constitutes our truths is not described *via* our cognition of it, it would be miraculous if we ever cognized the world.[11]

6 CORRESPONDENCE, IDEALISM AND EPISTEMIC CONCEPTS: EVIDENCE FOR THE VIEW

We are now better situated to appreciate the context in which questions about Correspondence naturally arise. I shall approach this topic taking the most extreme form for a Correspondence Theory – a form in which Correspondence does not require the truth of any, or at least very many, of the statements or beliefs we normally take to be true – and then seeing how this form of Correspondence interacts with a particular brand of anti-realism, idealism.

To begin with, Correspondence discloses what it is for a statement or belief to be true or false, but not whether it is true or, as critics are quick to note, how we are to decide on its truth-value. Thus, one can hold Correspondence without a commitment to any statements (/beliefs) not in the theory itself being true. If it is also held that a certain number or percentage of statements of type X must be true, that is not due to the requirements of the Correspondence Theory. As a result, Correspondence is compatible with some forms of idealism. Suppose we are suddenly convinced that the world which is the object of our beliefs and inquiries is cognition-dependent. This might alter our beliefs about the number and kinds of statements which are true while leaving Correspondence intact as a theory about what it is for statements to be true. For example, suppose that despite this second dose of mind-dependency, statements about minds or their contents that were formerly believed true remain so, while statements formerly believed true about what was taken for a mind-*in*dependent world are now deemed false. Perhaps this makes us vulnerable to a singular sort of scepticism in which we should no longer maintain most of what we had previously regarded as true. But this needn't effect Correspondence as an account of what it is to be true.

However, the above conjunction of affairs is highly unlikely. And in seeing why this is so we grasp more clearly the role of Correspondence in realist/anti-realist debates. Let us continue playing off Correspondence against idealism. In the more likely circumstance a commitment to Correspondence will be modified before the foregoing circumstances develop. This may be done in stages involving ever-increasingly radical mitigation of our views about truth: first by retaining Correspondence as compatible with idealism, but revising the interpretation of our truths; next by rejecting Correspondence in light of our acceptance of idealism; and finally by refuting Correspondence as a condition of accepting idealism. Let us look at each of these alternatives.

First, in the still unlikely event that an idealist found Correspondence compatible with his idealism and sought to preserve it, he will be more inclined to reinterpret allegedly true statements that had seemed to be about a mind-independent world than to declare them false for idealist reasons alone. Thus, if the statement that penguins waddle was taken as true under realism, it will remain so under the idealist's novel insight into the nature of things, but now as a statement about our new-found cognitively dependent penguins and waddling. This is the analogue in the sphere of truth to Mill's phenomenalism, cited earlier, and to Berkeley's proto-phenomenalism.[12]

But second, once idealism is instituted it is more likely yet that Correspondence will be abandoned. This need not occur because of any strict incompatibility between the views, but because once idealism is in place Correspondence may seem a less suitable account of truth than it would otherwise. If the world is mind-dependent, then wouldn't we want an account of truth more in accord with the way we actually divide up truths and falsehoods? What is the point of an account that makes truth mind-independent if the world about which we state truths is not so? Here we see one reason why the scepticism mentioned in connection with the extreme form of Correspondence is not usually bothersome in philosophical discussions: namely, because if the conditions for its occurrence obtain, Correspondence is not likely to be chosen as one's theory of truth.

However, finally and most importantly, the compatibility of idealism and Correspondence is unlikely to get as far as this. In establishing idealism or anti-realism, the advocate of the view will offer criticisms of realism, and when realism about truth or truths is in question it is precisely Correspondence that will come under attack. Put otherwise, the case against realism is likely to consist in the first place of reasons why truth cannot be constituted in a mind-independent way. Thus, the anti-realist's ability to overturn Correspondence is standardly a central part of his case against realism. Of course, not all realist/anti-realist debates are conducted in terms of truth or truths rather than in terms of things. But when truth is germane, Correspondence is among the important realist tenets that anti-realism rejects as part of its case for its own view.

This clarification of the respective debating positions has significance for our treatment of Correspondence. If the repudiation of Correspondence is a large part of the rejection of realism, then a defence of it is a rejection of a large part of what the anti-realist in general and the idealist in particular must prove. We shall be unable in the present work to moot all or even very many of the kinds of issues that divide realists and anti-realists. As I indicated earlier, these disputes cut a broad swath right through the middle of the history of philosophy, and in doing so they raise numerous side issues. Nevertheless, given the above, in defending Correspondence by distinguishing it from various misconceptions, answering objections to it and presenting a credible elaboration of it, we are treating a central part of the realist/anti-realist controversy.

Also, this puts into perspective another concern about Correspondence: namely, that it places the truth relation beyond our capacity to corroborate its obtaining. This is the problem mentioned in the last paragraph of section 4. One class of reasons for thinking that on Correspondence we could never confirm the actual truth of a statement would be those found in traditional epistemological scepticism. Other than further clarifying the relation of that form of scepticism to Correspondence (in Chapters 2 and 7) we shall not say much more about it, and certainly will provide little here to soften its impact. However, a doubt that does not rely on the sceptic's scruples seems to creep into discussions such as this; a doubt about whether we can be in contact with the sort of world envisaged in the Correspondence scheme. The most plausible grounds I can discover for believing we cannot are the anti-realist's typical views about the limitations on our cognitive capacities. However, if, as we have suggested here, the reasons for adopting Correspondence are to that extent reasons for rejecting idealism, or any other form of anti-realism that would impose such limits, the problem disappears. That the world or our view of it is not, in the anti-realist's intended sense, cognition-dependent does not automatically show that it is beyond our grasp. This would only be so if we had already acceded to some vital anti-realist assumptions. Of course, this also does not mean that we will be, or have the capacity to be, in contact with *every* truth-constituting situation. But there does not seem to be any principled barrier to grasping some of them that does not stem from certain distinctively anti-realist notions. Thus, forms of traditional scepticism aside, only if we accept views that are weakened by the plausibility of Correspondence need we worry about being able to have cognitive contact with many of the situations that Correspondence describes as making our beliefs true.

Is there any more definite sense in which Correspondence (/global realism) is related to epistemology? A typical anti-realist complaint is that since Correspondence rejects epistemologized truth, questions of justifiability and truth-constitution come apart. As Richard Rorty puts it, realism's notion of truth is 'something which needs have nothing to do with agreement'.[13] Even more overtly, Jonathan Dancy, although a realist *soi-disant*, claims that '[t]he theory of truth ought to fit the epistemology and not be allowed to ride independently of it'.[14] On these views, it appears that truth ought to be dependent on epistemological notions. The classical conception of truth does not wholly divorce epistemology and truth, but takes the dependencies to go in the opposite direction. On global realism, as classically conceived, truth is a regulator for testing standards of evidence or justifiability. A reliable standard increases or maintains a certain propensity toward truth. Alvin Goldman terms such criteria of justification 'truth-linked'.[15] The truth-link will of course be qualified by other considerations, such as the value of gaining truth over avoiding falsehood, and the needs for speedy answers and varying degrees of precision in different contexts. But the truth-link remains the most general regulating notion in these matters. (In Chapter 7 we shall examine in greater detail another of truth's roles in regulating evidence.) Moreover, truth may be of importance to epistemology because crucial epistemic notions such as *knowledge* require it for their characterizations. Thus, in a broad sense I would not claim that Correspondence makes truth irrelevant to the concerns of epistemology. Truth will still be of interest to epistemologists and will interact with our distinctively epistemic notions. The anti-realist protests that for Correspondence truth will not be delineated, say, in terms of (rational) agreement or justification. But, as we have seen, this is very different from divesting truth of epistemological associations.

Nevertheless, perhaps we have said enough about what Correspondence *isn't* to cause readers to wonder what methods could be appropriate for justifying the view. The strongest case for Correspondence now seems to be, as it has been for its many past defenders, its intuitive plausibility. A good part of the case for it thus rests on clearing up misconceptions and answering objections to it. But does its intuitive plausibility rest on anything? Perhaps we can base it on a thought experiment! In this respect it is helpful to compare the case for Correspondence with that for taking '*p*' or '*p* is true' as a necessary condition for the truth of 'S knows that *p*'. Whatever their official views about the place of intuitions in philosophy, those who accept this condition invariably do so because once we come *to believe* that *p* is false, we recognize that our grasp of the nature of knowledge prevents us from sincerely holding that S *knows* that *p*. Perhaps we will still say that S is certain that *p*, or even that she is justified in saying that she knows, and we may certainly say that she thinks that she knows that *p*. But we realize that continuing to say 'S *knows that p*' is a logically inappropriate way to describe S's cognitive state or relation to *p*. I have not claimed we are entitled to say that we *discovered* that *p* is false, and it is certainly no easier for S or anyone else to know that *p* is true than to know that *p*. One might even interject, consistently with this scenario, a form of philosophical scepticism that prohibits us from knowing or being justified in believing that *p* is false. But all this is beside the point; *p*'s *actual truth* (rather than its believed truth) becomes a condition for S knowing that *p* just by virtue of the fact that if it is no longer believed in, the original knowledge claim is no longer available.

The point is about the relation of our concepts, not about what has actually taken place with regard to p, and is thus shown by the inability to combine intelligibly 'S knows that p' and 'p is false', whether or not either is in fact the case.

The evidence for Correspondence is not dissimilar in kind. While convinced that the world is not as p states, I cannot sincerely affirm either that p or that p is true. I cannot both hold that p and reject that it is a fact that p (or, that the state of affairs that p obtains) and retain my grasp of the concept of truth. Scepticism may prevent me from knowing whether either is so, and various anti-realist views may seek to prevent me from escaping what Russell called 'the egocentric predicament'. But this in no way hinders what is disclosed simply by knowing something about the concept of truth we share. It is disclosed in various things we are committed to holding if our beliefs turn out one way rather than another.

What makes the case difficult to argue is that we are dealing with something that is so simple that it is hard to see how it could bear on our concerns. There are certain formularies which might be called laconic versions of Correspondence: such as, 'p is true only if it is a fact that p' or 'to say of what is that it is, is true'. Critics are not likely to reject such sayings in the most plain-speaking way (that is, by claiming that they are wrong, or patently false); rather, they are more prone to regard them as trivial, truistic or even empty. The charge is that they say less than the Correspondence theorist takes them to say. Thus, it is the charge of triviality or emptiness which confronts Correspondence, not that of intuitive implausibility. If we can show that such simple statements are neither trivial, empty nor, when properly under-stood, compatible with just any old view, we will have defended the intuition lying at the bottom of Correspondence.

A final warning. Now that we have eliminated the danger of conflating local and global realism and anti-realism, we can relax some of the sharp distinctions drawn earlier. A single local issue, such as the ascriptions of realistic truth-values to claims embodying scientific theories (scientific realism and anti-realism), may seem sufficiently important or paradigmatic to have the lessons drawn from it extended to truth generally. Scientific anti-realists have occasionally used their view as a springboard for global anti-realism.[16] But local anti-realism and global realism is a possible combination. For example, other philosophers have held fast to scientific anti-realism while allowing Correspondence to apply, say, to phenomenological laws or empirical claims.[17] They remain *global* realists. If we bear in mind the nature of our earlier distinctions, neither anti-realist tactic need result in confusion. The global issue can be approached through the study of a specialized language fragment. What we must look for are additional premises to make the connection.

7 PLAN OF SUBSEQUENT CHAPTERS

As recently intimated, Part I is devoted to a clarification and defence of Correspondence. Since it is the general idea of a Correspondence Theory that must be established, I shall hold off a detailed formulation of the view till chapter 5. This is done out of the belief that vagueness is easier to endure provisionally than are nagging doubts about one or another detail of the view formulated. That is, this approach is adopted to defer fraternal squabbles till we are assured that a view of this sort is worth pursuing. In Chapter 2 Correspondence is refined by distinguishing what is critical to it from other tenets with which philosophical debate has burdened it. Next, in Chapter 3, we shall look at some of the most common complaints against Correspondence, as well as a novel objection recently propounded by Hilary Putnam. The two most prominent alternative truth theories, Coherence and Pragmatism, are treated in Chapter 4. In the same chapter we also examine the Assertive Redundancy Thesis, which has been briefly introduced in this chapter and is mentioned again in Chapter 2. It occupies a special position in our considerations because of its dual role in criticisms of Correspondence: both as a straightforward objection to the view and as a premise in anti-realist arguments for epistemic notions of truth. Finally, in Chapter 5 we detail a version of Correspondence. It is a simplified successor to a version presented over 35 years ago by J. L. Austin, but one that seems to circumvent long-standing general concerns and to disarm the most devastating objections to Austin's view. It is offered as a plausible view, but not as the exclusively correct version.

Part II concerns, not standard theories of truth, as it were, but theories in which truth is epistemologized. The focus of our concern thereby shifts to global realism proper. Chapter 6 begins with an overview of certain generalized positions, including relativism about truth (veramental relativism) and related forms of qualifying doctrines. But most of Part II is devoted to the examination of three rather individualized attempts to epistemologize truth: those associated, in some cases perhaps inaccurately, with Michael Dummett, Ludwig Wittgenstein and Thomas Kuhn. I conclude that once Correspondence is better understood and the genuine insights of these views are clarified, global realism survives intact. The path to that conclusion is long and arduous, so with girded loins I proceed to take the first step.

II

THEORIES OF TRUTH: SOME PRELIMINARIES

1 THE STANDARD VIEW AND ITS STANDARD DOMAIN

For most disputed concepts in philosophy there are standard views, and for truth – whether framed in terms of a concept, the predicate 'is true', the sentential operator 'it is true that', or perhaps their respective contrasts-falsity, 'is false' and 'it is false that' – the standard view is Correspondence. Once again put crudely, it says at least that what is true is so by virtue of its correspondence with something in the not-essentially-mind-dependent world. The truth-constituter may be, for example, a fact, situation, state of affairs, ordered aggregate of individuals (or sequence of such), or a concrete chunk of spatio-temporal real estate; but at least *in general* this precludes such familiar alternatives as logical relationships between propositions (/statements/judgments/beliefs/sentences), states of satisfaction, verification procedures and approximations to theoretical ideals. Of course, some truths are *about* sentient beings or their sentient doings, and these will be in another way mind- or subject-dependent. But Correspondence maintains that this is because of the peculiarities of these topics, not because of the nature of truth. Correspondence's claim to being standard is twofold: first, it can be fleshed out from occasionally unsystematic and casual remarks in classical sources, and, second, there is the general impression that it is the commonsensical or plain man's implicit view.

In discourses such as this standard views are usually trotted out for flogging, albeit sometimes with a rueful sigh for their non-compensating attractions. But here I intend to elaborate Correspondence in ways designed to strengthen it. In this chapter I hope to show, by distinguishing Correspondence from certain things with which it may be confused, that some of the most up-to-date criticism is irrelevant and that Correspondence is responsible for many fewer controversial claims than is often supposed. In the next two chapters I argue that it evades the challenges of more direct leading objections and widely received competitors.

The minimal characterization of Correspondence omits many significant details. For example, on some versions the view is restricted, say, to a certain kind of empirical truth. In support of a restricted version, one may adopt reductionist accounts of allegedly non-applicable subjects, such as mathematics, mental entities and value judgments; either denying truth-values to statemental utterances in them, or finding beneath appearances a different kind of subject-matter tractable to truth-values. Also, questions have been raised about both terms said to correspond; the bearers of the property of truth and the state of the world in virtue of which the bearer is true. Although I shall for convenience start by speaking of 'statements' and 'facts', nothing said in these preliminary remarks *requires* those choices for terms. (And, when claims demand qualification, I shall adopt restricted expressions such as 'fact-based Correspondence'.) Moreover, *correspondence* itself has not escaped critical scrutiny. It has been understood in a variety of ways, both as a natural and as a conventional relation, and explained by means of the distinctions between our uses of a number of figurative and literal expressions such as 'copy', 'picture' (/'depict'), 'agree with', 'apply to', 'correlate' and 'refer'. There have also been explications of correspondence using satisfaction by all sequences of entities,[1] which in one stroke would specify the nature of correspondence while eliminating the much-mooted notion of facts in favour of particulars. Finally, some thinkers believe that metaphysical and epistemological requirements, as well as constraints on the conditions for acquiring and using language, dictate the form and likelihood of a Correspondence Theory. And as if these complications were not sufficient, consider Aristotle's *definition* of truth: 'to say of what is that it is not, or of what is not that it is, is false, while to say of what is that it is, or of what is not that it is not, is true.'[2] While some cite this as the very essence of Correspondence, yet others say it is a triviality that can be incorporated in any theory of truth; and, capturing the legitimate insight of Correspondence, it shows that the theory overstates its discovery. Such differences illustrate how even what is at issue can be controversial here.

Our treatment of the issues will be severely restricted. The lengthy historical quest for a theory of truth has led thinkers on to other paths, and original concerns are in constant danger of being overwhelmed by preoccupation with such branching issues. Not only do I slight, save for incidental comment, most of the topics mentioned in the last paragraph, but I set aside a number of alleged difficulties for Correspondence on the assumption that they turn out to be points of detail rather than problems of principle. I am hopeful that once the view is clarified and certain leading obstacles removed, those that remain to formulating a plausible Correspondence will not seem insurmountable. But since this distinction between points of detail and problems of principle is not sharp, perhaps a few illustrations of what I consider mere points of detail are in order.

First, there are disputes about the bearer of truth; some contending that, say, sentences, are not bearers of truth at all. Other philosophers have maintained what while many things such as beliefs, statements, propositions, judgments and sentences may be truth-bearers, certain among them are more fundamental and others derivative. And philosophers have disagreed about which fall into either category. None of this need be settled to show that Correspondence is not defeated by problems of principle. Such disputes would only be crucial if they served as evidence that *nothing* is a truth-bearer or that different bearers require different theories of truth. Neither of these is in the offing.

Second, there have been competing accounts of correspondence. Is it a natural or conventional relation? Is it something which can be given a general account or must it be understood only in terms of a variety of concrete instances? Can it be explained in terms of isomorphisms between elements of truth-bearers and elements of world-situations or do correspondences occur *en bloc*? These issues may be of great importance and interest. But settling them is unnecessary for what I seek to achieve here. Were there no suitable candidates for a correct account of correspondence – say, because of the incoherence of every proposal – this might be cause for alarm. But a surfeit of potential analyses is not itself an objection to a notion having legitimate instances. (Even if each of the candidates has some difficulties attached to it, as philosophical options generally do, this would not make them objections of principle to correspondence. The rule of thumb I believe we should apply for the occasion is that the proposals are not so defective that their plausibility would not be greatly enhanced were we to imagine the competing accounts removed.) If we supposed the mere existence of (attractive) competing analyses to be an objection to the concept itself, we would be implicitly sanctioning the general view that philosophical disputes over the correct account of *any* concept are grounds for doubting that the concept has instances. This is certainly an untenable principle. The existence of competing accounts of, say, personal identity, spatio-temporal continuity, human action, event-identity, thinking, causation, time or reference should not in themselves be evidence that there are no such things as persons, persisting physical things, actions, events, thoughts, causes, temporal occurrences or acts of referring.

We must first look more closely at exactly what sort of a beast a theory of truth is supposed to be. But we are confronted at the outset by a profusion of concerns, some only remotely related, which various so-called theories of truth have addressed. This has led to the all-too-familiar philosophical affliction of supposedly competing views that are really at cross-purposes. Perhaps the issues being tackled are incurably confused; that theorists have demanded a theory of truth to have consequences for metaphysics, epistemology, the philosophy of language, the conduct of inquiry, the goals of science and so on, not all of which could be encompassed by any clearly defined solution. If that is so there is no hope of getting reasonably clear about our question. But, in fact, I don't think we need despair so early in our quest. It does seem possible to state with greater precision than is customary just what one may expect of a worthwhile theory of truth. In this chapter I try to contribute to that goal by distinguishing various things one could want, and various questions one could ask, in seeking a theory of truth.

Let us begin with two parallel lists. The first contains characterizations, intended to be noncommittal between leading competitors, of the kind of thing any theory of truth may claim to supply.

On the second list are correlative questions specifying the different facets of truth to which such theories are taken as answers. The first characterization-question, (1) – (1'), is the most fundamental item for Correspondence. It will be the task of my commentary on the other items to show that this characterization is self-sufficient and detachable from other things that have been claimed about the nature and consequences of Correspondence. Thus, to begin, Correspondence is the view that purports to supply

(1) The condition *constituting* a statement's truth (or, the condition *making* a statement true)

and which answers the question

(1') What are the conditions *by virtue of which* a statement is true?

On this understanding of Correspondence, Aristotle gives expression to it when he says of the statement that a man exists that 'whereas the true statement is in no way the cause [reason] of the actual thing's existence, the actual thing does seem in some way the cause of the statement's being true'.[3] And although we may not wish to endorse additional details of Bertrand Russell's version, he is expressing little more than a fact-based Correspondence when he says that it is a truism that 'there are . . . *beliefs*, which have reference to facts, and by reference to facts are either true of false'.[4] Usually Correspondence, or any other theory of truth, is fleshed out in greater detail. We raise no objections to that. But we should note that the view has substance even if we say very little further in elaboration of its notions. In part this is because the view is non-vacuous just by excluding certain things. If we do not say more precisely what facts or states of the world are, nevertheless as a class they are distinct from, say, logical or quasi-logical relations of statements with other statements, ideal limits of inquiry, theoretical satisfactions, or clarity and distinctness. Correspondence does not claim that some or all of these features are not possessed by all and only truths, but only that they are not the features *making* statements true. Thus, whatever the shortcomings of Correspondence as an answer to (1'), it is not too thin to count as a theory of truth.[5]

Let us then proceed to a list of characterizations from which it is important to distinguish (1). Various writers, especially critics of Correspondence, have taken a theory of truth to satisfy one or more of the items on it, either in addition to or in place of (1).

(2) What statements refer to
(3) Our means of telling if a statement is true
(4) The criteria of or standards for a statement's being true
(5) The circumstances (linguistic, conversational, epistemic) in which 'true' may be used
(6) The purpose or point of saying that a statement is true
(7) The meaning of the phrase 'is true' or 'it is true that'
(8) The definition of 'is true' or of truth
(9) Necessary and sufficient conditions for a statement's truth
(10) The explanation of a statement's truth.

Specifications of these conditions are also answers to the following set of correlative questions:

(2') What do statements refer to?
(3') What means have we for telling if a statement is true?
(4') What are the criteria of or standards for a statement's being true?
(5') In what circumstances (linguistic, conversational, epistemic) may 'true' be predicated of a statement?
(6') What is the purpose or point of saying that a statement is true?
(7') What is the meaning of the phrase 'is true' or 'it is true that'?
(8') What is the definition of 'is true' or of truth?
(9') What are the necessary and sufficient conditions for a statement's truth?
(10') What explains a statement's truth?

No doubt some of the distinctions between items on these lists are more evident than others. And in some cases philosophers have argued that in spite of *prima-facie* differences, the issue raised by (1)–(1') cannot be resolved directly without first resolving one of the other items.[6] In later chapters I shall examine what I take to be the most serious challenges of this sort. But here let us confine ourselves to more basic distinctions. It is worth knowing that the characterizations themselves, and the ways in which they have been understood in philosophical discussions, provide us with sufficient material for distinguishing each of

(2)–(10) from (1). It helps us to understand how Correspondence as a specification of (1) can be independent by showing us why an answer to (1') needn't be significantly affected by its inability to answer any of (2')–(10') and how the answers given to the latter needn't affect a separate answer to (1').

A further preliminary remark. The review I am about to undertake is not intended to deny that on *some* interpretations of certain of (2)–(10) the relevant items may be construed to characterize no more than (1) does. I claim only that there is at least one natural interpretation of each on which it requires either more or something altogether different. Indeed, the capability of reading (2)–(10) in various ways, some of which overlap with the natural way of reading (1), is part of the difficulty. For, once something that might satisfy (1) is obtained under a different specification, the differences in the specification may lead us to impose additional or different requirements for success associated with that distinct characterization. Thus, we may find perfectly acceptable answers to (1') being expected to fulfil roles demanded of them by any of (2')–(10'). It is in large part for this reason, and not because the other characterizations on the list have no connection with (1), that it is important to emphasize their differences here. Thus armed against some possible misunderstandings, let us look at each of the items to be distinguished from (1).

2 WHAT STATEMENTS REFER TO

Our recent illustration of Correspondence from Russell appealed to what beliefs refer to in order to discover the fact relevant to a belief's truth. Although this is at worst a harmless inaccuracy, about which I shall say more below, it is more important to emphasize that *if* truth-bearers did not refer in any way this wouldn't impair Correspondence as we have understood it. It is important because certain objections to Correspondence have been based upon what Quine calls 'a tendency . . . to liken sentences to names and then posit objects [facts] for them to name'.[7] Strawson develops a similar objection by affirming *the identity* of the demand for 'that which the statement is *about*' (namely, what it refers to) with 'the demand for something in the world *which makes the statement true* [Mr Austin's phrase], or *to which the statement corresponds when it is true.*'8 According to Quine and Strawson the treatment of sentences/statements as compound names is misconceived. But it is this treatment which first introduces facts as referents, and then facts so introduced are enlisted to serve as truth-constituters. Strawson says that identifying the three demands above is 'an error of a logical type'.

Although the objection invites elaboration, we needn't probe deeper to see that Correspondence is not troubled by it. For the sake of argument let us grant that statements/sentences are not compound names, and that the mistaken belief that they are names is frequently responsible for philosophers adopting facts as their correlates. Even so, such mistaken beliefs are not the only or the best reason for pairing statements with facts. A more straightforward justification is that if there is a distinction between truths and non-truths – a natural supposition that neither objector would reject – *something* must account for it. The tarnished pedigree of facts would not disqualify them from being that something. Indeed, the objection gives rise to a curious discomfort; something in the nature of witnessing a post-mortem in which we are not sure yet that the patient is dead. For the objection is more apt for explaining why the view has gone wrong than for showing that it has.

What is the problem with statements referring? Of course, if the referents were the facts which made them true, false statements would be reference-failures. But to take false statements as such for this sort of semantic misfit would be to mislocate their shortcoming. Also, it is sometimes viewed as a condition of reference that the referential relation be uniform; but true and false statements bear different relations to the states of affairs constituting both truth and falsity. Perhaps these difficulties could be averted by making the referents of statements only *types* – what Barwise and Perry call 'situations'9 – rather than the concrete states of affairs whose obtaining is unrelated to the identity of the statement in question. But other problems await. For example, reference is usually taken to be a sub-function of formulae to which it contributes. Thus, in statements made with sentences of simple subject–predicate form, the reference we may suppose made with the subject expression serves only to identify what it is about which something further is said in the predicate expression. But for the references of statements the whole utterance is supposed to do no more than refer – which creates the impression that what is accomplished by this reference has been left incomplete. This may help explain why those who accept the reference of statements gloss the referential accomplishment of the statement that S by reformulating it as, for example, the statement that S *obtains*, thereby supplying the further predication missing in the strict formulation of the original. In addition, there is a popular, albeit disputed argument traceable to Frege which purports to show that all true and all false statements must have the same reference: namely, their respective truth-values.

However, for our purposes it matters not whether these objections are individually or collectively decisive. In either case statements bear a relation to states of affairs, situations, facts, or whatnot which satisfies the demands of Correspondence. For we can create a referring expression from any sentence, say S, used to make a statement by prefacing the words comprising S with 'the state of affairs such that'. Let us follow Fred Sommers[10] in adopting the convention of bracketing those words as a way of doing this. '[S]' is certainly a bona fide referring expression, but may seem to have the disadvantage of referring only on condition that the statement that S is true. However, this serves well enough for Correspondence's purposes, since even in the case of falsity [S] functions to direct attention to the aspect, part or constituent of the cosmos relevant to the determination of the statement's truth-value. Thus, even if statements fail to satisfy the formal conditions of reference, we can describe a function taking us from true statements to referents which are also truth-constituters and which is absent or fails to work for false (untrue) statements. If the acceptability of formulations of Correspondence, such as Russell's, which make use of the reference of statements or beliefs hangs on no more than the accuracy with which this relation is described, it appears the worst of which we can convict it is a harmless over-simplification.

3 OUR MEANS OF TELLING IF A STATEMENT IS TRUE

Various epistemologies maintain that the only world accessible to us is basically a product of or conditioned by our minds, ideas, language or conceptual scheme. Thus, we cannot check an essentially subject-independent reality to see that our statements are true. A less radical claim is that checking the world to see whether our statements correspond seldom, if ever, plays a role in investigations, perhaps not even when we are commonly said 'to look and see'. What is said below against the relevance of the more radical claims to Correspondence applies *mutatis mutandis* to this view as well.

Are any such epistemologies incompatible with Correspondence?

For some, these considerations lead to a thoroughgoing subjective idealism in which no subject-independent world beyond mental constructions can exist. It would be inappropriate to raise this brand of idealism as a side-issue to Correspondence, but a few words are in order. First, as we saw in Chapter 1, it is not strictly incompatible with Correspondence. The latter is only an account of what constitutes truth, not of which statements are true; though we also saw that by holding idealism one has a powerful inducement to seek a different account of truth. Second, subjective idealism itself seems to require much more potent support than its leading advocates have supplied, and, on the contrary, each version of it with which I am familiar confronts formidable objections. But I am interested here in a rather different consequence that thinkers often draw from the sort of epistemological outlook outlined above: namely, that it makes certain of Correspondence's would-be truth-constituters inaccessible to truth-staters, and that this is an objection to Correspondence. This too was mentioned in the last chapter, but here a different facet of it must be highlighted. Of course, the inaccessibility of the world that makes statements true often appears in the company of other considerations – perhaps considerations about what is meaningful – and is not meant to stand alone. But occasionally it has been thought that inaccessibility by itself is a forceful objection. Thus, if only for clarity's sake it is worth noting, and explaining why, the mere fact that what makes one's statement true may transcend our capability of direct confirmation (whatever one's conception of that) has no tendency to impugn Correspondence. Correspondence is not primarily a theory about ways of discovering that a statement is true, and any counsel of that sort derived from it is purely a bonus rather than a fulfilment of part of its direct obligation. Correspondence does not require that the relation making a statement true be an especially handy or helpful method for our discovering whether it is true. And while its uselessness for this latter task may be regrettable, it is not an objection to it as an answer to (1'). Critics may be correct in stating that to hold that a statement corresponds with the facts doesn't advance an inquiry into its truth; but as an objection to the theory this weathered observation is irrelevant. For all Correspondence has to say on the matter, truths might turn out to be inaccessible to anything we count as verification or direct evidence.

But it is also important to emphasize that Correspondence *does not require* inaccessible truths. If it can be shown by other means that nothing we affirm is beyond our ability to verify it, this would not weaken the theory's answer to (1'). Correspondence tolerates inaccessible truths because it addresses a question having nothing to do with that of accessibility. If it guaranteed accessibility, which it does not, this would have to be incidental. But on this basis we cannot rule out doctrines independent of Correspondence that may do so, and a Correspondence theorist is not debarred by other commitments from holding them.

The preceding paragraph also summarizes the extent of the vaunted connection between Correspondence and scepticism. Let us suppose that certain verificationist, or justification-condition, theories of meaning contain adequate replies to the sceptic (see Chapter 7). But they just as surely contain anti-realist elements in their constructivist theories of truth which render them incompatible with Correspondence. Were these the *only* guarantors against scepticism, the relation of scepticism to Correspondence might be of greater philosophical significance. But, once clearly expressed, the assumption that such anti-realist theories of meaning are the sole arguments against scepticism is not very plausible. The sceptic's use of concepts such as knowledge, certainty or doubt have also been questioned. Or, one may reject the Cartesian picture of the objects of knowledge. Correspondence may be as compatible with a critique based on those inquiries as with a host of others.[11]

35

4 CRITERIA OF OR STANDARDS FOR A STATEMENT'S BEING TRUE

Some may not distinguish this from (3), but I list it separately to leave room for views in which statement-making utterances have their sense (or meaning) determined by a proper subset of evidentiary conditions, variously entitled justification-conditions, assertibility-conditions or criteria. Several objections to Correspondence voiced recently by Michael Dummett and a number of Neo-Wittgensteinians[12] start from the contention that Correspondence is not developed consistently with the evidentiary conditions under which we learn to use and manifest knowledge of statemental utterances. There is certainly something to this. The conditions justifying one in asserting something or of accepting something asserted by another only occasionally coincide with those that Correspondence says make assertions true. And elsewhere we shall examine arguments purporting to show that the answer to (4') places restrictions on permissible answers to (1'). But first it is more important not to overlook the distinction between (4) and (1). On even superficial inspection one can see that they are specifications of different sorts of things, which may not coincide in particular cases. Even if criterial evidence for the truth of a statement is a central ingredient in its meaning, a statement may be false in the presence of an adequate justification or true though unjustified.

5 THE LINGUISTIC (/CONVERSATIONAL /EPISTEMIC) CIRCUMSTANCES IN WHICH 'TRUE' MAY BE USED

P. F. Strawson[13] once maintained that we use 'is true' and 'it is true that' to underwrite, support, concede or warrant what has been earlier said, considered or in some way placed before us. Thus, the illocutionary contribution of 'true' is much like that of 'ditto'. And while Strawson did not hold that this account answered the same set of questions addressed by Correspondence, he presumably did think that it could occupy the place of a philosophical account which was to be vacated by Correspondence. For the sake of argument let us suppose that unless someone has said, denied or been thought to have somehow considered a statement which could be made with the sentence 'the car park is empty', it would be appropriate to make that statement with the foregoing sentence rather than with the sentence 'it is true that the car park is empty' or with the sentence 'that the car park is empty is true'. I shall also suppose that these comments instance a genuine restriction on the correct uses of the truth predicate and operator. Nevertheless, a theory supplying (1) need say nothing about the matter, and it is rendered neither incomplete nor incorrect by not incorporating this restriction. The circumstances under which an expression embodying a concept may be used *need not* coincide with the circumstances under which that concept is instantiated. And it seems quite clear that in the present case they would not coincide. For if they did, then in this case there would be nothing further to inquire about the correctness of the use of 'true' once it had been settled that it conformed to restrictions such as (5).

6 THE PURPOSE OR POINT OF SAYING THAT, WANTING THAT, OR BELIEVING THAT SOMETHING IS TRUE

Dummett[14] claims that truth is the normal *telos* of belief and statement. He has suggested that 'a proper account' of the concept *truth* can no more avoid incorporating this fact than an account of *winning* can avoid pointing out that winning is the normal objective of competitions. But unguarded talk of 'accounts' of truth threatens to reintroduce just the confusion that our taxonomy of characterizations seeks to banish. Contrary to Dummett, if we confine ourselves to saying analogously what *constitutes* a win, we may be able to state winning positions without mentioning that it is the object of competitions to win. Thus, ignoring the fact that, say, in some chess matches the object is only to avoid losing, we might say that a game is won when the opponent's king is in mate, which is the position in which one may take it off on her next move and no moves by the opponent can prevent this. Such a description need not tell one whether the object of the game is to mate or get mated: that is, to win or lose. (Compare the case in which a player at a disadvantage seeks a stalemate by forcing his opponent to trap his pieces so that he has

37

no legal moves to make.) In like manner a theory of the conditions under which a statement is true can avoid mentioning the point of truth.

Nothing that I can detect in Dummett's preference for an account including the point of saying that something is true shows that attempting to answer (1') without providing (6) is logically defective. Perhaps traditional Correspondence theorists could have cast their nets wider, mentioning in their expositions the important observations about truth made by Strawson or Dummett. However, it would be a misunderstanding of the formers' project to suppose that what they in fact did is ill-conceived (rather than, on some standard to which they did not adhere, not the whole story) only because such topics were ignored. But Dummett uses his observation as a reason for rejecting a Fregean view that, for our immediate purposes, may be taken for Correspondence. And the objection seems to rest on no more than the assumption that in addressing himself to (1) Frege was, or should have been, considering (6) as well. But a tale unwhole is not thereby unholy.

7 THE MEANING OF THE PHRASE 'IS TRUE' OR 'IT IS TRUE THAT'

Under this heading we should also include *what we understand* when we understand one of these phrases. Thus, I shall speak of 'our understanding' of the phrase, meaning by this the content of our understanding. Frequently the issue is raised in terms of the *concept* or *conception* truth. This may also be treated under (7); not because concepts are no more than meanings, but because when philosophers set themselves to investigate the concept truth, they proceed by investigating the meanings and uses of the expressions incorporating that concept.

In order to know or understand an expression, one may need to know things other than the circumstances in which it would be truly applied. For example, one may not know the meaning of an expression such as 'gringo' unless one realizes that its predication of persons or groups is a racial insult *even if* it is true (as seems plausible) that 'x is a gringo' is true if and only if x is a non-Latino from north of the Mexican border. I want to concede, what is in any case at least arguable, that the meanings of our phrases or the word 'true' involve factors such as those cited by Strawson and Dummett in (5) and (6). Their knowledge is certainly part of the linguistic wherewithal of standard users of the expressions. What is even more certain is that a number of philosophers have thought so, and it has led to their requiring of an answer to (7') more than would be required of an answer to (1'). We place the issue in sharper focus if we see that nothing in these admissions concerning (7) adversely affects our ability to specify (1) without facing such complications.

Theories of truth, Correspondence in particular, have also been described in terms of

(7a) What it is *to say* that a statement is true.[15]

In comparison with other items on our list this terminology is imprecise. It could comprise any of the characterizations discussed under (5)–(7), but it might also include what the speaker (as opposed to her words) meant, or what is being referred to, or even what constitutes the statement's truth – (1). Both the contexts in which (7a) appears and the fact that (7a)'s way of describing its quarry is not directly about truth, but about the use of the word 'true', is some evidence that (7a) is frequently if not always regarded as a stylistic variant of (7). However, it is a formulation fraught with danger. This is not only because it allows us to answer the request for a theory of truth with one interpretation in mind while the dispute over it may then rage with others in mind; but also because its ability to be understood as no more than (1) may lure us into overlooking the important distinctions between questions (7') and (1'). I am unfamiliar with any reasons for preferring (7a) to (7) or (1), and henceforth I shall not comment on it further till Chapter 4, where its connection with deflationary conceptions makes it unavoidable.

Framing the central question, as (7') does, in terms of meaning or semantic content or what is said, seems to have had much to do with the celebrated Logical Superfluidity or Assertive Redundancy Thesis (hereafter, 'Redundancy'). We may approach the view through two equivalence theses: logical and semantic. Assuming only the two classical truth-values, Logical Equivalence states that p and p is true are always equivalent in truth-value: 'p' is true if and only if 'p is true' is. From this, meaning (or semantic) equivalence is inferred. As Frege puts it: 'One can . . . say "The thought, that 5 is a prime number, is true". But closer examination shows that *nothing more has been said* than in the simple sentence "5 is a prime number".'[16] And Ramsey writes, 'it is evident that "It is true that Caesar was murdered" *means no more than* that Caesar was murdered'.[17] For Redundancy one must proceed a step further, as the Ramsey tribe does, to the conclusion that *no property* is predicated of anything by the (grammatical predicate) expression 'is true'; or, in Ramsey's words, 'there is really no separate problem of truth but merely a linguistic muddle', and 'the problem is one not as to the nature of truth and falsehood, but as to the nature of judgment or assertion'.[18] Thus, we arrive at a deflationary view about truth and its theories.

We shall deal more fully with this challenge to Correspondence later (Chapter 4, section III), but because it makes evident the need for differentiating (7) and (1), a few remarks are in order here.

Philosophers are often accustomed to approach an account of any notion or concept by way of asking for the meaning of the predicate(s) expressing it. This seems to have had a sobering effect when the only alternative in the offing to asking for the meaning of the predicate 'is true' was asking a grandiose question about the nature of Truth. However, in the case at hand the semantic formulation obscures the goal. If we tenaciously think of a theory of truth not in terms of the use of a predicate, but in terms of the conditions that *make* something true, it will not be difficult to unravel Redundancy's original sin. Truth-making conditions are often relevant in the absence of uses of 'true'. Therefore, we slant our inquiry quite off-centre when we make the use of the expression its focus. Redundancy's metaphysical consequence that truth predicates no property – and, that thus there is no problem about truth – is obtained only with the help of its distinctive semantic equivalence thesis. But unless it can be shown that answers to (1') are conditioned by answers to (7'), which Redundancy merely assumes, it is difficult to see how the semantic, or even logical, equivalence of '*p*' and '*p* is true' can determine the illegitimacy or unanswerability of the former question.

Of course semantic ascent is possible for any notion. Rather than asking 'Is grass green?' we can ask 'Is "is green" truly predicable of grass?' Similarly, it may be innocuous to ask for the conditions under which 'is true' is correctly predictable rather than asking for the conditions making something true. But though the exchange of questions for 'is green' may be harmless, semantic ascent is not always so smooth. The earlier example of 'is a gringo' is ample warning that one cannot always infer from claims about the conditions under which an expression may be truly applied to accounts of the expression's meaning or semantics. And the observations of Strawson and Dummett illustrate how readily questions about the meaning or use of 'is true' are diverted from a focus upon features of the world that constitute accurate application. If we resist replacing theories that deliver the conditions making a statement true with those that deliver the meaning of 'true', Redundancy is left only with the claim that '*p*' and '*p* is true' always have the same truth-value (that is, share truth-conditions). This tells us less than deflationists require. For while saying that '*p*' and '*p* is true' mean the same may distract us from the issue of accounting for truth, saying that they have *the same truth-conditions* leads us directly to ask for the particulars of what they share. Truth-conditions – in the sense of the conditions making something true, not in the less robust sense of the conditions under which it is true – are just what specifications of (1) attempt to supply. And to say that two forms share them does not lead us to reject the need for such accounts, but helps make palpable just why one is wanted.

This set of distinctions also invalidates some related uses of Redundancy. For example, Dummett writes that a fundamental contention he had made earlier was 'that the acceptance of the redundancy theory precluded the possibility of using the notion of truth in a general account of what it is to grasp the meaning of a sentence of the object-language, and, in particular, of an account according to which an understanding of a sentence consisted in an apprehension of the conditions for it to be true'.[19] It is not clear which of our three steps Dummett takes here for Redundancy: logical equivalence, meaning equivalence, or the view that truth introduces no property (or relation) beyond the assertions of which it is grammatically predicated. But even if we grant him the step from logical to meaning equivalence, which some philosophers have plausibly contested,[20] unless we grant him the view that the truth of a sentence amounts to no more than the (asserted) sentence, this leaves room for an independent knowledge of truth-conditions, which can then be utilized in grasping or understanding sentences having them. That is, even the meaning equivalence of '*p*' and '*p* is true', if it does not prohibit Correspondence as an answer to (1'), is insufficient to show that there are no such things as truth-making conditions over and above the sentence asserted. What is then to prevent one from using knowledge of those truth-making conditions in understanding the sentences to which they attach?

8 THE DEFINITION OF 'IS TRUE' OR OF TRUTH

For those who understand the definition of an expression or concept to give its meaning, what has been said about (7) suffices for (8). But philosophers occasionally construe definition more broadly. For example, it is now common to recognize as distinct modes of definition reference fixings and stipulative definitions. While stipulative definitions yield meaning equivalences for their terms, reference fixings are introduced in part to avoid having the usual consequences of shared meaning between definiens and definiendum. Once again, reference fixing confronts us with a characterization too imprecise to stop at. It may overlap the territory covered by several other items on our list, especially (9), and may also introduce elements not covered by anything discussed elsewhere, such as the production of core cases to 'fix' the class under discussion. In any event, even when this characterization and question come close to singling out what it singled out by (1) and (1'), it should be obvious that the latter pair provide a superior method for zeroing in on this particular issue with clarity and precision.

9 NECESSARY AND SUFFICIENT CONDITIONS FOR A STATEMENT'S TRUTH

It appears that a specification of (1), the conditions constituting a statement's truth, always yields (9), necessary and sufficient conditions for its truth; but the converse need not hold, for example, *any omniscient being knowing that S* is necessary and sufficient for S being true. However, unless S has for its subject-matter the knowledge of omniscient beings, this condition doesn't *constitute* S's truth. As I am construing the example it doesn't presuppose the existence of an omniscient being. But even if the example were challenged on grounds having to do with the existence of such beings, it would not throw into doubt that were such a condition to obtain it would satisfy (9) but not (1). And this weaker claim is all we seem to need to establish the principle that having (9) is not, *eo ipso*, having (1).

It is not altogether clear whether Tarski's semantic conception of truth falls prey to the confusion between (9) and (1); but it seems certain that Tarski's own views about what his conception accomplished does involve it. First, let us briefly sketch the semantic conception.

In some places Tarski writes as if his *definition* of truth (for a given language) is just a list of all theorems conforming to the schema

(T) $\ulcorner$S is true in L if and only if $p\urcorner$,

in which 'S' is replaced by a structural description or name of a sentence, 'L' by a language containing that sentence, and '*p*' by the sentence itself.[21] Naturally, only languages that meet certain constraints will admit any such definition, the truth-predicate defined will belong only to the metalanguage of the object-language under study, and because languages have an infinity of sentences we could make this *list definition* finite only with the help of recursive clauses. Although this is not Tarski's ultimate definition of 'is true' (in a given language), it shares the spirit of his definition, and thus bears on later remarks.

It is best to begin Tarski's actual view with sentential functions or open sentences. The ones of interest to us are those which would become atomic sentences were their variables replaced by constants. A few examples are '*x* is bald' and '*x* is larger than *y*'. The crucial notion for defining truth, designation (/reference/ naming), definability and other familiar semantic notions, is *satisfaction*. Satisfaction is a relation between (sequences of) arbitrary objects and sentential functions. Shakespeare satisfies the sentential function '*x* writes' *because* Shakespeare writes. Of course, outside deductive sciences we seem more interested in (closed) sentences than sentential functions, but if we think of a sentence merely as a null-place sentential function it is included in the definition of truth as follows: a (closed) sentence is true just in case it is satisfied by every sequence of objects, false just in case it satisfies none.

Because satisfaction, in terms of which truth is defined, is a relation between the bearers of truth – in Tarski's view sentences – and the extra-linguistic elements of domains, it may appear that the semantic conception of truth is a form of Correspondence as judged by (1). I do not wish, or need, to deny this, but I am uncertain about it. Among reasons for doubt are the following. As far as the truth of closed sentences goes, the non-linguistic term in any satisfaction relation plays precisely the same role for each truth as it does for any one of them. Thus, the ordered pair <Caesar, Brutus> from our sequence contributes exactly the same to the truth of 'Enrico sings' as it does to 'Caesar trusted Brutus'. Both are satisfied by *every* infinite sequence of members of the domain, including this one. The ordered pair may play a greater role in the truth, *on a given assignment*, of the function '*x* trusted *y*'. But the individual, Aristotle, is no more relevant to the truth of any closed sentence than of any other.[22] Moreover, the way in which satisfaction figures in the truth of sentences seems to fall short of constitution. For recall that it is *only because* Shakespeare writes, the very thing the nature of whose truth we are after, that every sequence satisfies 'Shakespeare writes'.

The prime consideration for Tarski is not that his definition specifies (1) for sentences, but that true sentences can be found not to violate the general definition in terms of satisfaction: that is, that the definition built around satisfaction supplies *necessary and sufficient conditions* for the truth of sentences. Indeed, he shows positivistic disdain for any problem other than (9'). Thus, he writes:

> [N]obody has ever pointed out to me in an intelligible way just what this problem is. I have been informed in this connection that my definition, though it states necessary and sufficient conditions for a sentence to be true, does not really grasp the 'essence' of this concept. Since I have never been able to understand what the 'essence' of a concept is, I must be excused from discussing this point any longer.[23]

And elsewhere in the same essay he repudiates any attempt to 'contribute in any way to the endless, often violent discussion' of the correct view of truth.[24] The point is made even clearer by the first, what I have called the mistaken, interpretation of Tarski's definition. Schema (T) fails even more patently to link up the sentence S with anything extra-linguistic. To obtain theorems (not to prove them) we are given a recipe for replacing '*p*', but quite deliberately not told anything about what '*p*' is to *represent* other than a sentence.

Tarski is unmistakably clear about why a list of such replacements will not work as a definition: namely, only because there is no finite or denumerable number of sentences in a language.[25] Were there a fixed finite number of sentences, we could construct 'a correct definition of truth' in just this way. It does not matter, as some may want to argue, that it is essential to any language to have an infinite number of sentences (which would prohibit such things as simple Wittgensteinian language-games from being languages). For even if we admit the impossibility, it does not show that the features of truth-characterizations themselves require the infinity. Thus, schema (T)'s inadequacies as a definition of truth have nothing to do with the way it characterizes truth for sentences that it is illustrated to cover. Consequently, the 'partial' definition of truth it provides *for a given atomic sentence* is not inferior, *qua* partial definition, to that provided in terms of the sentence's being satisfied by an infinite sequence of objects. This demonstrates how ready one must be, in strict adherence to Tarski, to shelve altogether the role of satisfaction in an account of what it is that makes a sentence true. (T)-theorems are no more trivial or shallow, and satisfaction by a sequence of objects no more profound, in fathoming the nature of truth. Both provide lists, which in turn yield necessary and sufficient conditions for the truth of sentences of a language. The objection is not altogether novel. Critics have already described how Tarski's list characterizations of denotation and truth fail as substitutes for an account of the mechanism, as it were, of these notions.[26] I am only adding that just because the list yields necessary and sufficient conditions of truth, in some sense, its prospects aren't improved; for (1) and (9) are characterizations of distinct features of truth.

There is an additional, concise argument to show that the semantic conception cannot be identical with Correspondence. It requires a further assumption, but one that is easy to swallow. Defenders of the Coherence Theory of Truth claim that Tarski's definition does not settle the case between them and Correspondence because their own theory is consistent with the semantic conception. To show this would require further explanation, but experienced readers will not find it difficult to see the basis of the claim. However, Correspondence is incompatible with the Coherence Theory. It follows that the semantic conception cannot be identical with Correspondence. This succinct argument might seem unconvincing if we could not specify what it is about Correspondence that is missing from the semantic conception. But in conjunction with our foregoing remarks I believe it is easier to see why the argument is cogent.

The difference between (1) and (9) serves to illuminate the distinction we drew while discussing Redundancy: namely, that between the conditions making something true and the conditions under which something is true. Both have gone under the title 'truth-conditions'. But the former is a stronger use of the term. The possibility of having necessary and sufficient conditions for truth that do not determine truth shows graphically how truth-conditions of the second sort are not tantamount to those of the first sort.

10 THE EXPLANATION OF A STATEMENT'S TRUTH

There are notorious difficulties in attempting to give a single, all-purpose account of explanation. We need no excursus into the issues generated by proposals for the proper form of an explanation, such as the covering-law model, since the distinctions between (1) and (10) which need emphasis are more basic. Whatever else an explanation is, it is something that is suited by its form to 'fill a gap in the understanding'. (If something counts as an explanation only if it succeeds for its intended audience, we can say something stronger: namely, that it does fill a gap in the understanding.) But this can be accomplished to varying degrees. Thus, while one person may declare ø an explanation, another may deny it is one while not denying what ø states. The second person may be rejecting ø's claim to provide sufficient illumination of a critical aspect.

Accordingly, Davidson rejects fact-based Correspondence with the following remark:

Suppose . . . we distinguish facts as finely as statements. Of
course, not every statement has its fact; only the true ones
do. But then, unless we find another way to pick out facts, we
cannot hope *to explain* truth by appeal to them.[27]

This is not the claim, which we shall examine in greater detail in
the next chapter, that facts are not statementally independent
existents. Davidson is relying on some of the same evidence on
which this familiar claim rests: namely, that we identify a fact only
by way of the linguistic formulations by means of which we also
identify the statement used to state it. But Davidson's point is
that, even if facts exist independently of true statements, our
method of picking them out prevents us from using them *to explain*
the truth of statements. It is no explanation to be told that Hitler
died in the bunker is made true by the fact that Hitler died in the
bunker. For argument's sake let us grant this. But instead of
abandoning Correspondence as a specification of (1), it should
lead us to ask why Correspondence should be held accountable
for what may be the stricter requirements of explanation. If explanation requires a certain sort of illumination, then even if our
account is true, it may be insufficient for explanation. Thus, it
may fail to answer (10') while answering (1') quite satisfactorily.
We need not claim that explanations are in some sense intensional
and that statements of constitution are not. It suffices that if both
were intensional the points of asking (1') and (10') still would be
different; and thus we may expect that their ranges of acceptable
answers would vary even if they also overlap.

The variance will go unnoticed where, as in the usual case, we
want our answer to provide both the explanation and constitution
of truth. But it emerges in other cases. For example, if we are
discussing Hitler's death, then, archness aside, I may describe
what it is that makes the statement Hitler died in the bunker true
by means of the description 'what you just mentioned' (namely,
a certain fact). This will not normally be illuminating from any
perspective that makes conversations pointful. But that does not
impugn the truth of my remark. I am not saying that an explanation of truth might yield *something other than* conditions that
make for truth; but only that we need not inquire further into the
nature of explanation to note that on any account of it some

correct (true) specifications of those conditions can fall short of being explanations.

Thus, Correspondence may be an acceptable theory of truth even if it does not provide an explanation of truth on a legitimate understanding of the phrase 'provides an explanation'. Some may still be troubled by this conclusion because the evidence on which I said Davidson based his claim about explanation has also been used to argue that facts do not exist independently of true statements, and that the word 'fact', rather than standing for a distinctive type of thing, only supplies a stylistic variant for the word 'true'. Indeed, if this were so it would be a decisive objection to fact-based Correspondence on my interpretation. But that is a different matter, to be taken up in the next chapter. It should not lead us to undervalue the critical distinction here between attempted explanations and statements, which may or may not also be explanations, of what constitutes something.

None of this should obscure the point that would-be answers to (1') and candidates for (1) also normally (purport to) *explain* what it is for statements to be true. This emerges most clearly if, instead of the earlier particular 'explanation' 'Hitler died in his bunker is made true by the fact that Hitler died in his bunker', we take a general dictum such as 'a statement is made true by corresponding to a state of affairs (fact, situation and so on) in the world'. However, it is not the particularity or generality of the forms themselves that accounts for the crucial difference, but that they lend themselves to focusing our attention on what is beside the point in the first case and on what is crucial in the second. The particular formula, suited to answering questions about instances rather than 'illustrating' general truths, naturally draws our attention *not* to the relation that Correspondence claims subsists between the two, but to stating the value for the second member of the statement–fact pair that is set up by this relation. The question of how to generate such pairs is pushed in the background or ignored. But the general formula neglects case-by-case pairings to focus attention on the nature of the relation. This does not mean that *all* general formulae by means of which Correspondence is stated will be equally explanatory. For example, critics of Correspondence's explanatory role have remarked that 'true statements state facts' is unilluminating just because 'fact' is an internal accusative of what a true statement states. But not all formulations of Correspondence need be equally non-explanatory. Thus, we need not deny that some formulations of Correspondence which would be paradigms for (1) may explain truth as well as delivering what constitutes it. However, at present, it is more important to emphasize the other side of the matter: claims to which a Correspondence theorist may be committed by his theory are not disqualified just because they are not explanatory on some justifiable notion of explanation.

Let us also be careful not to confuse the complaint that 'Correspondence does not explain truth' with the equally common complaint that 'truth does not explain anything (or, anything about truths)'. When the latter is used as a criticism of Correspondence it is normally part of Redundancy's critique of any theory of truth – for which Correspondence is usually the exemplary culprit (see the quote from Michael Williams in Chapter 1, section 1, page 12). That sort of complaint is answered partly in the discussion of Redundancy under (7) in the present chapter, and will be elaborated in Chapter 4. But the matter of present concern is whether a certain view explains truth, whatever the explanatory value of truth itself.

11 SUMMARY

What has this taxonomy of questions and specifications accomplished? First, let us see what it didn't do. It didn't, and wasn't intended to, prohibit Correspondence theories as answers to any of (2') to (10'). It didn't even prohibit the use of Correspondence for answering one of these questions *in addition to* answering (1'), though it did provide an admonition against founding the resulting theory on a confusion of issues. But what the taxonomy did was to focus attention squarely where it belongs. A theory of truth is above all a specification of (1). Interests primarily directed to (2)–(10) should be plainly packaged as such. Whatever they produce, it will not be *a substitute* for (1). Once Correspondence is viewed as supplying (1) in contradistinction to any of our other specifications on some common interpretations, the odds against it decrease considerably. For, I hope it is now obvious, some of what has passed as fatal objection to Correspondence has relied on misunderstandings of what it is primarily a theory of. To repeat, this is not intended to close discussion on critics who realize this, but who nevertheless hold that straight answers to (1') are not attainable, and that what will take the natural place of Correspondence once its consequences are developed will be a theory or an outlook that rejects the question rather than attempting to answer it. But even in the expositions of several who claim this, the point is occasionally baldly stated and not shown. Both here and elsewhere in our subsequent studies, we will see things more clearly if we do not allow ourselves to slide unwittingly from (1) into any of the other characterizations.

III

SOME FAMILIAR OBJECTIONS TO CORRESPONDENCE – AND ONE NOT SO FAMILIAR

1 A LIST OF STOCK OBJECTIONS

Occasionally Correspondence is abandoned for apparently strong reasons supporting an alternative theory of truth. But in this chapter we are interested in a different order of reason philosophers have had for rejecting it: namely, its supposed difficulties. A number of familiar objections have been common coin. It would be foolhardy to attempt to compile an exhaustive list of them, but I shall enumerate and discuss what I take to be the most potent and popular ones. Very briefly, the chief objections of this sort against Correspondence may be summarized by the following claims:

A There are no such things as facts, states of affairs and so on.
B There is no single correct description of the world.
C Cognition always involves the use of concepts contributed by the cognizer.

This brief summary does not do justice to the force of the objections. Each has been taken by sizeable numbers of thinkers as a powerful, indeed mortal, challenge to Correspondence. They are addressed, respectively, in sections 2, 4 and 5. In addition, B is raised in connection with a somewhat different set of considerations introduced by Hilary Putnam and discussed here in section 3. Putnam supplies a battery of non-traditional arguments for rejecting the metaphysical picture of which Correspondence is a part. Although he raises B among his objections, it occurs in the context of a yet larger argument devised to refute a rather different sort of doctrine. While discussing this doctrine he produces a theorem which says, roughly, that if there are any correct descriptions of the world, there must be a multiplicity of competing ones. This argument for B leaves us with a restricted form of the claim. (The restrictions are discussed later.) Other problems connected with B will be discussed elsewhere.

Although C is also promoted by Putnam, that objection will be treated largely independently of his other concerns.

2 WHITHER FACTS?

The first objection to be considered is that the world-relatum in the correspondence relation – let us provisionally call it a 'fact' – is not available for truths to correspond to. The claim here might be either (1) that *we cannot know* that there are facts or (2) that there are no facts. As explained below, it matters which of these is argued. But either claim might be a way to sum up a few more specific theses held by critics of this cast. The first is that facts, if there are such things, are (or are known to be) no more than truths (true statements). This is to claim the reductive identity of facts (or, its identity as far as our knowledge goes) with truths or true statements. The second thesis is that while certain idiosyncratic forms of expression may prevent us from holding that facts are strictly identical with true statements, nevertheless facts are not items logically independent of (true) statements. This is a vaguer claim, but the general idea is that facts are really variants of true statements (or what are claimed to be true statements), but with a few recalcitrant forms of expression whose untranslatability disguises this dependency. '(I)f you prise the statements off the world you prise the facts off it too.'[1] While less than strict identity, the logical dependency of facts on truths is sufficient to deprive facts of their role in Correspondence as truth-constituters. (Although this second thesis is obscure, the points I shall make about the generic objection do not require us to become clearer about its details.)

A quick way with the objection would be to frame Correspondence in terms of states of affairs, situations, or some other notion in place of facts. Of course, some of the alternatives are vulnerable to objections like those brought against facts, though perhaps not so obviously. However, I shall argue that the objection fails for facts and, since this was the critic's strongest case, it frees the theory to test each of the candidates, including facts, to see which would serve best as a truth-constituter for Correspondence.

The basis for the objection is the same sort of linguistic evidence cited earlier in Davidson to show that the notion of fact could not be used *to explain* that of truth. We specify or identify a given fact by means of a set of phrases, factative-clauses. But the very same set of phrases is used to identify the statement stating that fact. For example, the statement *that bears exist* states the fact *that bears exist*. To say 'it is a fact that bears exist' seems to say no more or less than 'it is true that bears exist'. The fit is too good. There are not statement-exclusive ways of identifying or individuating facts. We conclude that our 'fact' vocabulary, instead of providing a means for discoursing about an independent realm of potential non-linguistic correlates for our utterances, merely supplies a stylistic variant for presenting the contents of statements claimed to be true. Of course, this is fatal for fact-based Correspondence. A statement is not made true by corresponding to itself, but to something distinct. If facts were the right sort of distinct item, they would be identifiable independently of specifications that were also identifications of their correlative statements. The evidence indicates that this cannot be done.

Although there are minor variations between its adherents, the basic objection is familiar in the literature. Some instances were cited in the last chapter, and I list several more for illustration.

> We could . . . eliminate the word 'fact' from the language altogether, and substitute for it the longer expression 'true proposition.' . . . In ordinary usage they are surely identical, in that whenever we assert that something is a fact we could assert that it is true without change of meaning.
>
> A. D. Woozley (1966), p. 12.

> There is no nuance, except of style, between 'That's true' and 'That's a fact'; nor between 'Is it true that . . .?' and 'Is it a fact that . . .?' [Facts and statements] were made for each other.
>
> P. F. Strawson (1950), pp. 196–7.

only indirection results from positing facts, in the image of sentences, as intermediaries. . . . In ordinary usage 'fact' often occurs where we could without loss say 'true sentence' or (if it is our way) 'true proposition'.

Willard Van Orman Quine (1960), p. 247.

['Corresponds with the facts'] gain[s] a use only by being allowed as a substitute for 'is true'.

Simon Blackburn (1984), p. 225.

Let us use the title 'differentiating formulation' for a method of identifying a particular fact that would not also be, *mutatis mutandis*, a method for identifying the statement which states it. What the argument, either for (1) or (2), requires is that if facts are (known to be) independent entities with the ability play their role in a fact-based Correspondence, they must have differentiating formulations. Otherwise 'fact' just seems to be a word to stand proxy for 'true'. Since there are no differentiating formulations, it is usually concluded that, (2), there are no facts over and above true statements.

My first complaint about this argument is that the conclusion is too strong for the evidence; for there are too many other potential explanations for the absence of differentiating formulations. For example, the absence may be due to a scarcity of vocabulary and syntactic structures, or to an inflexibility in our language for inventing and incorporating new forms of expression. Or it may result from our own limitations as users: either because we lack the capability of inventing such forms or because the purposes to which we put language are unlikely to have prompted us to have invented them. To expect that differentiating formulations would be at hand, without regard either to the language in question or its users, is to harbour unwarranted expectations about the expressive resources a language must have and about the forms of expression in which speakers are likely to have been tutored.

(1), that we *do not know* that there are facts, and this because of the absence of differentiating formulations of facts, is a properly modest conclusion, and may be more plausibly inferred from the evidence cited. Unfortunately, it is also too weak to support the objection against fact-based Correspondence unless it can be used as a warrant for (2), the thesis that there are no facts. However, the above-mentioned competing explanations for the lack of differentiating formulations robs (1) of its power to support that objection. Thus, the objection seems to fail.

But is there any reason to believe that an explanation other than the objection's is actually correct? I think so. Various philosophers have remarked that the causes leading us to note facts are largely the same as those for which we could be expected to utilize statements. We heed facts because of our pressing concern for what is the case, or at least because of a number of concerns that require us to determine what is the case. We make and obtain statements for similar reasons. This characterization is certainly too sketchy for many purposes, but the crucial point is that any way which one would want to elaborate it, its further development would be applicable to facts and statements alike. If so, it is understandable why, even if facts and statements were distinct, it would be difficult to find forms of expression appropriate to relating a particular fact that would not also be appropriate to relating the statement stating it. This explanation of the similarity of the two vocabularies does not support the denial that facts and (true) statements are distinct items. It is not that *talk about* facts and *talk about* statements are talk about the same things, but rather that talk about facts and statements themselves (not talk about them) talk about the same things. This explanation for the lack of differentiating formulations strikes me as more promising than (2). Of course, one reason it seems more promising is that it is consistent with the intuitive appeal of the belief that there are facts. But that can be allowed without begging the question against the objection. The objection would be that, notwith-standing the intuitive appeal of a world with some non-linguistic facts, there cannot be any facts as distinct from truths if we cannot identify facts by formulae that would differentiate them from the statements stating them. The rejoinder made here is that the last conditional clause is mistaken. We might be unable to so differentiate facts, but we can account for this in a way that does not injure the claim that they have a distinct identity.

Let us look at the problem from another angle, as it develops. Initially we wanted to know what it is that makes something true. We seem driven back to the answer that something is true if and only if things are as it says they are. As Strawson writes: 'a statement is true if and only if things are as one who makes that statement thereby states them to be. A belief is true if and only if things are as one who holds that belief thereby holds them to be. . . . Thus if someone says that Peter is bald, what he says is true if and only if Peter is bald.' And he adds, 'in raising the general question we wanted something more substantial than this trivial-seeming formula'.[2] In the light of the last chapter we can see that Correspondence is more substantial. For, while the connective 'if and only if' only need express necessary and sufficient conditions, or it might mark any number of things less clearly, Correspondence says, for example, that Peter is bald *is made true*, or *its truth is constituted by*, a certain fact, state of affairs, situation or satisfaction of the property baldness by Peter. Introducing the world-item as the reason, cause or constituter of truth, and going on to say (at least, with a list of candidates including facts) what the similar-sounding form of words on the right side represents makes a great difference. Taking seriously the implications of these changes seems to me to leave us with a substantial claim, if anything does, not the one disparaged as trivial by Strawson. However, Strawson would no doubt retort that what makes the formula trivial-sounding is not the connective 'if and only if' or the absence of the mention of facts, but that the specification of the content of the statement on the left side of the equation is homophonic with the specification of the content of the fact (or whatever) on the right side. And unless this can be overcome, the formula will remain an insufficiently substantial answer to a theory-inviting question.

It is here that we must reflect on what we should expect if fact-based Correspondence were true. Whatever general point there may be in having language users specify facts, it surely overlaps to a great extent, if not entirely, with whatever general point there may be for making statements. Why should we expect there to be salient vocabulary for doing the one that wouldn't be just the resources for accomplishing the other? And if by some chance there existed for a brief period a fragment of vocabulary or syntax that could be used, say, to specify particular facts, but not to formulate statements stating those facts, given the way language changes and the latitude for contriving new forms, have we any reason to expect that this situation would persist for very long? Finally, given that this is just what we should expect if fact-based Correspondence were correct, its obtaining surely cannot be converted into an objection to Correspondence. It may lead us, in the desire for a more elaborate account, to pose questions that are offshoots of our original one: say, questions about the meaning of 'is true', or the point of a truth-predicate. Correspondence need have no quarrel with such inquiries, but the spirit in which they are undertaken is often mislocated. They *are not*, as so often advertised, the basis for substitutes for Correspondence or replacements for a defective question. Rather, they are the subjects to which we turn because the initial question (1') of Chapter 2 has been satisfactorily answered, and we thus now find it is time to pursue a deeper understanding *via* elaboration.

Even those who maintain the objection being discussed may be expected to recognize that the fit between facts and truths (or true statements) is not perfect. We can utter sentences such as the following:

The fact that the airline went bankrupt caused me to miss my vacation.

She gathered he was nervous from the fact that he spilled his drink.

There were facts before any languages were around with which to utter truths.

Here 'truths' or 'true statements' are not adequate substitutes for 'fact'. And 'brute facts' are not 'brute truths', while those who favour the objection under discussion do not believe that because the world contains no facts it thereby contains no truths. Moreover, true statements can be made in English, facts cannot, and the contradictory of a false statement isn't a fact.[3] But the objectors may be sufficiently impressed by the similarity of the formulations in which particular facts and statements are identified as such to minimize the significance of these differences. They may be dismissed as marginal variations, or taken as grounds for maintaining only the reduced claim that facts are not logically independent of true statements. However, I think these various differences may be refashioned into an improved rejoinder to the original objection. They can be considered not so much as things we may say about individual facts (statements) that cannot be said about the individual statements stating them (the individual facts

57

which they state); but rather as *general* features of facts or statements that the other member of the pair lacks. For example, facts cause things. And while this is true of true statements also, it is a statement in the sense of *what is stated* (= its content) that has a chance of identification with facts, but a statement in the sense of the stating of it (= the act) which can be a cause. And we may mount an additional challenge to the demand for differentiating formulations by holding that it is sufficient to distinguish facts *in general* from truths or true statements *in general* in order to show that similarly formulated particular facts and the statements stating them need not be identical.

No doubt it is equally true that desks and crates are not identical in general, but this does not prevent my desk from being (identical with) an old crate. However, this does not alter the main point. It is the distinction between facts and statements as classes of items that is at issue. Whatever the merits of claims that some particular fact and some particular statement are identical, as long as this is the same sort of random occurrence as the conjunction of a particular desk and an orange crate, the objection to facts as candidates for truth-constituters is defeated.

Another objection to facts, which to varying degrees had influenced Russell, Ramsey, Ayer and Prior,[4] is based on the view that the clauses specifying facts are not names of those facts. If facts are items 'in the world', shouldn't we be able to name them? But sentences such as 'It is a fact that p' and 'p is a fact' cannot use 'p' as the name of a fact, for they have the same significance when they are true as when they are false. But when they are false there would be nothing to name, and thus statements made with these sentences should manifest reference-failure, which they evidently do not.

If this objection were cogent, it could also be used to show that there are no truths; for similar remarks could be made, *mutatis mutandis*, about 'It is true that p' and 'p is true'. However, adequate rejoinders to this objection can forgo relief from that quarter. The main point is that, because the objection trades on moot uses of such notions as object and name, it cannot be taken to show anything of significance. Let us call what can be named an *object*. Let us also admit, for the sake of argument, that facts cannot be named (at least in an interesting way) and that they are therefore not objects. But, *over and above what has been conceded*, what does it mean to deny that facts are 'in the world'? It may be admitted that, although there is some sense in which facts can be 'referred to', they are essentially the sort of thing that can be *stated* rather than named.[5] But if that isn't just a way of repeating what has been conceded, it is still wholly unilluminating. On the other side, facts *involve* objects in a very familiar way: the fact that bears exist has as a constituent bears. This is not to say that facts are just compound objects; they are more like complexes of objects. But structure counts. That Othello loves Desdemona is a different fact from that Desdemona loves Othello, although on any promising scheme all the same objects are involved in both. But although we may want to distinguish facts from compound objects, it is difficult to see how anything having objects as constituents could fail to be part of the same world as those constituents. In addition, there is an admittedly unexplicated sense in which a world unlike ours *only* in being shorn of the facts to which we lay claim is much less profuse than ours. Of course, this does not mean that it contains *fewer objects* than our world, for we have conceded that facts are not objects.

But why should the difficulty of elucidating this kind of profusion in terms of objects be charged against this persuasive observation rather than against the ontology that forces us to explain the remark in terms of its narrow notion of an object? Moreover, whatever sense it is in which it is true that a certain fact has bears as its constituent, it is *not* equally true that the sentence 'Bears exist', or the statement made with it, also has bears as a constituent. The sentence (statement) may involve the word 'bears', or even a *word for* bears, but the fact does not require such intermediaries.

This exhausts, to my knowledge, the grounds on which it is held that the vocabulary of 'facts' is nothing more than a stylistic variant for that of 'truths'. Let us then turn to a rather different kind of attack.

3 BRAINS IN VATS AND REFERENCE: PUTNAM'S CHALLENGE

Hilary Putnam has recently objected to what he calls 'the copy theory of truth'.[6] It maintains that '(t)ruth involves some sort of correspondence relation between words or thought-signs and external things and sets of things' (p. 49); in brief, Correspondence. But the objection also touches upon other matters. Putnam first attacks a sceptical hypothesis that we might be disembodied brains in vats, kept alive in a nutrient fluid and obtaining through an artificial and possibly purposeless means experiences mistakenly regarded as resulting from contact with an external world very unlike the vat in which, *ex hypothesi*, we would be contained. In the course of the argument he states a few principles about the nature of reference and belief that start the objection to Correspondence. We begin by displaying the anti-sceptical argument.

Let 'S' abbreviate a statement made with the sentence 'I have always been a brain in a vat'. Putnam argues:

1 I can hypothesize that S.
2 If I can hypothesize that S, I can refer to brains and vats.
3 Necessarily, if I can refer to brains and vats, I have had genuine (namely, non-hallucinatory) experiences of brains and vats.
4 If S is true, I have not had genuine experiences of brains and vats.
5 I can refer to brains and vats (from 1 and 2).
6 I have had genuine experiences of brains and vats (from 3 and 5).
7 S is false (from 4 and 6).

(Alternatively, we might use the argument to show that *either* S *or* step 1 is false.) The steps of this argument that concern us are 2 and 3. 2 generalized affirms, in effect, that beliefs *presuppose* reference (or the ability to refer). Putnam clearly intends a hierarchy, with belief, and we might add *intentions to refer*, resting on the ability to refer. 3 generalized implies that 'mental presentations' alone are insufficient to account for reference. To illustrate, Putnam asks us to imagine an ant whose path in the sand happens to trace an outline resembling Winston Churchill's profile. It is no more a *representation* of Churchill than the man in the moon is a representation of a man. Thus, pure resemblance, in mental as well as physical images, is insufficient for representing something beyond the medium itself. Moreover, words or mental-signs have similar inadequacies. Putnam uses the setting of

Turing's imitation game to argue that apparently intelligent discourse which is not properly sensitive to changes or unrealized possibilities in its would-be referents cannot contain actual references to the external world, and thus cannot express beliefs about that world. The kinds of connections Putnam believes are missing will be discussed later.

To get from steps 2 and 3 to an anti-Correspondence conclusion requires a further manoeuvre. Putnam offers as a theorem, put informally, that for any *standard* interpretation of singular terms and predicates yielding an assignment of truth-values to statements of the language, there are a multitude of alternative interpretations (call them *non-standard*, though this deviates from the usual model-theoretic use of this term) which will preserve all assignments of truth-values in all possible worlds (namely, specifications of truth-conditions). He illustrates it in the main text and sets out a proof in an appendix. One way to report Putnam's lesson would be to say that assigning statements (/sentences) truth-conditions does not uniquely determine what they refer to. Another is to say that referring expressions have *many different word–world connections*, each of which has an equal claim to be called the referential relation and no one of which can reasonably be claimed to be the exclusively correct one. Given 2, beliefs will vary with interpretations of reference, and thus many different sets of beliefs will provide true total descriptions of the world. But, according to Putnam, Correspondence and the metaphysical (or global) realism it embodies require that there be a uniquely correct description of reality. Since standard and non-standard interpretations supply distinct but equally adequate descriptions of the world, Correspondence must be mistaken. 3 is important in eliminating a popular rejoinder to this conclusion. We seem naturally inclined to believe that we know what we mean by our words and that from mental resources alone we can show that the correct interpretation of our words is the standard one. The objection to the sufficiency of mental and verbal signs for reference is used in several instances to show that these beliefs are mistaken.

I shall not discuss in any detail whether the argument refutes this form of scepticism. But to evaluate its claims against Correspondence we must scrutinize its contentions about the nature of reference, belief and the relation between them. As for reference,

Putnam has located a genuine problem. When we place ourselves in a certain frame of mind it is remarkable that with verbal and mental signs we can cast out mental hooks, as it were, to grab on to things beyond them. Indeed, in *Gulliver's Travels* Jonathan Swift satirized just such a frame of mind. He created academicians of Lagado who went everywhere burdened by large pedlar's packs containing everything about which they might have occasion to discourse. In that way, while discussing something they could have it before them, which presumably relieved their bewilderment at how communication could be accomplished. Despite Swift's ingenious lampoon, the concern need not be silly. But although Putnam has located an issue, I shall argue that he hasn't resolved it. He disparages what he calls 'magical theories of reference', presumably those that hold that this can be done by basically mental resolve. But I shall hold that if Putnam is not radically sceptical about the possibility of reference, he is committed to a view that is equally 'magical' on his own requirements. It turns out that the connections between belief, reference and intention are more complicated than the asymmetry for which Putnam opts: in particular, their relations are symbiotic rather than parasitic.

Let us begin by considering Putnam's proposed solution to the referential puzzle. To repeat, he uses the setting of Turing's imitation game to argue that mental presentations and words have no intrinsic relation to their references. Any token which would have such a connection must be supplemented by two kinds of *rule*, which Putnam describes.

> There are 'language entry rules' which take us from
> experiences of apples to such utterances as 'I see an apple',
> and 'language exit rules' which take us from decisions
> expressed in linguistic form ('I am going to buy some apples')
> to actions other than speaking. Lacking either language entry
> rules or language exit rules there is no reason to regard the
> conversation of the machine . . . as more than syntactic play.
> (p. 11)

It is not immediately obvious how we are to implement these requirements. An internalized rule is no doubt realized as an *ability*. And Putnam seems to think of these rules as so embodied (pp. 18–20). An ability is, very roughly, something like *a disposition to behave* in certain ways and under certain circumstances, rather than a particular manifestation or set of manifestations. But if Putnam's entry and exit rules are, on the psychological side, only dispositions or abilities, a brain in a vat might have such rules. We may illustrate the point with language entry rules. If we are not to beg any questions, Putnam must imagine the utterance of 'I see an apple' not as a sentence of English, together with part of its significance already determined by references, but as a mere string of (mental) noises. A brain in a vat can certainly have that: 'the people in that possible world can think and "say" any words we can think and say' (p. 8). Moreover, they can have an experiential life that is phenomenally indistinguishable from ours, even if it is only of what Putnam calls their *notional* world. Such brains may not have senses that enable them to see apples. But since they have the same disposition towards notional apples as actual speakers of English are supposed to have towards real apples, and since, *ex hypothesi*, they are in the phenomenal state of someone who thinks she is experiencing a real apple, it would appear that they have just the same disposition and ability to utter those words if they should (actually) see an apple as have speakers of English. In fact, without changing the envatted brain's mental contents at all, but only putting it in a body, its linguistic behaviour upon sighting an apple would be indistinguishable from that of a native speaker. Both are equally likely – which isn't very likely – to utter those noises upon seeing an apple. A similar case could be made for the possession by brains in vats of language exit rules. Thus, the presence of such rules wouldn't distinguish English speakers from brains in vats.

The way round the foregoing objection would be to construe the embodied rules as other than abilities, or abilities as more unlike dispositions. There are a few hints that Putnam would press one of these alternatives, as when he approvingly discusses Wittgenstein's treatment of 'rule following', and says, for example, that 'it is the practice that fixes the interpretation: signs do not interpret themselves' (p. 67). But these are casual remarks, which do not even begin to sketch a genuine alternative to a dispositional view of rules. If Putnam would associate the rule only with its manifestations, how could he formulate *any* definite rule covering unmanifested cases, since, as he emphasizes, our practice is always compatible with an infinity of different rules? If having the rule is more than has been manifested in our practice, what could the rule be if not a kind of disposition? These questions are difficult enough in themselves and Putnam doesn't indicate a tendency to address them. Thus, it seems better to construe his discussion of these Wittgensteinian points (like the discussion of Kant) as illustrations of historical precedent for his views rather than as serious evidence for interpreting them. The only point in Putnam's discussion which we can rely upon is that, when rules taking us into and out of the language are present, we can be assured that our words have reference.

Apart from difficulties just mentioned, the solution simply doesn't work. Putnam has certainly described cases in which, should they obtain, it would be absurd to deny that the speaker was referring. But both the exit and entry rules do this by employing a level of description that presupposes that the speaker has the kinds of *beliefs* which Putnam maintains can only be accounted for by the ability to refer. This may have escaped his notice because the beliefs in question are not presupposed by the utterances, but by the experience and actions, respectively, with which the utterances are paired. Thus, these rules *presuppose* the very abilities which they are supposed to account for.

This is easily seen for *exit* rules in which we are asked to describe the agent's movement as an intentional action (such as buying apples). Not all human physical movements are actions. The most widely received view is that actions are distinguished from mere physical motions by combining them with, broadly construed, relevant wants and beliefs. For example, suppose the agent takes a coin out of his pocket and extends it in an open hand to the grocer. Unless the agent *believed* that this constituted payment for an apple, would this count as buying an apple? Of course, Putnam might want to replace the orthodoxy with another analysis of action. But in lieu of a concrete suggestion, I see no way of avoiding attributing beliefs as a condition of agency. Thus, the scene Putnam describes does not take us from non-reference to reference, *if*, as he asserts, *we cannot have belief till we have reference*, but rather it presupposes both belief and reference.

However, since Putnam says we only need exit *or* entry rules, let us see whether we fare better with the latter. For entry rules we do not require an action, but only an experience. However, the experience cannot be so thin as a mere sensory exposure to apples. If we are to have the right connection between the experience and the utterance 'I see an apple', it must be something we *take* for an apple. And taking is a form of believing. The type of experience Putnam requires once again presupposes belief.

It is evident that Putnam's entry and exit rules work *not* because he has supplied the missing ingredient that makes reference work, but because he has described a situation in which reference is already an ongoing enterprise. This is a situation which contains a mixture of reference, belief, intention and so on, a mixture which the account of reference was supposed to elucidate.

The second objection was that the relations between belief and reference must be more complicated than step 2 suggests. Putnam argues that we cannot have a belief without reference, but there is an equal difficulty in seeing how we can make a reference without belief. This point is connected with the previous one. We may begin with Putnam's insistence that reference cannot be secured by mental or verbal signs alone. What is lacking? Although he raises various objections to what he takes to be a causal theorist's solution to this sort of problem, and even rejects a certain kind of causal connection as too 'weak a connection to suffice for reference' (p. 11), what suggestions he does make have to do with experiential connections between our use of language and, loosely speaking, non-linguistic practice. It is through perceptual experience that we can capture best what it is that allows us to use terms referentially.

Putnam's discussion of the actual practice of reference may be seriously flawed in its details, and in particular may underrate the central role of second-hand referential expressions. (How many people who use the word 'brain' to refer to brains have first perceived one?) But for our purposes we may overlook the details of the account, and take as our example his most favourable case: the ostensive learning of an expression. Wth regard even to these cases some philosophers now realize that it is not what one actually sees that matters, but what one *believes* one sees.[7] Once again, the kind of 'experience' in question here cannot be mere sensory exposure: for it is *how one takes* the experience that will determine the use made of the referring expression. Thus, it would appear that one could learn the use of the term 'water' as effectively from a series of illusions as from a series of legitimate specimens.

It must be emphasized that this *need not* conflict with Putnam's anti-realist point that the objects of our reference are those we experience, and that they are not affected by an inaccessible noumenal realm whose nature our referential expressions may misdescribe (for example, pp. 50–2). Even the non-realist would want to draw a distinction between veridical and non-veridical experiences. And nothing in Putnam's argument against the possible truth of S warrants the claim that our experiences could not be systematically misleading. That is, we can imagine a run of cases in which a language learner was regularly deceived into believing that the things she experienced were, say, real skeletons. Indeed, if it weren't for humanitarian constraints on human experimentation we could easily devise such a case. Such an individual might have a perfectly normal ability to refer to skeletons by the expression 'skeleton' if, counterfactually, she ever encountered one. Conversely, without any *beliefs about skeletons* – for example, that such-and-such is an instance of one – it is difficult to see how we could ever develop the ability to refer to skeletons. Now it looks as if it is reference that presupposes belief rather than vice versa.

Other examples in the literature seem to reinforce this point. Gareth Evans[8] noted that Marco Polo's naming of the present Malagasy Republic as 'Madagascar' depended on his mistaken belief that this was his informants' name for that island. If we discounted Polo's beliefs, and those of the Europeans to whom he subsequently taught it, we would be left without any plausible explanation why 'Madagascar' didn't continue to refer to a part of the African mainland.

Thus, Putnam's theses that belief is posterior to reference and that connections with non-linguistic experience and activity *account for* referential abilities should both be scrapped. Moreover, assuming that we are not envatted brains, in the fact that an envatted brain whose experience is phenomenally comparable to ours would have just our tendency to vocalize 'apple' if it could be brought to experience an apple, we have some basis for holding that the brain is 'speaking' English, albeit *sotto voce*, despite its extraordinary way of acquiring the language. Is there any further reason to suppose that an envatted brain, with phenomenally comparable experience, does not refer? One argument may be culled from Putnam's notorious Twin Earthians, who use the word 'water' for a phenomenally indistinguishable but chemically distinct liquid from water on Earth (pp. 22–5). An initial explanation for the difference of referents is that the Twin Earthians' use of 'water' is causally yoked to a substance different from ours. But the case does not readily transfer to that of a brain in a vat. It is not simply that the Twin Earthians lack the appropriate causal connections to our water: they also have an appropriate connection to a different sort of substance, and moreover one which is not preceptually misconstrued and has a scientific account that differentiates it from water. None of this is true of the envatted brain, which 'notionally' believes it is *not* 'notionally' perceiving 'notional' water. In brief, it is deceived. Moreover, there is no chemistry of its notional water. The compelling reasons for distinguishing the references of the Twin Earthians from those of the Earthians do not apply here. For these accumulated reasons, this stage of the argument against Correspondence fails.

An overview of Putnam's argument for a generalization of step 3 – 'necessarily, if I can refer to something, I have had genuine experiences of that thing' – is revealing. It exemplifies a type of appeal which has a wider popularity in philosophy. I shall call it an 'additive strategy'. Because Putnam falls into a common trap to which the strategy is particularly susceptible, looking at his argument in this light may be even more generally useful.

The first stage, or point of departure, of the strategy is seldom stated explicitly, but it is vital. It is some depiction of the paradigm situation in which it is taken for granted, and uncontroversial, that the practice to be explained occurs. The strategy is, in other words, decidedly non-sceptical. The next stage takes us backwards, by stripping away the vital elements, to a more primitive situation, which others may have mistakenly thought was sufficient to give rise to the phenomenon under study. For reference (according to Putnam), at the first stage the language user interacts with its environment, as encapsulated in the entrance and exit rules, and at the second is the mental sign or image which is taken to secure reference. In Wittgensteinian discussions of rule-following or, related to this, private language, the first stage is the social setting in which a community of users check one another's practices, while the second stage is, once again, a lonely mental episode which, some allege, fixes the course of behaviour on a rule or the meaning of a name. In discussions by contract theorists of the source of legitimate authority, the first stage is the ongoing state with its apparatus in place, while the second stage is the state of nature in which individuals exact concessions from one another, often by force. It is the third stage for which the additive strategy gets its title; for it raises the question 'What has to be added to the inadequate solution of the second stage to get us from non-Xing to Xing (from non-referring to referring, from not following rules to following them, from brute force to political obligation)?'

From now on let us concentrate on Putnam's problem. He makes a few brief suggestions, discussed earlier, that fail. From their failure he proceeds to the fourth step: his own solution. But, lo and behold, the solution at this step is simply to return us to the paradigm case which was the point of departure! Putnam regards this as the successful end to his quest, but, for reasons given earlier, I regard it as a tacit admission of failure. Perhaps now we can see *why* it is failure. It is the inner working of the paradigm we wanted explained. In effect, Putnam has used the failures at stages two and three of the strategy to return us to the explanandum, but to present it as an explanans. However, the paradigm only set us looking for explanations because it already contained all the interesting mechanisms of reference, whatever they may have been, in their opaque and tangled complexity. There is no fear of falling short of sufficiency here, but for the wrong reasons: namely, the same sort of reasons that make anything a sufficient condition for itself.

Why does the quest at stages two and three fail? My view is that Putnam was looking for the wrong type of thing, *a manifestation*. Manifestations include mental images or signs, actual causal connections, performances of the imitation game, and uses of entrance and exit rules. Only a kind of *disposition* – the kind we might more particularly call a 'sensitivity' or 'responsiveness' to changing circumstances – could even be a candidate for success. No manifestation alone will assure us (even in practical terms) that reference has taken place. Putnam verges on stating this point, but the passage in which he toys with it is a casual remark, thrown out but not used again when he puts forth his official solution. He says of a machine playing the imitation game:

> Not only is it logically possible, though fantastically
> improbable, that the same machine *could* have existed even
> if apples, fields, and steeples had not existed; more important,

the machine is utterly insensitive to the *continued* existence of apples, fields, and steeples, etc. Even if all these things *ceased* to exist, the machine would still discourse just as happily in the same way. That is why the machine cannot be regarded as referring at all. (pp. 11–12)

And notice, once again, that *possession of* entrance and exit rules is a disposition (or a set of dispositions), not to be confused with a manifestation of such a rule. No particular manifestation could secure sensitivity to the continued existence or non-existence of apples and so forth, any more than a solitary performance of Turing's imitation game could do so. Accordingly, the failure of 'apple' to be referential in the envisaged circumstances is explained by the speaker's insensitivity to changes and unrealized possibilities. Nor need these be changes in real apples and so on, for we are concerned not with the accuracy of the speaker's responses, but with their appropriateness. If a wax apple should trick the speaker into saying 'apple' incorrectly, that is still the sort of manifestation of a referential ability which we sought. But accurate or not, the ability is not discoverable in a manifestation alone. Thus, it is not a mere accident that the solution Putnam ultimately defends is the possession of a certain disposition. In sum, what must be added to the 'episodic' solutions run through at stages two and three of the additive strategy is not a further episodic something or a series of episodes. What is critical is that it be an instance of something that cannot be read off from its phenomenal features: namely, responsiveness to certain kinds of situation.

This has dire consequences for Putnam's strategy, for his denial of referential abilities to the envatted brain, and, ultimately, for his argument for the generalization of step 3. First, the question of the privacy of the mental sign has nothing to do with its inadequacy. The mental sign, being a manifestation, cannot exhibit in its immediately graspable features its sensitivity to changes and unrealized possibilities. Nevertheless, it might be the manifestation of such a responsiveness. No inspection of an episode will show this, but the same is true of the entrance and exit rules themselves.[9] Second, it is unimportant whether the responses are to real or to notional apples. In normal cases interaction with real apples still must fall far short of the unlimited sensitivity which

69

referential abilities are supposed to encompass. But it is also ordinarily supposed that these interactions are sufficient evidence for the presence of the unlimited sensitivity. There is no reason why an envatted brain's responses to notional apples should not provide similar grounds for ascribing to it whatever level of responsiveness to changes and unrealized possibilities is good enough for reference. Of course, its responses have been to notional apples. But is there any reason, short of a scepticism powerful enough to upset any dispositional solution, to suppose from the cases that it would not be equally responsive to changes and unrealized possibilities in real apples? Whatever reason might have existed is undermined by the way the topic is introduced: at least initially, the hypothesis is that *we might now be* brains in vats. If, without its knowledge, the envatted brain is embodied while asleep, and thus continues its existence as a genuine perceiver and agent, I can find no grounds for supposing that its responses to real apples will prove to be less reliable than those of any English speakers. The point to emphasize is that it is sensitivity to (potentially) changing circumstances which is a better guide to a vocable being used referentially than anything Putnam provides in its place.

Let us conclude this discussion by looking at two things Putnam might say in response to this counter-proposal.

First, he mentions that if two Turing machines played the imitation game with each other, no matter how proficient at it they were, without entrance and exit rules we would have no reason to regard them as engaged in anything 'more than syntactic play' (p. 11). But whatever force there may be to this intuition seems to stem from doubts about machines as genuine language users rather than lack of contact with the world. For the envatted brain the question is not whether its expressions are only syntactic rather than semantic: the question is the nature of its semantics. Does it refer to apples or only to notional apples? There is no question that without any alteration to the brain other than placing it in a functioning body, the resulting individual could be a fully fledged language user. The reason is that the original brain-in-a-vat hypothesis asked us to imagine such creatures as enjoying as fully complete a conscious and emotional life as embodied persons. Thus, they are intrinsically, as it were, semantic creatures. The only kinds of reasons we might have for wondering

whether the interacting Turing machines were language users
would have to do with the fact that we might want to know
whether we have something more *in kind* than complex pocket
calculators. Thus, the problem here is whether we have semantics,
and not just syntax. I do not wish to become embroiled in this
dispute; but only to make it clear that Putnam's apparent grounds
for doubt about the imitation game do not intuitively transfer to
brains in vats.

Next, let us return to the Twin Earthians. Putnam might reply
that if responsiveness is all that matters, and not genuine contact
with, say, apples, when the Twin Earthians arrive here, shouldn't
their word 'water' denote our water? Recall that the Twin
Earthians use the vocable 'water' to refer to something with chemistry XYZ, rather than, as Earthlings, something with chemistry
H_2O. But whereas apples have a chemistry, notional apples have,
at most, a notional chemistry. Moreover, we cannot suppose the
notional chemistry to be fixed at the time of the first notional
appearances of apples. Therefore, brains in vats do not stand to
persons as Twin Earthians stand to Earthlings. Envatted brains
do not refer to a different kind of thing, for notional apples are
not a kind of apple, but only the illusions of (real) apples. And,
indeed, if we suppose (for the sceptical hypothesis) that everything
is otherwise the same for envatted brains, we must allow them
(as we would initially describe it) the belief that their apples have
the chemistry of real apples, not a notional chemistry. When Twin
Earthians and Earthlings finally meet, after making some mistakes
about each other's liquid called 'water', they can realize their
mistakes and agree that they were referring to different things.
But when envatted brains become embodied and enlightened, the
most they might concede is that they didn't come to learn what
apples were like through seeing, tasting (and so on) real apples.
The content of their instruction is in fact indistinguishable from
that of those who learn what brains are through pictures or
descriptions – that is, from the vast majority of users of the term
'brain'. The one difference is that envatted brains thought that
their mental pictures were real apples. If Putnam is still willing to
maintain that the envatted brains could not refer to real apples,
having never confronted or reacted to one, we may say that it is
no worse a position in this respect than Putnam is in referring to
(talking about) the Twin Earthians' word 'water'. This is not, as

it may first appear, a mere *ad hominem*. Putnam's scenario seems a perfectly good one, and its convincingness is a concrete demonstration of how we can manage to refer to things we have not encountered. (I don't believe there is an escape clause or special dispensation here to be applied to our philosophical musings but not applicable to its subject-matter.)

4 ONE WORLD, MANY DESCRIPTIONS

We have yet to examine Putnam's alleged proof that the truth-conditions of our sentences and mental signs do not determine a unique interpretation of our statements and beliefs. As Alvin Platinga has observed,[10] the argument rests on the peculiar assumption that the expressions of our language receive their meanings or their extensions by virtue of a set of models of first order formalizations of our beliefs. Whatever the failings of competing semantic theories, this is an independently implausible view. Not only is there no initial reason supporting it, but there also seem to be excellent reasons for rejecting it. The ability to map countable anythings on to equinumerous anything-elses assures us that there will be as many isomorphic models for a theory with a countable domain (having at least one non-universal, non-empty predicate) as there are possible permutations of predicates. Indeed, it is unclear why we need restrict ourselves to isomorphism. We are guaranteed that any theory with a countable model for n members has a model for every domain with at least n members, including a model of every infinite cardinality.[11] This means, among other things, that a theory A – say with a certain number of elephants – can be mapped by a permutation of the relation between its elephant predicate and the predicate's extension on to the domain of any theory A* with a property whose extension is at least equinumerous with elephants – say, natural numbers. But it is difficult to see why this shows that our referring expressions are indeterminate between elephants and a subset of natural numbers. Indeed, all it seems to show is that the beliefs in the theory form a consistent set. If it shows more, this has yet to be explained.

This is not quite the way Putnam puts his conclusion, though it is not far from the actual use he makes of the point. What he says is that this result follows *if we fix reference only by fixing truth-values of whole sentences*. Even that is not strictly what he shows. For his theorem presupposes a fixed domain of a set of possible objects for each possible world in order to obtain a permutation on the relation forming the extension of its predicates. But what could this domain of objects be if not *fixed referents*? The whole procedure depends upon introducing strategies from philosophical contexts in which this doesn't matter (for example, proofs of meta-theorems for formal systems) into contexts in which this is just what is at issue.

In fact, we can see by using an illustration how the philosophical consequences of Putnam's proof misfire. His argument is generated only if we are able to pick out different sorts – say, elephant and natural number – to be paired in distinct interpretations. But if the only way to arrive at a denotation for elephants is radically indeterminate, where do we get the determinate predicates needed for the argument's different interpretations? Thus, we might wish to begin by saying that we don't have different interpretations, but an all-embracing one in which the members of the domain have any or all of the characters we are able to ascribe to it in what we originally thought were its distinct models. But we cannot even say this, for any conjunction or disjunction of our former predicates still requires that the conjuncts or disjuncts (our former predicate expressions such as 'is an elephant') be understood determinately. How, then, are we to characterize our predicates, and, by extension, the 'bare particulars' of our domain? We cannot even invent a name for some of them, such as 'blurgs'; for then we can permute the extension of this predicate into, say, 'grulbs' and 'glurbs', thereby reinstituting the problem that led us to abandon 'elephant' and 'number'. In our effort to explain the problem, we are finally reduced to an inarticulate cry. Isn't this just a *reductio ad absurdum* of the peculiar assumption about the way to determine meanings and extensions?

However, the argument betrays a deeper and more traditional concern: namely, the multiplicity of correct descriptions of what the global realist takes to be a single reality. This is a stock anti-realist objection and, despite the model theoretic wrapping, it is also basically Putnam's complaint.

The name Putnam gives the view under attack is 'external

realism'. (He takes his own view to be a form of realism, 'internal realism', but on our taxonomy it is a version of global anti-realism.) External realism is characterized as follows: 'the world consists of some fixed totality of mind-independent objects. There is exactly one true and complete description of "the way the world is" ' (p. 49). Although Putnam may not countenance a distinction between the two statements, a little reflection makes it obvious that they do not say the same thing. Nevertheless, his attack rests upon their relationship. Therefore, let us have a canonical, slightly modified, formulation of each:

(1) The world consists of a fixed totality of objects, at least some of which are mind-independent.

(2) There is exactly one true and complete description of the world.

In subsequent discussion the author seeks to discredit not (2) directly, but a companion claim about referring expressions.

(2') There is exactly one correct interpretation of our referring expressions (all other, extensionally equivalent interpretations being mistaken).

But, for simplicity, we can examine the case as if it concerned only (2). It might be supposed that, since (2) mentions 'true and complete descriptions', our two statements would be more congruous if we replaced mention of 'objects' in (1) with that of 'states of affairs'. But again, we can let our original formulation of (1) stand. It is worth noting that we could replace either (1) or (2) or both if the need arose. It won't for our limited purpose.

(1) is a fair, succinct summary of metaphysical realism, framed about things rather than truths. (I shall presently express a scruple about the mention of a 'fixed totality' in (1), but we can overlook that for the nonce.) Moreover, it would not be unfair to allow the fate of global realism to weigh in its balance. In Chapter 1 we suggested that Correspondence could survive the rejection of the world's mind-independence by sharply distinguishing its task of delivering the nature of truth from that of claiming that any statements are true. However, this would be a Pyrrhic victory, for two reasons. First, advocates of Correspondence would be much less devoted to the theory if they did not also believe that an overwhelming majority of our ordinary 'truths' could be salvaged

without reductive analysis. Second, Correspondence has always been a large part of the defence of claims such as (1); in some cases perhaps a sufficient ground for the latter. Thus, in striking at (1) Putnam and others are aiming at a vital part of the view which we are in the process of defending. The looming problem here is that the rejection of (1) goes through an assault upon (2), and it is in the relationship between these two claims that we encounter difficulties both of understanding and credibility.

At a minimum, the objection to metaphysical realism is committed to the view that (1) logically implies (2). Thus, by arguing for the falsity of (2), through (2'), it implies the falsity of (1). To elaborate, if the world contains determinate, mind-independent objects, as in (1), then one of its potential descriptions must be the correct one. However, we are confounded by a multiplicity of equally applicable descriptions, with no grounds for declaring one objectively correct and the others wrong. Therefore, the world cannot be as (1) claims it is. (This conclusion is really the confluence of this and another sort of consideration: namely, that all description is emblematic of a conceptual scheme. And if our descriptions are mediated by conceptual schemes, reality is not merely being labelled as it is found, but is 'to some extent shaped by our concepts' (p. 54). We shall examine this additional consideration in section 5.)

The objection collapses because (1) does not imply (2); thus, a multiplicity of descriptions shows nothing about the subjective or non-subjective nature of what is described. Earlier I parenthetically alluded to a scruple about the phrase 'fixed totality' bearing on this. Anti-realists seem to rest the argument on our inability to *complete* an inventory of objects; and this, I shall argue, is irrelevant to the issue of mind-dependence. It may at first seem more relevant to obtain a *unique* characterization of some fragment of reality. But, I shall also argue, even this may not bear on whether the world being described is mind-dependent. That is, we may be unable to complete descriptions of the world, or uniquely describe any part of it, for reasons having nothing to do with the mind-dependence of what is being described. The metaphysical realist could, and I believe should, hold that the fixed objects in the world may or may not be exhaustively describable. Thus, the question of 'totalities' drops from consideration. What must be determined is not whether our descriptions are completable or unique, but whether their not being so is assignable to the mind-dependence of the subject-matter. If not the argument fails.

As a prologue, consider an obvious way, having nothing to do with the issues dividing realists and anti-realists, in which a complete description might be thwarted. Perhaps a finite complete description would have to be so general that it was empty, and the only alternative would be, *per impossibile*, an infinite formula. This failure to complete a description would not dim the prospects of realism. At first it may appear more to the point that there be a *unique* description of any given mind-independent portion of the world. It is unclear why this need be so if it is a question of preferring description A to B, where neither description is included in the other. But even if we grant that there must be a unique description of some sort, this may fail again for the reason that the description is not completable. Under these circumstances, we may be justified in regarding the failure differently than the anti-realist. With that in mind, let us turn to the kinds of competing descriptions to which an anti-realist might appeal.

To get a firm grasp of the notion of an alternative description it is best to begin with familiar cases. Controversies surrounding the more exotic specimens prevent us from drawing clear morals. The one requirement of our review is that all the descriptions in a set be ones we are inclined to say are *correct*. (There is no threat for realism from a multiplicity of incorrect descriptions.) Given that, it appears that there are two sorts of relatively commonplace cases in which we have correct descriptions that are in competition:

(a) descriptions differing in amount, degree or level of detail;
(b) descriptions cross-classifying what are in some sense the same set of phenomena.

Although (b) seems more pertinent to (2), both reveal something about the nature of our supposedly non-unique descriptions. Thus, we shall begin with (a).

An occupant of a certain location is described as a Swiss Army Knife. 'It' might also have been described as a collection of blades, implements, casing and so forth, with no mention of a knife. No one supposes that metaphysical realism requires these sorts of descriptions to preclude the other. The same would seem to hold for all descriptions related in this way by amount, degree or level of detail. A first thought might be that we could craft a *unique* description by conjoining these, together with any others related to them in the same way, to form a single description. But a second thought is that the detail of any fragment of the describable world is inexhaustible; thus no finite description could have the required uniqueness. If this is so, it shows what is wrong with (2), but has no implications for the realism expressed by (1). The description couldn't be unique because it couldn't be complete. But that part of the world might still be mind-independent, even if too luxuriant to be captured in a single description. And the Swiss Army Knife might, for all that, be there, independently of the ability of any sentient creature to conceptualize or perceive it. An anti-realist is not likely to deny this. After all it only concerns (a). My contention is that the problems arising for (b), though perhaps more complex, are really not of a different order. Let us then turn to (b).

Nobody disputes the possibility of classifying animals, normally sorted phyletically, by size, diet, geographical distribution, colour, as tailed or tailless and so on, or even without regard to their being organisms (say, by weight along with other objects having rest mass). Apparently these possibilities are unproblematic for realism. But they are also too mundane, cross-classifying as they do the same individuals. Let us then turn to one of Jorge Luis Borges' fictions – fictional even within his tale – about a planet Tlön.

> The literature of this hemisphere (like Meinong's subsistent world) abounds in ideal objects, which are convoked and dissolved in a moment, according to poetic needs. At times they are determined by mere simultaneity. There are objects composed of two terms, one of visual and another of auditory character: the color of the rising sun and the faraway cry of a bird.[12]

This greatly increases the possibilities for cross-classification, but just the same prospects for a unique description of any fragment of this reality (on a given description to determine its boundaries) exist. It is perhaps now easier to appreciate how a unique description obtained by combining all the possible ones can be hindered by the difficulty of completing it. But this has no tendency to show that each of the legitimate descriptions we could muster are not descriptions of mind-independent objects, things 'out there'. This brings us close to Putnam's original argument. His extended possibilities are perhaps even more recherché than those of Borges'. But even if we allow the model-theoretic determination of ordinary denotation, his theorem shows no more than the Borges examples. We may be unable to get a unique description of a fragment of reality because we cannot get a complete one. This has no tendency to show that what we do describe contains subjective or mind-dependent elements.

It may be objected that we have overlooked the gravest threat to metaphysical realism: competing, equally applicable but *incompatible* descriptions, descriptions that cannot be combined into a larger conjunction. If such cases existed, they would indeed be food for thought. But before asking whether there are such cases, let us note that they would not lead directly to anti-realism, and might more appropriately lead to a form of scepticism. They would not immediately lead to anti-realism because the explanation for this phenomenon might not be that we are only describing a mind-dependent reality. And such an explanation might even seem unlikely when we ponder a typical anti-realist tactic. To elaborate, when confronted with putative cases, the realist may relativize the frameworks in which the descriptions are given, and thereby remove the incompatibility. Thus, working with a crude example, when the anti-realist says I am sitting still, but moving (with the earth), the realist may reply that I am sitting still relative to the earth, but moving relative to the sun. A typical anti-realist response is that this palliative loses something in the 'translation'. And, as I shall explain presently, that is very likely a just observation. However, if the anti-realist rejects this counter-move, it is difficult to see why the anti-realist's own counter-move, which could be viewed as relativizing the description to the describer or her community, does not fail for roughly the same sorts of reasons. Relativizations will change things, and it is hard to believe that this problem troubles only the realist's non-subjective relativizations.

But perhaps we should first ask if there really are cases of equally applicable, incompatible descriptions. The proposals for them with which I am familiar do not seem to work. They hinge, whatever their other faults may be, on the dubious maxim that certain descriptions (or predicates) which would be incompatible on some occasions will be incompatible on all occasions. Consider, for example, Jastrow's duck-rabbit. Kuhn identifies a duck, Quine a rabbit. We assume both are correct. But the figure itself is neither; and while nothing can be both a duck and a rabbit, something can be a representation of both a duck and a rabbit. Similarly, consider two cases of continuous motion on a screen. The first is projected by a film which consists of discrete images, the second by a linear series of lights flashed in rapid sequence. For on-screen continuous motion, it *just is* a rapid succession of discrete images. That is how cinematic motion occurs. Nothing is inconsistent here. Compare this, for example, with the motion of a bug crawling without halt across the screen. Though in another sense it happens 'on' the screen, I would deny that its *continuous* motion was any series of static discrete occurrences, though it might perhaps be 'composed of' such a series.

How does this differ from relativization of motion to context? Broadly there is no difference. But we do not require any translation of the original into a counterpart that may begin 'In the context of a screen image (or, the earth as fixed point) . . .'. Such translations are likely to be futile for many of the same reasons that reductive analyses have proved so overwhelmingly unsuccessful. And, there is an added reason here. Screen motion came only with screen technology, just as my motion while sitting quietly entered vocabularies only with the belief that the earth moves. It was a very natural convenience, which scarcely required a constituting convention, to extend a predicate such as 'moving' to the on-screen imitation of the only kind of continuous motion we had known beforehand. And this applied as well to extending 'is a duck' to a drawing of a duck. This does not mean that these predicates must be synecdoches, and in this way not quite accurate.

'Moving' applies without qualification to cinematic images. But there is no reason to suppose that the convenience which led us to extend a predicate so naturally would also introduce a precise vocabulary (or necessitate one) to capture just the parameters of the situation in which this extension is usable. Consequently, in deciding whether 'there are a number of discrete images in rapid succession' is incompatible with 'x is continuously moving', we must go on a case-by-case basis. In the case of cinematic movement continuous motion just is a series of rapidly succeeding discrete images, but we may or may not want to accept this for off-screen or video motion. If Descartes is right, everything is like screen motion, a rapid succession of instants, 'each one of which does not depend in any way on the others'[13] and is caused by God. We might take any of several attitudes to this result: revising our notion of continuity (*per* Descartes), revising our view about things actually persisting, or combining the first with a distinction between supernaturally and naturally caused sequences in order to preserve common discriminations. But the main point is that even if Descartes' view should prove to be necessarily false, and ordinary off-screen objects couldn't move continuously if their motion was a series of discrete instants, this would not show that *on-screen* motion was incompatible with its being a series of rapidly flashing discrete images or bulbs.

To see more clearly how (2) misses the core of the issue expressed in (1), we may note that not even the anti-realist is committed to rejecting (2). Of course, an anti-realist is not likely to accept (2), largely due to the kinds of arguments that have been traditionally bandied about. However, were someone to hold that the one uniquely true description of reality contained ineliminable subjective elements, contributed by the describers, this would be a form of anti-realism, not realism.

We have here a forceful reminder of how very peculiar metaphysical realism or Correspondence would be if it required (2). Ordinary cases of (a) and (b) are enough to thwart (2), and thus we might wonder what sort of conception of the world a metaphysical realist or Correspondence theorist must have in order to be committed to such a view. Indeed, it would need to be so far from what we ordinarily conceive that different levels of specificity or generality for describing things would be prohibited. Quite obviously, this is not a condemnation of realism, but of the attempt to characterize it in such clearly inadequate terms.

Perhaps others believe that the prime difficulty in this area is the incommensurability of scientific theories containing competing descriptions of their respective phenomena. This problem deserves fuller treatment, and we return to it in Chapter 9 when we discuss Kuhn's views. For now, suffice it to say that much more must be said before it can be taken as support for statement (2). Moreover, the different models used by Putnam to illustrate the possibility of redescription do not suit Kuhn's enterprise; for they all require the same sentences to remain true on the different interpretations. Such interpretations would not be, for Kuhnians, competing theories.

If (2) does not capture a basic realist commitment, why do anti-realists so commonly father this view on metaphysical realism? A natural thought might be that since metaphysical realism is committed to a single world, it is committed to a single correct description of it. Any shift in description seems to depend upon a shift in our perspective, and our perspective shouldn't matter to a mind-independent world. But relativizing our schemes of description to our interests needn't have this consequence if we see that the world is too luxuriant to be exhausted by any preferred, non-inclusive way of describing it. However, 'luxuriance' is just a metaphor. It is one of a set of rather feeble tools for trying to explain why a mind-independent world needn't be harnessed to a single set of relatively narrow descriptions. We may try to blame the inability on the world by calling it disorderly, inexhaustible, luxuriant or analogue; or on the limits of our powers of describing by calling our descriptions selective, abstract or digital. But all of these are mere pictures. The world is, in yet another trope, multi-faceted. Any number of cross-classifying descriptions can correctly fit a fact; but for reasons we have just reviewed, it is almost certain that no exclusive set of descriptions we could come up with will exhaust all its facets. This, it seems, is the most appropriate characterization of the metaphysical realist's outlook, and nothing in the arguments examined in this section has provided reason for overturning it.

5 CONCEPTUAL SCHEMES AND ASEPTIC DESCRIPTIONS OF REALITY

Not unrelated to the foregoing anti-realist complaint is the objection that Correspondence and metaphysical realism wrongly assume that there is a God's eye-view of the world. This would be a *neutral* way of describing things, or a 'description' that captures the world independently of any observers of it. The reasoning behind this verdict might run as follows. All cognition of the world involves cutting it up in certain ways. We may call this 'classification'. Humans do this by way of *description*; but

description clearly requires classification. Classification in turn just
is *conceptualization*, or the adoption of a *conceptual scheme*. But
once we employ a conceptual scheme, we are mixing what is
cognized with our own subjective contribution to it. As Hume
observed, 'the mind has a great propensity to spread itself on
external objects'.[14]

Once again, the view is held by Putnam, who writes that
' "objects" do not exist independently of conceptual schemes. We
cut up the world into objects when we introduce one or another
scheme of description' (p. 52). In fact, his earlier objections may
have been in part efforts to state this one. On this interpretation
the chief point of emphasizing alternative descriptions is that their
existence is symptomatic of the fact that cognizing things always
involves description, which in turn rests on classification and
conceptualization. Indeed, Putnam also attributes to Correspondence (and 'external realism') a God's eye-view of the world
(pp. 49, 50) and a kind of truth viewed 'as independent of
observers altogether' (p. 50).

It is not easy to cut through this thicket of claims. For the
objector the fact that we cannot describe the world without classification is decisive: all classification is conceptualization, and the
assumption is that all concepts are subjective contributions of the
cognizer. Concepts help the believer to organize the 'manifold'
rather than being elements of what she cognizes. Because this has
been generally taken to be the role of concepts since Kant's day,
and largely due to Kant's work, we may call the view Neo-
Kantian. On the other hand, the realist will no doubt agree that
cognition involves classification, and may even allow that classification is the imposition of concepts. But he will demur from at
least the last step in the argument; that is, he will contend either
that classification does not require subjective kinds of conceptualization or that conceptualization need not be the contribution of
the cognizer. As knowledge-gatherers our faculties are attuned to
the environment in which evolution places us, and the categories
under which we come to know parts of the world really are as
much a part of the world as anything else we may grasp. For such
a thinker the world may be an inexhaustible collection of just such
aspects or perspectives. This is not to claim that no classifications
will be overlooked, or that they will not be overlooked by some
language-groups while noticed by others. But among the various

arrangements into which the world is divided, many may actually do no more than reflect the world, and the significance of competing arrangements is no greater *within* a single conceptual scheme than it is as between such schemes. But the realist will insist that none of this clutter is grounds for denying the mind-independence of lions, copper beeches, crowns or tides.

If our task were to choose between these views, we would require further argument. All we have above are two pictures of the nature of classification, without supporting reasons for preferring one of them. But we need not make that choice in order to evaluate the objection against Correspondence. For the very possibility of constructing an alternative realist view compatible with the evidence shows that the Neo-Kantian conclusion begs the question. If the fact that we describe the world, or that this involves our classification of it, leaves room for the realist view just sketched, then these facts cannot imply that part of our cognition of the world must be imposed by the subject. Thus, the objection fails. As it stands it *assumes* that our descriptions contain a component contributed by the peculiarity of our constitutions, but it would require further argument to make a case for it.

The supposition that the realist demands a God's eye-view, or a neutral description, is predicated on an argument of roughly this nature. The mere fact that our cognition requires descriptions, or that it is always from our perspective, must be sufficient to show that our knowledge or information about our environment is tainted by our mentalities. Thus, if there is a mind-independent world, at least part of which we grasp, there must be a different sort of description, without the impurities of ours, against which we could measure for proximity the various descriptions supplied by human artifice. But of course there could be no such neutral description that we could understand; for the moment we grasped it, it would become *ours* and thus just another facet of our local viewpoint. However, we can see how this sort of objection can be evaded by the realist if he simply refuses the Neo-Kantian's initial gambit. Characteristics and their similarities really may be found in the world. At least nothing produced by the objection under discussion shows why they should not be part of the cognized manifold. But they needn't therefore be so salient and so unavoidable that all capable cognizers must incorporate each of them into their system of description, regardless of those cognizers' larger purposes or functions in obtaining knowledge. Thus, there is the possibility of a number of complementary ways of describing things, each of which *could*, so far as the argument here goes, be nothing more than grasping the way things are. Perhaps *not all* of the way things are! That may be an unattainable ideal. But it does not invite the hypothesis that this is prevented by an ineradicable subjectivity in the ways in which we describe the world. What is subjective may be only the adopted purposes that lead us to emphasize one rather than another of the things that, for all that has been said, really may be there.

The belief that conceptualization, which has judgment as an ingredient, contributes something not 'given' to the world has various sources, with varying degrees of credibility. To take one example, it may stem from a preconception of what the world must be like; say, that it is an undifferentiated Bergsonian flow. I cannot find any other construal for remarks such as the following, presented in support of the Neo-Kantian objection: 'to see a situation as one containing or illustrating or displaying a fact is *just* to judge and interpret. Even such a low-grade judgment as that my typewriter is on the table involves recognizing that the elements of the situation are spatially external to me, that they are objects with a temporal history, that they have various physical properties such as solidity, and so on. Judgment just *is* the isolation of facts.'[15] The presupposition of the argument is that reality doesn't come in discrete units before we divide it, which is precisely what the realist would want to deny.

Another source for a belief in the subjective contribution of all cognizing emphasizes the anthropocentrism of our classifications.[16] This criticism incorporates a legitimate historical insight. Although the basic facts of cultural anthropology on which it rests seem to have been known already by Herodotus, till recent times – that is, before the advent of modern anthropology brought them to the forefront of the educated public's consciousness – classical realists wrote as if the set of distinctions embodied in familiar vocabularies would be roughly the set of distinctions embodied in *any* conceivable cognizer's articulation of the world. But even if this confidence proved misplaced, there is a problem in translating the fortuitousness of our purposes or classifications into an argument that conceptualizations are subjective contributions. In fact, it is even hard to state the issue as anti-realism seems to conceive it. We may illustrate this with the example of the division of sounds into musical and non-musical. Let us ignore here the local dispute over whether sounds are secondary qualities. The only relevant issue for us is whether this way of dividing up sounds *introduces* a subjective element. Moreover, even when critics of this stripe deign to give examples, which isn't as often as one might hope, they may disagree on the case. But the example just given sufficiently illustrates the problem for any classification they might have in mind.

The nub of the difficulty is that if the distinction is not purely imaginary, there must be some basis in the world for the differentiation between the two sets of sounds. But then what do we contribute? To begin with a clearly unsatisfactory answer, let us say that we take pleasure in the one and are either jarred by or indifferent to the other. But surely a realist isn't likely to suppose that pleasure or jarring is part of what is cognized. Then perhaps what is subjective is our regarding this distinction as salient or important independently of the interest taken in it. But, again, it would be a distortion to attribute to a realist *as such* the view that what is important to us is so to the cosmos independently of our purposes. If it has achieved nothing else, the attempt to solve the traditional problem of evil has indelibly stamped on our consciousness the distinction between human interests and higher concerns. Thus, let us ask what it is about this distinction that shows either that it is not really there, or not there *as* we believe it to be, independently of our mental contribution. The problem is in seeing *both* how there can be a basis in the world for the distinction (for example, 'the given', 'the manifold of intuition') *and* at the same time how this basis doesn't exhaust whatever a realist must claim belongs to the world. On the other hand, if the critic holds that there is no basis in the world for the distinction, what is maintained fits not Neo-Kantianism but subjective idealism.

The fact that more than a single set of concepts might genuinely characterize the world shouldn't be supposed to imply that no system of describing things is inherently defective. In particular, nothing we have said suggests that the scientific world-view – as we tend to call the temperament of deliberately leaving one's most venerated beliefs vulnerable to the accumulation of evidence – must be on a par, say, with medical opinions in hunter–gatherer civilizations or with the theistically influenced outlook suffusing a community of religious devotees. Indeed, describing someone as a witch may always be mistaken, and the description of an event as a miracle may be incompatible with, and not merely exist alongside, its description as a natural occurrence. Thus, in allowing that the world is capturable in more than a single system of distinctions, we should not be thought to have fallen into the indefensible view that it is describable by any possible set of 'concepts'. That would of course have subverted the purpose in section 4 of detaching Correspondence from claim (2).

However, here the question has not been the existence of more than one set of concepts, but whether the use of any concepts at all distorts the reality we grasp. Kant held, in so many words, that it did. But despite the fact that philosophers since Kant have acknowledged that his arguments rested on outmoded views of mathematics and logic, many of them have adopted his outlook without seeking new ways to show that concepts must be subjective contributions. In other words, the view under attack has survived the demise of the arguments for it, and now appears as an assumption or as too obvious to warrant defence. Whatever the historical or epistemological reasons for this, I have been arguing that the view is neither obvious nor well defended. It cannot simply be presented as an objection to the existence or even the knowledge of a mind-independent reality.

IV

COHERENCE, PRAGMATISM AND REDUNDANCY

1 LEADING COMPETITORS OF CORRESPONDENCE

In this chapter we shall consider the leading alternatives to Correspondence. Thus far, I have argued that much of its opposition rests on either a misunderstanding of the nature of its claims or objections to which there are adequate rejoinders. Still, if another view should be more promising than Correspondence, the latter would forfeit its hold on us. This leads us to ask about possible alternatives. We shall not be able to discuss Coherence and Pragmatism in the detail they deserve, and we shall have to satisfy ourselves with corporate views that contain tenets from which some of their supporters will demur. None the less, even a brief survey will advance the discussion if, as I argue, each view reveals fundamental defects. Of course, an adherent of either view, supposing he conceded the objections, could redescribe his doctrine in terms of one of our other characterizations, (2)–(10), rather than abandon it altogether. That is all we require. It is sufficient for our purposes if Correspondence turns out to be the lone candidate for what it is that *makes* a statement or belief true and the only plausible answer to the companion question 'What constitutes the truth of a statement or belief?'

Let us then begin our inquiry with the Coherence Theory of Truth (Coherence).

2 THE NATURE OF THE THEORY

Coherence maintains that the truth of a belief or statement (a combination which coherentists typically sum up with the term 'judgment') is constituted by its inclusion in a certain kind of system of such judgments. Also, its precise relation to the other judgments is crucial in creating the proper system. In arguing for this, Coherence frequently relies upon a claim that we recently criticized: namely, that since experience is infected by the conceptual contribution of the believer, it is already judgmental in character. Thus, 'agreement' between judgments and facts turns out to be an intrajudgmental business. Two forms of the view differ over whether coherence is the name of the relation between judgments making them suitable for inclusion or merely the character of a properly constituted collection of such judgments. We shall distinguish these versions where necessary, but much of our investigation can ignore this detail. For we shall want to know more about the exact nature of the appropriate relationship between judgments in such a whole, whether we regard this as fleshing out what the relation of coherence comes to or as just discovering the details of a different relation. And we shall also be interested in the more specific character of the whole set that can serve as this sort of truth-constituter, under the title 'coherence' or any other.

To begin, let us inquire about the mandatory relation between judgments. All coherentists hold that it is one or a set of logical and evidential relations, but this still leaves considerable room for disagreement. At one extreme *entailment* may be demanded. That is, a group of judgments coheres if each is entailed by a conjunction of the remainder. (Few maintain the even stronger requirement that each judgment in the set entails *all* the rest, although this would be a suitable formal counterpart of the doctrine of internal relations favoured by some prominent coherentists.) On most accounts, this is an ideal to be achieved only by complete knowledge. At the other extreme it may be required only that the members of the class be *consistent*.

The entailment view won't do as stated. For example, imagine a system with statements A, B, C, D, E and F, and an entailment relation symbolized by '@→'. Every judgment will be entailed by a conjunction of the remainder if A & B @→ C, A & C @→ B, B & C @→ A, D & E @→ F, D & F @→ E, E & F @→ D, and no other entailment relations that are not consequences of the above hold. But there is little reason to have one unified system here rather than two systems (A, B and C contrasted with D, E and F), and although no single judgment could be removed from the system without having consequences for the remainder, various triads of judgments could be removed without logical consequences for the remainder. One might solve the specific difficulty, as Ewing suggests, by adding that 'no set of [judgments] within the whole set is logically independent of all [judgments] in the remainder of the set'.[1] But the problem is only an example of the kinds of further technical problems that will be encountered by attempts to formulate the view adequately.

What of those who maintain that the members of a coherent system need only be consistent? Coherentists generally prefer to speak of the 'compatibility' or 'harmony' of judgments in a coherent system, and even when they use 'consistency' and its congeners we cannot assume that it is intended as rigorously as formal logic has accustomed us to read it. But if Coherence is not merely providing a mysterious title for the vital relation between judgments in such a system, strict logical consistency must at least be an ingredient in it. We are certainly not sacrificing any plausibility by making it a *sine qua non* of any system of coherent judgments. But is it sufficient? Here the coherentist is confronted by the spectre of two or more systems of conflicting judgments, each of which may be internally consistent. This is a stock objection to Coherence, and it is almost as frequently met by a few stock rejoinders. One is to declare that consistency is supplemented by other relations between judgments (perhaps entailment, but not only that). Another is to require that any judgment which is included in the system contributes further to the relevant character of the system. Since it cannot contribute any more consistency, perhaps what it contributes is greater *comprehensiveness*. Thus, to finish off the reply to the objection, we may eliminate competing coherent systems by demanding that the truth-constituting system be the most comprehensive such system in the offing. More will be said about this, but this brief excursion into the polemics surrounding Coherence should illustrate the need to elaborate 'coherence' both in the sense of a relation between judgments and as a character of the system containing such judgments.

When coherentists demanded entailment it was frequently because they were drawn to modelling coherence on what they believed to be the character of deductive systems such as Euclidean geometry. For various reasons coherentists nowadays are more inclined to conceive of their system on the model of a theory in the physical sciences. The judgments in such a system, they may aver, mutually support one another, but this is an evidential relation falling short of entailment. On some accounts of scientific theorizing the bedrock considerations for testing, or even adopting, a theory are matters of simplicity, fecundity, economy, predictive power, scope, elegance, strength and precision (quantifiability). (We discuss these further in Chapter 9.) Continuing with this account, there is no higher court, such as a direct confrontation with nature, to which to appeal. Not all varieties of Coherence are developed in this way, and some of the views that do make such appeals are theories of justification (= criteria of truth) rather than theories of truth. But this sort of view is sufficiently prominent nowadays to be worth mentioning.

Motivations for Coherence range from the devoutly metaphysical to the zealously anti-metaphysical. Each finds it impossible to compare judgments with anything other than judgments, and the only comparisons relevant for truth are then the logical or evidential relations comprising coherence. Absolute Idealists, such as F. H. Bradley,[2] reject non-linguistic facts, as we have said, on the grounds that perceptual experience is already replete with judgment, being conditioned by the conceptual apparatus always present in it. This argument, which looms large in the more metaphysical camp of Coherence, supposes that our experiences can be somehow fully exhausted by implicit judgments contained in them. On the other side are philosophers such as Rudolph Carnap and Otto Neurath, who hold that any pretension to compare our language with non-linguistic reality is itself metaphysical, and, not being verifiable, (cognitively) meaningless. They limit relevant meaningful relations of our speech to logical ones with other judgments.[3]

This summary omits a number of collateral doctrines about truth favoured by absolute idealist supporters of Coherence:

doctrines such as degrees of truth, the actual ascribability of truth only to the whole, internal relations, identity in difference and organic unities.[4] In various discussions these tenets and Coherence interpenetrate, as only befits a view which regards its total theory as a seamless web. But I believe we can avoid further elaborations of the collateral views for two reasons. First, regarding the introduction of Coherence, as several commentators have noted, the absolute idealists' theory of truth is a beachhead, rather than a rearguard, in their assault on the issues. Second, none of the other doctrines seems to afford needed relief from the objections we shall raise against Coherence.

Support for Coherence often begins with a critique of foundational theories of knowledge. Coherentists claim that foundationalism serves Correspondence by providing an exit from language at which judgments confront extra-linguistic reality for their veracity. Other judgments' truth may depend on their relationship to further judgments, but here a judgment such as, say, 'the cow is dead', is made true or false by a world *sans* conventions. Coherentists claim otherwise; that the experienced empirical world cannot avoid having our categories imposed on it. Two points raised in earlier chapters undermine this source of coherentist support. First, in Chapter 2 it was argued that Correspondence does not require in any sense an ability to inspect directly the truth-constituter, or even knowledge that a judgment is true. Distinctions between characterizations (1) and (3) or (4) were meant to drive home the distinction between what makes a judgment true and our means of discovering truth. Next, in Chapter 3 I argued that dividing the world in accordance with what might be called 'concepts' is insufficient to show that the world thus organized does not actually manifest those divisions. However, we are at present more immediately interested in Coherence's nature than its plausibility. That it rests on such support is a key to its understanding: that is, Coherence is intimately involved with considerations about how knowledge is obtained and how sentences acquire meaning. This makes it all the more crucial to disentangle Coherence from certain coherence-like doctrines of belief and meaning that neither support nor need it. Let us look in more detail at these other doctrines.

One popular coherence theory concerns *criteria* for truth:[5] alternatively, it is about justification or justified belief. Let us refer to it as Belief Holism. It says that individual beliefs are justified (= can be taken for true) just in case their incorporation into an acceptable system of beliefs contributes to the latter's coherence. The system itself either needs no justification or is justified by being coherent. Just what the relations between the beliefs in the system must be to give rise to the coherence, or what the coherence amounts to, are further questions that must be addressed, but about which belief holists may differ among themselves. We might say, as before, that beliefs in the system give rise to coherence by mutually supporting one another. (This comes dangerously close to saying that they *justify* one another, but it is not our purpose to evaluate the view here.) A coherence theory of *meaning* – hereafter, Meaning Holism – might maintain that the sense of a sentence or word is determined by the larger language, or part of it, in which it is contained. In a familiar version Meaning Holism claims that we cannot draw a principled distinction between statements expressing beliefs about, say, dogs and statements purporting to convey the meaning of the word 'dog' (between synthetic and analytic truths about dogs). In this version it is the same conglomeration, the entire system of our beliefs, which is responsible for both the justification of individual beliefs and the meanings of meaningful elements. Of course, for Meaning Holism patently false sentences may have meaning though they do not express justified beliefs. And this may be sufficient to distinguish the views. But the distinction it is our present concern to insist upon is that between both of these views and Coherence. It is primarily Belief and Meaning Holism, rather than Coherence, that have motives for rejecting foundationalist theories of knowledge.

Belief Holism quite naturally appeals to the previously listed virtues of explanations, such as simplicity, precision, fruitfulness and comprehension, as ways of supporting some beliefs with others. But in finding our way about the thicket of claims resulting from this, it is helpful to make some distinctions. Belief Holism, as characterized, is compatible with global realism as well as with more than one form of non-realism. For example, some philosophers may regard the possession of a sufficient number of such virtues as a symptom of a judgment or theory possessing them capturing the world. This could be realism combined with a coherence theory of justification. Its theory of truth could be, for all we have said, Correspondence. Others may regard the list of explanatory virtues as a substitute for truth, say, with regard to scientific theories. In abandoning truth for this fragment of discourse this view is non-realist, but it rejects Coherence along with Correspondence. But if confined to an isolated language fragment, it may only be *local* anti-realism. Yet others may regard the formal virtues relating judgments in a system of mutual justification as constituting truth. This would be a form of Coherence. If, as I have suggested, we take global realism to be represented by Correspondence, this is also a non-realist theory. Unlike the previous non-realist theory it yields the sort of theory of truth delineated by (1) and (1'). But the three options show that the core of recent discussion about the justification of beliefs does not have one unvarying consequence for a choice of truth theory.

This also suggests that a number of the issues which have crept into coherentists' attacks upon Correspondence, such as foundationalism and the criteria for theory acceptance, concern not so much the character of truth, but meaning and justification. But even if what a sentence means is a function of its relation to a language or set of beliefs, its truth might consist only in agreement with a non-sentential configuration of things in the world. And even belief holists maintain that we, quite legitimately, hold some things to be true, and the account of what it is we are holding about those things may be Correspondence. Of course, we just conceded that it is possible to use the holistic theories to support what some see as the correlative theory of truth, Coherence. But it is not necessary to do so, and in fact there are a few good reasons for not doing so. One is that certain pernicious faults of Coherence do not impair the holistic views. Consequently, tying the holistic views to Coherence is offering unnecessary hostages to fate. The other is that, however strong the case is for Meaning or Belief Holism, neither extricates Coherence from those objections. Thus, in sum, the holisms may be weakened by an association with Coherence while the association does not strengthen Coherence.

Our next task is to list and evaluate the best objections to Coherence.

3 OBJECTIONS FROM MULTIPLY COHERENT SYSTEMS AND CIRCULARITY

Earlier we mentioned the familiar charge that there can be more than one equally coherent system of judgment, each of which is incompatible with the others. We cannot have incompatible truths, and nothing more than the coherence of the system is a determinant of truth (on this view). Thus, since there is nothing to favour one system over the rest, none of them could constitute the truth of its judgments. We also noted a stock reply: namely, only a system which is *comprehensive* as well as coherent creates the truth of its judgments. But what is a comprehensive system of judgments? Is it, for example, a maximally consistent set of propositions, containing one member from each pair of contradictory propositions up to the limit of impossibility? Such a system would ignore the likelihood of the propositions in it being held by anyone and whether there was evidence for them. It would be very uncharacteristic for a coherentist to appeal to this sort of system rather than one of actually held beliefs. But in asking whether our own system of beliefs is the most comprehensive, we cannot ignore the capacity to construct other systems out of mere possibilia. And if we are comparing judgments we actually make with those we might make, it is difficult to see what grounds there are for the claim that none of our system's alternatives is both coherent and equally comprehensive.

Moreover, why can't we increase our system's comprehensiveness, without impairing its coherence, by adding to it one of a pair of propositions for which there is no evidence either way? For example, suppose I add to my current doxastic system the belief that Thales did not have more than two brothers. Isn't the resulting system more comprehensive? But if it is, then so would be the system which added, instead of that belief, the belief that Thales had more than two brothers. This would expose two faults: (a) that the method would make gratuitous suppositions true, and (b) that we could once again have two or more most comprehensive systems which were incompatible. Bertrand Russell[6] raised this sort of objection to Bradley's version of Coherence.

Bradley's reply[7] was that the addition of fanciful suppositions to the system violated principles of evidence validated by Coherence, such as those requiring reliable procedures, including memory or

eyewitness testimony, for the acceptance of a belief. These principles are themselves included in the system of beliefs. Thus, any
change created by the inclusion of a fanciful supposition would
not be minor, but cataclysmic; including the modification or elim-
ination of such principles, and affecting all the beliefs accepted
on their basis. On the other hand, accepting this one belief without
altering anything else (including the aforementioned principles)
would destroy coherence.

If we are not to confuse Coherence with Belief Holism, the
principles of evidence of which Bradley writes must be made true,
not merely justified, by their inclusion in a coherent whole. And,
as we shall argue in Chapter 7, truth cannot be no more than
justifiability. Thus, it must be a different facet of the coherent
whole that makes a proposition true from the one that makes it
justified. All this is possible, but Bradley's comments on the topic
do not encourage confidence that he has not merely run together
these issues. However, even if we overlook the potential for
confusion here, there is reason to believe that the additions we
have fancied could not violate any principles of evidence to which
a coherentist is committed. For if the inclusion in a coherent and
comprehensive system makes the proposition, say, that Thales
had no more than two brothers true, mightn't we gerrymander
the relevant evidential principle to permit this one exception? This
altered principle would be clearly *ad hoc*, but what it sacrificed in
streamlining it would compensate in completeness: that is, it
would allow us to have more truths and to have them justified.
And how could we say the additional judgment is not true if the
only determinant of truth is inclusion in that system? I am not
claiming that the proposition *is* justified, but that it is difficult to
see what basis the coherentist has for denying that it is.

Recently, Jonathan Dancy[8] has proposed the following novel
defence: although we cannot show that Coherence is invulnerable
to the prospect of a plurality of equally coherent systems, the
same prospect threatens other theories of truth, including Correspondence. He does not say much about Correspondence. Since
its truth-constituter is the world, it would appear that we would
require either two worlds or two equally good relations of correspondence to it (other than the kinds scouted in the last chapter
that cross-classify things). It is difficult to judge without further
details how either threat materializes. But this is not the chief

problem with Dancy's rejoinder. Its most serious difficulty is that, even if what he said was correct, it would drag the other theories down with Coherence, not lift Coherence up with them. The plurality condition is fatal, whether for Coherence or for other views that share it.

It may be noticed that the objection seems to ignore relations other than consistency that must subsist between judgments to form a coherent whole. It doesn't seem that a consideration of these relations improves the prospects for comprehensiveness, though it may allow us other ways of forming uniquely coherent wholes. In the next objections we shall consider, *inter alia*, two leading candidates for such relations: namely, logical relations – including, but not restricted to, consistency – and, in section 4, evidential ones.

A second objection to Coherence is that it must presuppose for its account the very conception of truth it seeks to elucidate. We shall show this for *consistency*, since this is at least a *sine qua non* for a coherent system; but any other logical relation, such as *entailment*, with which Coherence conjures, will present a similar difficulty.

As normally understood, a consistent set of sentences is one in which *it is possible for all the members to be jointly true*. This immediately introduces truth as an ingredient of consistency. On this account, and regardless of the other elements in a complete account, truth could not be *a product* of a set of judgments that requires this relationship between its judgments.

There may be a temptation to circumvent this objection by offering a syntactic-viz. non-semantic-definition of consistency. We might say that p and q are consistent just in case *not-q* is not derivable from p: more generally, set S of sentences is syntactically consistent iff, for all wffs A, it is not the case that both $S \vdash A$ and $S \vdash \sim A$. However, this will not serve the present purpose. As a syntactic notion *derivability* is relative to a set of rules of derivation. Of the indefinitely many possible sets of such rules, only the rare ones are of interest to Coherence: namely, the *truth-preserving* ones. An arbitrarily selected set would be useless for explicating truth. Therefore, if one's ulterior interest is in truth – or, for that matter, most other virtues of system which logicians have sought – the concept of truth still enters, albeit in concealed form: namely, it is written into the process of selecting the particular set of rules of derivation to obtain the relevantly coherent sets.

Let us put the point another way. Formalists may characterize logical operations as transactions between meaningless symbols. But, for the coherentist, *truth* must emerge from the construction; thus we cannot describe the earlier elements too thinly. If we were perfectly faithful to the syntactic restrictions a formalist could place on these notions, we might wonder how anything like truth could be an achievable result. It seems inevitable that we shall have to import it surreptitiously. Truth cannot be presupposed, even as a limiting condition on our selection of rules, if it is to be explained as resulting from the system constructed in accordance with such-and-such requirements.

We might mention that there is little reason to believe that coherentists would avail themselves of the syntactic defence. They regularly conceive of coherent systems as containing fully interpreted judgments. Even the logical empiricists from this group, who Russell claims regard truth as a syntactic rather than a semantic concept,[9] believe that the relations between, say, protocol and other sentences hold in part because of what these sentences mean. Thus, it is unlikely that they would make use of this apparent way out of their difficulties. However, I do not know of any other ways they might have to avoid it, or to dispense with consistency (/compatibility) in their elucidation of coherence.

4 RELIABILITY VOCABULARY AND THE TRUTH-LINKED NATURE OF JUSTIFICATION

The next difficulty implicates a number of popular forms of global anti-realism along with Coherence. It begins from the previously noted fact that, in Goldman's phrase, justification is truth-linked. This means not only that a belief's being justified requires a certain propensity for truth, but also that theories of justification are themselves held accountable for having truth-yielding proclivities. Consequently, there is no epistemic advantage in a belief's being justified if this does not signal a greater tendency or probability for truth than the belief would have had had it lacked this property. However, we cannot restrict our attention to 'justify'; for this is not intended as an observation about parochial usage. There is a larger vocabulary – I call it a 'reliability vocabulary' – of expressions that indicate just the same sort of epistemic advantage. Its expressions are applied to evidence, methods of gathering it, and propositions thought certified by it; and they signify that a distinctively epistemic approval is conferred. The reliability vocabulary includes, as prominent examples, 'justified', 'reliable', 'rationally acceptable', 'warranted', 'trustworthy', 'assertible', 'probable', 'plausible', 'supportable' (or 'supported'), 'reasonable' and 'probative'. But it also includes a host of less conspicuous expressions (occasionally, neologisms coined in an attempt to sever the truth-link of traditional vocabulary). Thus, when William James writes of the species of 'good in the way of beliefs, and good, too, for definite assignable reasons',[10] and when John Dewey mentions 'the satisfaction of the needs and conditions of the problem out of which the idea, the purposes and method of the action, arise', and promptly adds that this is 'not to be manipulated by whim or personal idiosyncrasy',[11] they are devising circumlocutions to convey what less guarded epistemologists speak of with standard expressions of the reliability vocabulary. But it is the epistemic advantage sought, and not the particular term used, that necessitates the truth-link. Thus, I am claiming that the application of each of these expressions requires, *inter alia*, that the property expressed be viewed as probabilifying, retaining, or somehow enhancing the chances of whatever has it being true. If the truth-link were not extendible from justification to the remainder of the reliability notions, the former would not deserve the interest it has held for epistemologists.

We must say more about the truth-link, but first let us detail why it is a problem for Coherence. We have noted that the judgments in a coherent system must have more in common than being mutually consistent, and that entailment seems too much to demand and is nowadays generally disregarded. But otherwise we have not probed deeply into the relations that must subsist between individual judgments in a coherent system or that qualify a judgment for inclusion in one. Coherentists themselves haven't been prodigal with detailed suggestions about the ways in which judgments in such systems are related. When they do spell out the relations, it is with notions from our reliability vocabulary, such as justification and mutual support. '[A] candidate belief [must] have some relations to our accepted beliefs such that, if it were rejected, the credibility of some other beliefs would be put in question.'[12] But a truth-linked notion raises special problems for this view, since truth is supposed to emerge from the coherence of the whole system, and thus apply to individual judgments only in consequence of this systemic property. How are we to understand the justification, support or 'credibility' of judgments independently of their propensity to truth? But what could that propensity amount to if they are only true because the system they belong to is coherent?

Not all coherentists find the truth-link unwelcome, but this seems to be because they have in mind an aspect of it other than the one just cited as troublesome. For example, Dancy,[13] once again, begins with a coherence theory of justification (Belief Holism). But since, on Correspondence he believes we would have trouble showing why the character of a belief that accounted for its justification would tend to increase its chances of truth, and the truth-link requires that there be this connection, he concludes that this warrants Coherence. We haven't the space to assess properly the view that one's theory of justification and truth must mesh in just the way Dancy suggests, though I shall simply dogmatically state that the putative incongruity of Belief Holism and Correspondence tends to evaporate when we pose the relevant questions in more detailed, less abstract terms. Nevertheless, such an inducement to adopt Coherence does not absolve any theory making use of justifactory links between judgments in a coherent system of the difficulty. The problem of forming the system on the basis of a justifactory relation between judgments that makes no surreptitious use of truth not only remains, but is amplified, on Dancy's premises. Moreover, he has an additional problem. For it appears that the nature of the system creating justification is, aside from a few inessentials, no different from that creating truth. If there is any distinction between the systems, it is only that justification is reserved for *believed* propositions while truth is applicable to a larger pool of propositions. The alleged truth-link thereby becomes empty; truth and justification are linked only because the former is virtually reduced to the latter. Later (Chapter 7, sections 4–5) we shall show why truth cannot be reduced to the elements that constitute justification. But even without that difficulty, the truth-link loses its intended force if truth is instantiated by nothing beyond the features that instantiate justification. For the reason behind the link was to give justifications a point by showing that they approximate to something non-epistemic to which our epistemic attitudes may be directed. If truth introduces no property over and above the one constituting justification, there is as little point in certifying justified belief in terms of its tendency toward truth as there would be, say, in certifying justified belief in terms of its tendency toward warranted belief.

Returning to the truth-link itself, what evidence is there for it? Proof is elusive, but grounds for a strong *prima-facie* case are at hand. Concerning our familiar notions of epistemic reliability, it would be no more than reporting accurately on customary practice to say that discussants freely and frequently draw upon the notion of truth to ground the reliability of an indicator. Although this does not demonstrate that the intended force of the reliability vocabulary could not be preserved without the truth-link, it gives some reason to suppose the connection vital. The opponent of the truth-link is thereby handed a challenge to show that we can have our reliability notions without grounding them in truth. In discussing this challenge, perhaps we must consider two cases: that in which the notion of truth is preserved, though the link is severed, and that in which truth, and not merely its link to justification, is abandoned (or eliminated via reduction).

The first scenario is most unpromising. The places of both truth and justification are mystifying if both notions are preserved, but a belief's justification carries no commitment concerning its truth. Discarding truth altogether, as in the second case, relieves one of this last difficulty. But in this case one must still produce a value-giving standard, other than truth, to explain why justification of our beliefs is something we should want for purely epistemic reasons. Attempts to provide such standards have thus far supplied additional epistemic values, which have left the unconverted with nagging doubts that truth must still be there, albeit in purdah, to sponsor the whole venture. That is, grounding one reliability notion in terms of another is no help, and the only reason it may have seemed otherwise has been the refusal of defenders to countenance a need for a further explanation of why the grounding notion is of value (and so on).

One way to put these doubts to rest might be to offer an analogy for non-truth-linked justification. Much of our reliability vocabulary, including 'justified', is predicated of activities, such as social measures or reforms, that are not even candidates for being truth-bearers. Perhaps the analogy in political terms for truth is something equally permanent and ideal, such as utopianism. Thus, one might say that a justified measure does not have to be sanctioned by a utopian scheme, but simply by satisfying a present need. Similarly, we might argue, a belief is justified by satisfying the needs of the immediate inquiry, without any further question of its leading to something eternally true.

But does the analogy work? Of course, utopianism can mean different things to different theorists, so it is unhelpful to place too much emphasis on a particular interpretation. But truth's function is not like that of a distant ideal; and even if truth, once attained, is final, the fact that we are fallible cognizers prevents us from closing off an inquiry from the possibility of further evidence just because we believe we have achieved the truth. Truth is less a highly abstract ideal than it is a regulator of any particular line of inquiry that may be current. Just as, in practical affairs, we would not think a measure justified if it threatened greater disaster in the foreseeable future, so also we would not settle intellectually for a solution to a particular line of inquiry if results incompatible with it were likely to appear as soon as the practical reasons motivating this particular inquiry expire. Otherwise, we could not avoid considering ourselves satisfied with agreeable delusions. Indeed, is there even such a thing as 'the immediate purposes of an inquiry' that is itself divorceable from a truth-link? Once again, aren't we confronted with an apparently under-described value-giving standard? The truth-link was originally proposed because something had to provide the normative epistemic force that attaches to justification. The need is not eliminated once we disqualify truth from providing it. And it is doubtful that we make any progress toward providing it if all we have done is to make justification subordinate to a further notion from the same reliability circle that, as a whole, needed this sort of support.

Another way to show the inadequacy of the analogy might begin by conceding that methods (for changing light bulbs, cooking pasta, satisfying people's wants and so forth) are *reliable* because they work. But we cannot stop there. There must always be a further explanation of what working consists in. A reliable way of changing a light bulb may work because it doesn't lead to shorting the bulb, getting a shock and so on. It is because 'working' is a part of the reliability vocabulary that such further elucidations are called for. Thus, it will not do simply to say that a belief works or meets the needs of a present inquiry. It is not merely that a further question can be asked, but rather that the question is of exactly the same order. We have not got anywhere by offering those answers to a question about the source of the epistemic value of justifiability.

Truth too is valued, though there is no necessity in this. However, it is not a notion of epistemic reliability. There is no further *distinctively epistemic* goal which the acquisition of truth must help us achieve. On the other hand, if a belief were *just* 'justified' or 'reliable', but there was nothing further to be said about what it was reliable for or what its justification did for it, this would sharply estrange these uses of 'justified' and 'reliable' from our current understanding of these words. I suspect this is the reason why the truth-link provides a kind of anchor for justification which we cannot replace by using other terms of epistemic reliability. But my explanation of the difference is not as important as the obvious fact that the difference exists. And it poses a serious obstacle to forms of anti-realism that must make intelligible a notion of justification that precedes the introduction of truth.

These criticisms aren't the only ones that have been brought against Coherence, but they have the advantage of displaying weaknesses in the view without requiring too distractingly detailed an exposition of the various idealistic doctrines that enter indirectly into its exposition and support. Among the further sceptical questions we should want to raise of any developed coherentist position is whether it allows room in the universe for *chance occurrences*. Reports of such occurrences, it would appear, could not be supported by other judgments in the system. Of course, there may be no chance in the universe, but I don't see how it could be excluded just by one's theory of truth. Thus, if chance and Coherence are incompatible, it would appear that the blame falls upon the latter doctrine rather than the former. We have also cited in passing how evidence regularly employed by Coherence is undermined by the distinctions of Chapter 2 of this part, as well as by the discussion at the end of Chapter 3. This is perhaps even more apparent with the next theory of truth we shall discuss,

Pragmatism, the proponents of which suggest drawing their conclusions about what makes something true from various epistemological and semantic views from which they begin. Let us now turn to that doctrine.

II Pragmatism

5 THE NATURE OF THE THEORY

Taking into account substantial differences between its proponents, the theory of Pragmatism may be very generally summarized as saying that the truth of a belief consists in its working. Before clarifying and elaborating this formula several exceptions should be noted. Some pragmatists have intended working to be only *the criterion* of truth and some restrict their view to empirical truth. Moreover, although we find formulae conforming to my preferred characterization for a theory of truth, (1) – for example, F. C. S. Schiller's remark, 'social usefulness is an ultimate determinant of "truth" '[14] – usually pragmatists' claims are phrased in terms of what is *meant* or what *we mean* by truth. Thus, Peirce writes that 'the opinion which is fated to be ultimately agreed to by all who investigate, is what we mean by the truth'.[15] And James maintains that '*true ideas are those we can assimilate, validate, corroborate and verify.* . . . That is the practical difference it makes to us to have true ideas; that, therefore, is the meaning of truth, for it is all truth is known-as.' James next inquires into 'what the words verification and validation pragmatically mean' and answers that in our investigations 'transitions come to us from point to point as being progressive, harmonious, satisfactory. This function of agreeable leading is what we mean by an idea's verification.'[16] Next, Dewey writes 'that which guides us truly is true – demonstrated capacity for such guidance is precisely what is meant by truth'. And by such guidance, he adds, he intends 'confirmation, corroboration, verification'.[17] Finally, a contemporary fellow traveller, Richard Rorty, has discussed the issue in terms of a 'sense' of 'true' in which truth amounts to such things as 'what it is better for us to believe', 'warranted assertibility', 'what we will believe if we keep inquiring by our present lights'.[18] In Chapter 2 we distinguished questions about the constitution of truth from those about the *meaning* of terms such as 'is true', but we cannot automatically superimpose this distinction on the philosophical tradition. For in the past hundred years it has been commonplace to raise questions about constitution by framing them in terms of expressions from the (multiply ambiguous) meaning family. I am not suggesting this has always been a mistake, though it provides an opportunity for the confusions cited in Chapter 2. Pragmatists in particular, whose prose styles were characteristically effusive rather than terse and scrupulous, have not been notably exercised about precise formulations of their views. Nevertheless, they certainly took the pragmatic theory of truth to displace Correspondence and Coherence. Thus, to begin, we may treat their pronouncements without undue distortion as proposing the features which *make* beliefs true.

There are a few prominent themes common to pragmatist treatments of truth. For one, they all would have us regard truth primarily as a *process* for finding our way about in the world. It is also something that is forever vulnerable to tests of further experience. This is sometimes signalled by a disparagement of what they call *static, abstracted, absolute*, or *final* truth. Truth for them is an evaluative notion, and is valued because it leads us smoothly to future behaviour. Success in belief is associated with *satisfaction*. Some writers are more careful than others in restricting the contexts in which the relevant kinds of satisfaction occur (for example, contexts of theoretical inquiry). We shall say more about this shortly. All, however, agree that it is in the relation of a belief to future experiences or verifications, rather than in its relation to a possibly mind-independent fact or to a network of other beliefs currently held, that truth resides.

A warning is in order. For our purposes we must settle for the outlines of a general view. Commentators have claimed that one or another of the pragmatists quoted above have not been addressing the question of the constitution, or even the meaning, of truth, but rather, say, describing the process of inquiry. Moreover, some of them have changed or radically modified their views over their lengthy careers. But even if they are not each and at all times truth theorists, they are sources for much of that view's later support and understanding; and it is that general outlook with which we must come to grips. We take up questions of the interpretation of a particular writer only to the extent that it helps us to arrive at the most refined version of Pragmatism possible. As for the view that pragmatists wanted to show that the question to which Correspondence and Coherence are answers should be jettisoned in favour of a different sort of inquiry altogether, if reasons for this are not treated here or in Chapter 3, it appears Correspondence may evade this critique by drawing upon the distinctions of Chapter 2.

We should also add a brief remark about the role of *satisfaction* in Pragmatism. Although all pragmatists take it as a psychological phenomenon – for example, it is not the sort of thing mentioned in phrases such as 'satisfaction of graduation requirements' – it still admits distinct construals. These differences emerge clearly by way of what might be considered each interpretation's natural associations. The two I have in mind may be described as follows. First, satisfaction may belong to our stock of pleasure-concepts whose natural associations would then be notions such as happiness, pleasure, contentment and so on. Or, second, it can be viewed more on the order of 'fulfilment of expectations', whether such fulfilment is desirable or not. Both seem to have figured in pragmatist writings, and naturally the use of a single term has aided their conflation. It is obvious that only the second could play any role in the understanding of an epistemologized truth. But to avert confusion, let us say something about each.

On the first construal there is something paradoxical about being satisfied but displeased. To regard truth as what leads to satisfaction in this sense is to require truths to subserve a kind of happiness, although perhaps only a very mild contentment. In light of these remarks, if we take James's claim that 'Our passional nature not only lawfully may, but must, decide an option between propositions, whenever it is a genuine option that cannot by its nature be decided on intellectual grounds'[19] as determining the appropriate kind of satisfaction for truth, we have an instance of this view. Morton White claims that James is talking about methods of belief acceptance rather than the nature of truth. (White should have said '*justified* acceptance', for James certainly isn't engaged in a narrowly sociological study of belief acquisition.) And, White continues, this makes it more difficult 'to lampoon [James] as the patron saint of wishful thinking'.[20]

However, the ridicule doesn't thrive upon taking James's proposal as being about truth rather than justified belief, but on using 'satisfaction' with its pleasure-concept associations.[21] It is no less perverse to say of every belief's *acceptability* – White says only 'acceptance', but this is clearly too weak for what James needs – that it 'should not clash with moral feelings or with moral beliefs that may occupy a well-entrenched position' than it is to say it of every belief's truth. Well-entrenched moral or religious views may make a conflicting view difficult to believe, but they are not thereby justifications of a belief for which they are not otherwise evidence. Similarly, satisfaction construed as 'not disturbing tenets we favour for other than evidential reasons' is patently irrelevant to truth.

Satisfaction in the sense of expectation fulfilment need not concern contentment. What fulfils our expectations may depress us, infuriate us or confirm our worst fears, while what violates our expectations may be a pleasant surprise, a relief or a godsend. It is in its capacity to prepare us to meet something in the future that this sort of satisfaction evaluates beliefs as true or false. This is the only interpretation on which it seems satisfaction can have even the remotest plausibility as a truth-constituter.

But merely eliminating exceptionally implausible interpretations does not show that Pragmatism is a promising view. Let us now turn to some charges against the doctrine that cannot be so easily dispatched.

6 RAISING FORBIDDEN QUESTIONS

Upon what evidence does Pragmatism rest? Considerations on behalf of the view are generally directed towards showing only that working is a test – perhaps *the* test – for truth, and readers are left to puzzle out for themselves how this shows that working constitutes truth. It is more in character for James to 'turn [his] back' upon questions about what makes a belief true than to address them. We must then ponder how this could be intended as an objection with philosophical force rather than as a confession of temperament. All this lends substance to claims of recent commentators that pragmatists weren't offering competing answers to the old question, but displacing the old answers more indirectly by showing that we had asked the wrong question. But these explanations have not aided plausibility. For example, Rorty, interpreting Pragmatism so that it excludes Peirce, Schiller and much in Dewey, approvingly argues that the pragmatists not only found Correspondence unilluminating, but also found that those who raised the questions Correspondence answers neglected the central fact that truth is valuable. Such neglect rendered all such views deficient; to wit:

> James' point was that carrying out this exercise will not enlighten us about why truths are good to believe, or offer any clues as to why or whether our present view of the world is, roughly, the one we should hold. Yet nobody would have asked for a 'theory' of truth if they had not wanted answers to these latter questions.[22]

And to reinforce his last claim Rorty adds: 'nobody engages in epistemology or semantics because he wants to know "this is red" pictures the world'.[23] These are patently weak grounds for rejecting Correspondence, or for thinking of Pragmatism as a successor to it. There are questions to be raised about things that are valuable other than whether they are of value or why they are so. No doubt, that sapphires are valuable to us explains our fascination with their topic and has led us to devise refined views about sapphires. But it shows nothing about the legitimacy of lapidary inquiries into the nature of sapphires. Rorty confuses what prompts our interest in truth with the focus of our interest. Inquiries can be into matters other than the tail-chasing one of what prompted the inquiry. No doubt, it is the fact that truth is good to believe that leads us to want an account of what exactly truth is, but a detailed account of what possesses this distinctive brand of goodness is not thereby rendered illicit or deficient.

We may hope that our inquiries into the nature of truth will also shed light on why we value it. But this shouldn't blind us to the fact that an inquiry into the nature of what it is that we value so much and for such-and-such a reason is likely to be worthwhile enough. Moreover, I find Rorty's glib generalization about the motives of such research egregiously mistaken or, because it is so vague, overstated about my own case and almost as certainly about the cases of some others with whose motives I am familiar. As for his caricature of what Correspondence discovers – the trivialized formula ' "this is red" pictures the world' – we have already answered subtler forms of essentially the same objection in Chapter 3, section 2.

Since the attempt to replace the original question doesn't enhance the plausibility of Pragmatism, let us see how Pragmatism fares as a view about what *makes* a belief or statement true. Even if not many would now accept Pragmatism's claims in this regard, it is important to locate its basic failures. Briefly, it seems to reside in its determination to stop short in its explanations. It leaves mysteries for which it has not the internal resources either to allay or to declare illegitimate. Let us elaborate.

According to pragmatists, philosophical treatments of truth may be divided into two classes. A metaphysical treatment, rejected by them, takes truth for a static, eternal or transcendent property or relation. This sort of truth obtains independently of the adequacy of our means for acquiring it; and, then, in top-down fashion we use it to design or formulate cognitive practices that will give us the best chance of acquiring it (though without guarantees). Evidently, the truth-linked notion of justification exhibits this pattern. A moot question, which we shall re-examine presently, is whether all the relevant data for conceptions falling within this broad ambit are themselves top-down. The second treatment is, as Rorty puts it, a 'workaday' notion of truth. It is formed in close connection with our verification procedures and emerges from our practice of acknowledging successful inquiries. But in order to confine themselves to this second conception, pragmatists routinely disallow what seem to be legitimate investigations into the further nature of this palpable success that is recognizable when it obtains. Since the questions cannot be easily dismissed, we are entitled to know how the pragmatist can countenance them. For they appear to demand answers that Pragmatism is incapable of providing. I shall cite three examples.

First, concrete success does not yet distinguish *truth* from *justified belief*. Despite a regular pragmatist conflation of truth and knowledge, the former two notions are certainly distinct. This is perhaps made clearest in the case of defeasible justifications (Chapter 7, sections 4–5); but it is sufficient to point out that when we change our minds in light of further evidence, we might still hold that our original belief was *justified*, but not that it was *true*. Nothing in Pragmatism prepares us for this distinction or has articles for explaining it. If these are different features, why is Pragmatism's account of each exactly the same in the cases where both notions are applicable (that is, where beliefs are justified *and* true)? Second, truth, as Peirce has written, is the opinion 'fated to be ultimately agreed to by all who investigate'. (He does not even say that it *should be* agreed to, but that it *will be*.) But what makes convergence, rather than divergence, of opinion inevitable? And why should it matter to truth? Moreover, there are many kinds of potential convergence which Peirce would no doubt want to exclude as irrelevant: such as the emergence of a hypnotic thinker who converts everyone by dint of her character, or a mind-altering chemical in the water supply that creates intellectual zombies. Narrowing convergence to the relevant sort makes it all the more puzzling why it should be 'fated'. Of course, Correspondence could explain the likelihood of convergence in terms of the nature of the world on which the evidence of all inquirers is ultimately triangulated. And while it might be too hasty to claim that this is the only explanation, certainly Pragmatism seems to owe us an alternative account. Finally, Pragmatism also seems to require a type of synchronic convergence of inquirers. In responding to critics about its unfortunate adoption of the term 'satisfaction', pragmatists are prone to reply that the satisfaction is not merely personal, but is a kind that is available to each similarly equipped cognizer. This is not merely an optional response for pragmatists: the perennial undergraduate favourite 'true for me but not for you' is not a serious contender in the truth-theory sweepstakes. Thus, how could the relevant verifier be something a cognizer doesn't share generally with other cognizers? Once again, while Correspondence can appeal to an experience-independent world on which experiences of certain sort can be expected to converge, and Coherence can appeal to a system of common judgments with which the one in question must fit, it is difficult to know what Pragmatism might say. Why, for example, shouldn't truth satisfy only half of an otherwise indistinguishable group of cognizers? Does Pragmatism supply any reason to believe that satisfaction should converge upon truth-gatherers as such? Here it does not even appear that pragmatists can give a non-psychological explanation that wouldn't violate their prohibition against truth theories of the first sort.

It is important to realize that these lines of inquiry are merely natural attempts to extend descriptions of our practices which pragmatists themselves would tender: thus, whatever might be used to complete the inquiry gets introduced bottom-up. This is critical because it seems to be widely accepted by pragmatists that all evidence-transcendent concepts of truth start from an *a priori* notion that has pretensions of dictating, in top-down and wholly unempirical fashion, to the empirical sciences. To see us as merely extending an inquiry initiated by Pragmatism makes it much more difficult to tar and feather all versions of Correspondence with the same broad brush wielded against certain other non-epistemic conceptions of truth. And this makes it difficult for pragmatists to reject the question itself by condemning all other possible answers to it on this single ground. (It is not essential here that Correspondence supplies the needed answers, but only that Pragmatism doesn't.) In fact, Pragmatism is in a peculiarly unfavourable position for rejecting the question. Verificationists have a principled basis for disarming an embarrassing question by declaring it meaningless (because metaphysical). But pragmatists have no such systematic theory of meaningfulness. Their *pis aller* may be to stand up squarely for practicality in philosophizing. But that is totally ineffective here. We should render some credit to Disraeli's observation that the practical man is the man who practises the mistakes of his forefathers. But, if this is too harsh, this is still an insufficient basis for settling disputes in which each of the antagonists has a detailed view; for one man's practicality is only another's lack of vision.

The above are not the only instances in which pragmatists decline to provide explanations for which their remarks seem to create a need. For example, James accepts that truth is a kind of agreement with reality only because 'Pragmatism defines "agreeing" to mean certain ways of "working", be they actual or potential'.[24] But if we ponder the implications of *potential workings*, we quickly realize that they stand as much in need of a ground in something as does convergence. If something about the world supplies the ground, isn't it more reasonable to take that as our truth-constituter rather than the experience (possible or actual) resulting from it?

A related difficulty is connected to a tension within Pragmatism to accommodate two incongruous tendencies: namely, the tendency to make truth reside in an experience accessible to an individual cognizer and the tendency to escape from a subjective conception of truth. These could be called the satisfaction and convergence tendencies, respectively, because these are ways in which prominent pragmatists have characterized each of them. According to pragmatists such as James, placing truth beyond something that is spelled out by a termination in sensible experience is 'going beyond experience' in just the way that absolute and static truth-concepts do. However, if the truth-constituter must be understood *via* the actual or possible experiences of *all* cognizers, then the individual stands in just the relation to this state of affairs that she would to the supposedly mind-independent state of affairs to which Correspondence appeals. What, then, has happened to the supposed advantage of Pragmatism? Why is the community of experiences, to which no single cognizer (and perhaps no group of *actual* cognizers) has direct access superior to a mind-independent world of facts? We might surmise that pragmatists were selective, for no apparent reason in their scepticisms: taking scepticism about the external world seriously, but discounting scepticism about other minds. I can find no other reason for their belief that Pragmatism has an advantage in the accessibility of truth to practise over Correspondence.

These defects seem to have a common root: the attempt to devise a notion of truth out of epistemic justification rather than beginning with a truth-linked notion of justification. When we try to fix up our notion of satisfaction to seem less personal and subjective, we run afoul of new problems about why it works that Pragmatism seems incapable of handling. When we attempt to make satisfaction self-sufficient, we see that broader considerations from our prereflective, and no doubt truth-linked, notion of justification prevent it from operating on its own. I fail to see how any version of Pragmatism can avoid these kinds of difficulties.

Moreover, ignoring difficulties of inaccessibility and interpreting satisfaction sympathetically, it is simply not the case that true beliefs always lead to satisfactions and false ones to dissatisfactions. Whether our beliefs lead to satisfactions or dissatisfactions will depend, in part, on what other beliefs we hold. Chisholm succinctly sums up the problem:

(T)he belief that there are tigers in India, even if it is true, need not lead to satisfaction (the man may encounter tigers, but mistakenly think that they are lions or that he is not in India) and it may even lead to dissatisfaction (he goes to Syria, finds no tigers, and mistakenly believes that he is in India).[25]

This illustrates a point insisted upon by the Belief Holist: our beliefs do not confront the world separately. Satisfactions concern only what we expect given our other beliefs, not given what is so. Therefore, we must be ready for satisfaction to vary with the beliefs creating those expectations, regardless of the truth of the beliefs we want tested.

III Redundancy

7 REDUNDANCY'S SUB-THESES

Although the Redundancy (or Logical Superfluidity) Thesis is a view *about* truth, it would be, at a minimum, misleading to call it a theory *of* truth. *Prima-facie* Redundancy rejects all theories of truth. By its choice of examples it suggests that if a substantial theory of truth were possible, it would be Correspondence. But if we are not considering some of the further uses for which it has been commandeered, Redundancy affirms that no such theory is possible.

We discussed this thesis in Chapter 2, and some of what is said in this section merely elaborates points raised there. But in Chapter 2 Redundancy was only an illustration, and it deserves separate attention, since, for many, it is the chief obstacle to Correspondence. For it has not only discouraged some from trying to achieve a substantial truth theory; it has also spurred efforts in other directions. It has been used as an anti-Correspondence weapon in arguments for Coherence. And it has been employed to suggest altogether different approaches to the basic questions involving truth: for example, to produce justification-condition semantic accounts as bases for the notion of a truth-condition, or to replace questions about what makes a statement true with questions about the illocutionary force or purpose of predicating 'is true'. This protean nature of Redundancy in the service of disparate, occasionally incompatible, views indicates its centrality in the thinking of those who tackle the questions outlined in Chapter 2. Save in the odd case when it has been pressed into the service of Coherence – a case so rare that we shall henceforth ignore it – its view of truth is deflationary: to say that a statement is true does not amount to what is prereflectively believed, for it says nothing more (assertively) than the statement does. The common thread in all of the roles of Redundancy is that it is incompatible with Correspondence, for it denies to our common forms of speech any power to affirm the word–world relations that Correspondence requires.

As I understand Redundancy, it involves three theses, though these are often confused with one another and with the total view. As a rule, its proponents do not recognize such distinctions, but I hope that doing so here will aid us in avoiding confusion and will illuminate arguments for Redundancy. The subtheses are as follows:

(A) *Logical Equivalence.* A statement made with a sentence of the form '*p*' is true if and only if one made with a sentence of the form '*p* is true' is true.[26]

(B) *Semantic Equivalence.* A sentence of the form '*p* is true' means the same as (or, nothing more than) one of the form '*p*'.[27]

(C) *No Truth.* There is no traditional problem of truth. (Sometimes this is formulated by saying that truth is neither a property nor a relation, or that the only thing left to the problem of truth is that of the nature of judgment.)

(C) leaves what can be said about truth to the other theses. Although some have regarded (B) as Redundancy itself, I take (C) as vital to it. At a minimum, if Semantic Equivalence had not been perceived to have as a consequence No Truth, Redundancy would play a relatively marginal role in these controversies.[28] To see this, first note that various Correspondence theorists cheerfully concede Logical Equivalence, (A), and are not thereby numbered among adherents of Redundancy. Why, then, should they be considered Redundancy theorists if accepting Semantic Equivalence also does not deter them from accepting a full-blooded

Correspondence Theory? (A) too is necessary for Redundancy – though, for reasons just given, not sufficient. We may also remark that (A)'s equivalence is more than *material* because it must hold for any two sentences related as '*p*' and '*p* is true'.

The role of (B), Semantic Equivalence, is singular. Not only have various thinkers taken it (wrongly) for Redundancy itself, but it seems indispensable to the inference to (C). This is not to say that all Redundancy theorists have used, or even approved of, the idioms of *meaning* and *sense*. Some have instead envisaged a complete *account, explication* or *analysis* of the concept of truth.[29] But all have been after appreciably the same sort of thing sought by those who pursued the meanings or senses of words which they supposed expressed that concept. Still others have framed their views in terms of *what is said, asserted* or *stated* when one says something of the form '*p* is true'. Again, despite a serious ambiguity in 'what is said (etc.)', the contexts of these remarks makes it clear that what is intended is that the linguistic forms in question be conventionally proficient for expressing the same information – which is close enough for present purposes to saying that they have the same meaning. The basic point in all the cases mentioned is that there is a reduction of the semantic content or information in sentences of the form '*p* is true' to the semantic content or information of those of the same sentence *sans* the predicate 'is true'.

The argument typically proceeds as follows. The question of truth is a *Scheinproblem*; for, once (B) shows us that 'is true' contributes nothing to the semantic content of sentences in which it occurs, there is no longer a reason for holding that it expresses a property. We cannot have learned that truth is a property anywhere but from ordinary expressions such as 'is true'. But if there is no property of truth, efforts to elucidate the worldly conditions for its application accomplish nothing. And similar reasoning shows, *mutatis mutandis*, that the sentential operator 'it is true that' is no better off.

8 MEANING AND TRUTH-MAKING CONDITIONS

Redundancy has been challenged at a number of junctures. For example, Logical Equivalence has been rejected on the grounds that there are more than two truth-values. Certainly, if there are undefined values, a statement made with '*p*' could be undefined (neither true nor false), while one made with '*p* is true' would be false. (A) relies on bivalence, or *tertium non datur*, if those are distinguishable.[30] Alternatively, the inference from Logical to Semantic Equivalence might be questioned. It has been claimed that although the logical equivalence of sentences may be necessary for their semantic equivalence, it is not sufficient. Were it sufficient, all logical truths would mean the same thing, as would all logical falsehoods. Moreover, sentences such as 'This object has size' and 'This object has shape' would mean the same, although clearly 'has size' and 'has shape' mean something different.[31] Although these objections deserve attention, for the sake of argument I shall question neither (A) nor the inference from it to (B). This is so that we may concentrate on the role of Semantic Equivalence in supporting the No Truth Thesis, which touches more closely upon the concerns of theories of truth in general. I shall venture two claims. First, the argument from Semantic Equivalence against classical theories of truth is misguided; second, none the less, without (B)'s role in this erroneous reasoning, Redundancy has not even the semblance of plausibility.

I have maintained all along that Correspondence addresses the question

(1') What are the conditions by virtue of which a statement is true?

(B) does not attempt to answer this question, but the use to which it is put indicates that it takes an answer to another of our earlier questions

(7') What is the meaning of the phrase 'is true' and 'it is true that'?

to exhaust whatever might be of interest in an answer to (1'). In particular, the use of (B) to defend (C) implies that a deflationary answer to (7') eliminates the possibility of a substantial answer to (1'). Thus, let us look more closely at the reasons given in Chapter 2 to show that a thesis about the meaning of 'is true' is no substitute for one about truth-constituters.

Even if the truth-conditions for the sentential function '*x* is a gringo' could be separated for purposes of analysis from the predicate's derogatory tone as an ethnic slur, it is clear why we might not want to accept those truth-conditions as a complete account of the predicate's *meaning*. In ignoring the potential for derogation, it ignores something vital to the term's current use. But this has no tendency to show that there is no legitimate work to be done by the earlier account of its truth-conditions.

Similarly, Correspondence seeks something within the domain of truth-conditions for truth. That characterization is too broad because, as noted in Chapter 2, sections 7 and 9, truth-conditions may be either

(a) conditions making a statement true

or

(b) conditions under which the statement is true: that is, necessary and sufficient conditions for the statement's truth.

It is (a) rather than (b) that Correspondence attempts to track. For, although all total specifications of (a) are specifications of (b), the converse does not hold. One can specify (b) without thereby supplying the conditions that account for the statement's being true. Accordingly, a demand for the meaning of 'is true' may yield (b) *and* fail to yield (a). But that may be because a demand for the meaning of 'is true' yielding (b) may be a different and independent demand than one for (a). The former neither renders nugatory the need for an account of (a) nor provides a substitute with any semblance of accomplishing (a)'s task.

Of course, there are vital differences between the hypothetical case involving the predicate 'is a gringo' and the situation of Redundancy. In the former we were concerned with *surplus meaning* going beyond the predicate's truth-conditions; but if Redundancy is correct, truth-conditions supply the whole meaning of 'true' and they are present *before* 'is true' is attached to a sentence or statement. Moreover, with 'gringo' we have two essentially semantic accounts; one concerning its meaning, another its truth-conditions. But the crucial difference for Redundancy is between any semantic account, of the meaning or truth-conditions of 'is true', and the constitutive conditions for a statement's being true (whether or not the term 'true' is used in the object-language

116

whose account is being given). Despite these differences, both cases seem to rest on a similar mistake: namely, supposing that the conditions for applying a concept can only be understood through a full account of the semantics of the linguistic formulae used to express that concept. Perhaps this works for a host of cases. But when it is transformed into a general, meta-philosophical maxim directing our practice, it leads us to overlook important distinctions.

To see this, let us try to bring to light that instance of the maxim which we could expect to be employed by those who infer, without further explanation, from Semantic Equivalence (B), to No Truth (C). The only 'principle of inference' I can imagine might be expressed as follows: anything worth saying about conditions for the application of truth is discoverable in the semantic features of the expressions whose primary office is to introduce the notion into our languages. Of course, when stated this baldly, few would be tempted to accept it. But it does conform to a general philosophical practice concerning a number of concepts, and we are looking for something that would explain what it is that induces philosophers to infer (C) from (B) without being struck by a need to explain this step further. If there is another explanation very different from this one, I am unacquainted with it. However, the maxim fails in the following critical instance. According to Redundancy there is no difference worth noting between *saying of a statement* S that it is true and simply making S *without saying of it* that it is true. But this non-difference fails to capture the genuine distinction between S having the property of being true and S not having that property: in other words, between being true and not being true. Here is a vital difference between truth and its absence not at all reflected, according to (B), in the semantic difference between a saying about truth and the saying's absence. The failure is critical because it is precisely the difference between being true and not being true toward which Correspondence's efforts have been traditionally directed. It is the difference for which Correspondence purports to account. Rather than resolving this issue, we see how the Thesis of Semantic Equivalence is designed to overlook it. But that is fatal. Reformulating a question in such a way that the original issue cannot be sensibly stated does not show that the issue, in this case (1'), is bogus, much less that one's favoured issue (7'), settles it.

Let us see more exactly the nature of this objection to Redundancy. It is not being claimed that Semantic Equivalence translates the original issue badly, but rather that it is no translation at all. When we engage in semantic ascent what we discover is that the particular differences for which Correspondence sought an account cannot be captured by our new way of phrasing questions. The closest semanticized formulae which Redundancy allows conceal the old issue rather than rendering it more perspicuous. We cannot suppose that the old issue disappears just because it no longer occurs in our reformulations. This might have been more evident were it not for the philosophical blinkers put on by allowing ourselves to be tacitly guided by the maxim of the last paragraph.

Since this attack has been aimed at the role of Semantic Equivalence in Redundancy, is there perhaps a hope for the latter view without (B)? This would not be an altogether outlandish expectation. After all, Correspondence has frequently been proposed as a theory about what 'true' means, and we have seen that it has survived this misstatement. We would not wish to reject Redundancy just because of a similarly misleading way of framing a valuable insight. However, although semantic claims may be mere window dressing for Correspondence, Semantic Equivalence is indispensable to Redundancy. In order to see this, consider once again the import of (B).

In saying that '*p*' and '*p* is true' mean the same, (B) denies that 'is true' contributes anything to the semantic content of sentences in which it appears; but it does not deny that sentences of the form '*p* is true' have any meaning. Rather, it says what meaning, if any, that they have: namely, the meaning that '*p*' has. We must here emphasize the obvious point that (B) would be an inappropriate vehicle for arguing that sentences of form '*p* is true' have no meaning: for the argument it exemplifies begins from the assumption that the sentence to whose meaning it is reduced *may* have a meaning.

Thus, suppose we attempt to establish No Truth on the basis of (A), Logical Equivalence, without going through the semantic claim. Let us call this Revised Redundancy. On it, what do '*p*' and '*p* is true' have in common? No more, it appears, than their *truth conditions*. (We may provisionally overlook the fact that this is only for type (b) conditions, not for those of type (a).)

Consequently, 'is true' adds nothing to the truth-conditions of *p*. However, just as Semantic Equivalence did not attempt to deny that the equivalent sentences each had meaning, this can be no attempt to deny that each has truth-conditions. And rather than leading us to believe that there is no problem for a theory of truth to treat, this highlights it. For the question 'What are these truth-conditions (that '*p*' and '*p* is true' share)?' does not have the same authority to dissipate the problem of what it is that makes them true that we get when we turn from the question of truth-conditions to that of meaning. Indeed, the question sends us directly back to our original issue.

To concentrate on the last point, we overlooked the distinction between truth-conditions of type (a) and those (merely) of type (b). But if we keep in mind that, as argued in Chapter 2, (b) is no substitute for the possession of (a), we close off what appears to be the last remaining escape route for Redundancy. For the adherent of Revised Redundancy might argue that what '*p*' and '*p* is true' share in the way of truth-conditions can be specified innocuously – say, by theorem schema (T). But I hope that it is perfectly clear by now that all this does is to paper over the original problem without providing any demonstration that it is not a legitimate one.

The point may be further reinforced by seeing the more precise moral of Logical Equivalence: namely, that 'is true' makes *no further contribution* to the truth-conditions of propositional clauses to which it attaches. But this does not show, as Redundancy would have it, that 'is true' is vacuous. A repeated sentence makes no further contribution to the discourse of which it is a part, but it is not thereby vacuous. It has the same meaning that the sentence did on its first occurrence. We may expect that if 'is true' had any contribution to make, it would include one to the truth-conditions of the propositional phrase preceding it. But, as (A) tells us, that propositional phrase has already made that contribution. Thus, 'is true' has the peculiar misfortune of always arriving too late. Nevertheless, what it would have contributed is genuine. Though not many phrases are in this position, the situation is not so counterintuitive when we realize that this is because that contribution must be built into the nature of the propositional clause. Thus, we need not even take (B), Semantic Equivalence, as saying that 'is true' has no meaning: it is more plausible to hold that it expresses explicitly part of what is only implicit in any asserted sentence to which it is attached. This robs us of whatever motivation we might have had to conclude (C) from (B).

9 SUMMARY

Let us once more take stock of what we have accomplished. We began Chapter 2 with a skeletal form of Correspondence, which was then distinguished from other sorts of views with which it has regularly been associated. This enabled us to distinguish it from other sorts of commitment by which it has been erroneously supposed to be bound. Next, we detailed (in Chapter 3) leading objections of principle to Correspondence. We discovered adequate rejoinders to each. Finally, in the present chapter, we discussed the alternatives with which Correspondence might be replaced. The first two, Coherence and Pragmatism, are substantial theories of truth; but they have serious flaws not matched by anything in Correspondence. The last, Redundancy, would reject all forms of classical theories of truth. However, it was argued that this view suffers from a special case of the confusion between accounts of meaning and constitution first uncovered in Chapter 2. With that behind us, we may now proceed to consider a more detailed specification of Correspondence.

V

CORRESPONDENCE

The central task of this chapter is to frame a defensible detailed version of the Correspondence Theory of Truth. Though I stand by its plausibility, I do not claim that it is the exclusively correct version. But it serves us to have a demonstration that Correspondence can be given a more elaborate formulation – one that even addresses some persistent doubts mentioned, but not treated further, early in Chapter 2. However, before introducing this version, let us interject a few remarks about our defence in the previous chapters and possible additions that might be made to it.

1 APOLOGIA

The preceding case for Correspondence can be divided into stages. First, a thought experiment in Chapter 1, section 5 served as our initial inducement for adopting the view. But, in addition, we remarked that Correspondence is the commonsense truth theory, the one from which reflection on the issue arises. This, it appears, places the burden of proof on those who would reject it. Some may think the supposed commonsensicalness of Correspondence gives it no such advantage. But its *prima-facie* acceptability can be strengthened by recalling another observation of that section: namely, that even those opposed to Correspondence seldom reject it outright, but rather seek to show it is vacuous or can be incorporated as a trivial element of their favoured views. Thus, few if any, when confronted with what may be considered minimally informative, concise statements of the view – such as 'a statement is true when it corresponds to the facts' or ' "*p*" is true if and only if *p*' – simply dispute such claims. Rather, they are more inclined to object that these statements are unhelpful, or empty, or trivial, or neutral between competing views, or. . . . Consequently, a proper tack for a defender of Correspondence would be to show that such formulae are, say, neither vacuous nor trivial. We have defended Correspondence against the charge of vacuity in several places (e.g., Chapter 3, section 2; Chapter 4, sections 7–8). In future chapters we shall defend it against the charge of triviality by showing that various conceptions of epistemologized truth cannot satisfy these formulae. But this defence overlaps with the second stage of the case for Correspondence, so let us explain that.

With the initial reasons for adoption in place, at the second stage we defended Correspondence, first by sharpening the doctrine, thus pre-empting misunderstandings and potential objections (Chapter 2), then by replying to the weightiest remaining objections (Chapter 3), and finally by showing that the most promising alternatives have basic shortcomings (Chapter 4). This work continues in Part II, where we shall examine the most prominent recent doctrines of epistemologized truth.

Thus far our batteries have been aimed quite generally. But we must not neglect those who, while rejecting Correspondence for what they regard as its irremediable flaws, remain equally impervious to the blandishments of alternative truth theories and to any version of cognition-dependent truth. They may reconcile themselves to this by accepting Redundancy as the last word on the subject and continuing to believe themselves basically realists because this stops short of epistemologizing truth, or they might simply plead agnosticism. For such reluctant realists there is a further consideration to persuade them that, if any account of truth is possible, it must be Correspondence. It is worth our while briefly to explore it.

Certainly, a substantial portion of our statement-making utterances employ singular affirmative subject–predicate sentences. Anyone countenancing a distinction between true and false (/nontrue) statements cannot avoid taking them as a central case. But since we have eliminated, *ex hypothesi*, across-the-board cognition-dependence, such utterances, among others, will contain elements having realistic word–world connections necessary for their truth. These are, of course, the referential or denotational uses of certain of the sentence's expressions. Now earlier (Chapter 2, section 9) we distinguished some necessary and/or sufficient conditions for truth from those actually contributing to a statement's truth. The former are not always contributory conditions. But what is crucial here is that contributory conditions *can be*, and commonly are, necessary or sufficient. Referential elements are, where relevant, invariably *contributory* necessary conditions for the truth of the statement in whose making they occur. These are conditions that associate singular terms, as used, and predicate expressions, as used, with individuals and sets (or properties), respectively. If such relations are necessary for truth, it is difficult to see how any account of the matter other than Correspondence could succeed. How, for example, could Coherence, Pragmatism, or even Redundancy, incorporate this sort of contribution to truth? Just as significantly, if the condition is admitted at all, it is difficult to see how its contribution could be other than central. Thus, even if it is not sufficient, it certainly looks as if Correspondence is the only handy solution, if not an inevitable one. At a minimum, if we have such a central ingredient of truth that is incompatible with the other leading views, how could there be a successful *principled* objection to Correspondence, whatever the particular faults of a given version? Thus, realistic referential and denotational conditions, if accepted, are a strong inducement to adopt Correspondence.

We might attempt to formulate this contributory necessary condition as follows, specifying the condition schematically for a statement S made with sentence S+. (Because of scope complications, we restrict S+ to *affirmative* subject–predicate sentences.)

> S is true *only if* there is a function, f, mapping singular terms and predicates in S+ onto things and sets, respectively, such that S+'s singular terms, as used, denote the things and S+'s predicate(s), as used, express the set(s) assigned by f.

Aside from the fact that this condition is explicitly designed to be contributory, it also differs in certain other respects from what may be found in well-known semantic accounts of truth. What it demands for closed sentence S+ is not satisfaction by sequences of individuals, but relations with particular individuals or sets. Semantic accounts modelled on Tarski's satisfaction relation may also incorporate necessary conditions for truth, but they should not for that reason be confused with the one above. Moreover, since it is only a necessary condition, it does not commit us to taking sides on certain controversial questions concerning truth – such as whether an utterance can be true containing a description that misdescribes what it refers to.[1] But if we are given this much, it is easy to see how Correspondence is, as we have said, the only feasible account of truth, and it may even look unavoidable. Anti-realists who know their business obviously needn't be reminded by us of these facts. But it is useful in critical discussions like this to keep plainly in view that global anti-realists of every stripe seem committed to the rejection of even this much realism in their accounts of reference.

2 *A QUOI BON* A DETAILED FORMULATION?

A good philosophical theory, like a good scientific one, should have a key feature of a Kuhnian paradigm: namely, its general thrust should be plausible enough to outlive flaws that may undermine particular formulations. For that reason I am suspicious of the air of finality that too often envelops discussions of precise or detailed versions of Correspondence. The danger here is that merely local problems of formulation may be taken as grounds for abandoning a view, many of whose virtues are independent of, and thereby should outlast, the fortunes of its articulation in question. Partly for this reason, and partly to avoid distracting squabbles over the natures of bearers of truth-value and 'facts', I have thus far avoided attempts to improve upon our bare-bones characterization of Correspondence, which, in Chapter 2, section 1, read 'that what is true is so by virtue of its correspondence with something in the not-essentially-mind-dependent world'. This is not an apology for vagueness. Any view, however unmeritorious, can appear defensible if we are allowed to overlook every failure in its formulations. Thus, even our minimal characterization of Correspondence must be correct as far as it goes if there is to be any hope for more ample theories elaborated on its basis.

Despite this, there would be something untoward about a view that could not be elaborated beyond our sketchy characterization. Thus, it is also important to chart the progress that can be made with a more detailed account. We can make headway in this endeavour. An elaborated version of Correspondence can not only, as mentioned above, address certain misgivings raised early in Chapter 2, but also can be made resistant to previous attacks on similar formulations. The remainder of this chapter is devoted to fleshing out this promising, if not exclusively correct, version of the account.

3 AUSTIN AND MACKIE UPDATED

The best-known version of Correspondence since the Second World War is contained in an article by J. L. Austin, aptly entitled 'Truth', published in 1950.[2] It has been much bruited about in a series of papers by P. F. Strawson, who takes issue both with Austin's original essay and with refinements suggested by G. J. Warnock.[3] In 1970 J. L. Mackie published a modified version of Austinian Correspondence.[4] The version I shall offer builds upon foundations laid by Austin and Mackie; therefore, I shall begin with a summary of their proposals and of some central obstacles to their acceptance.

Austin's variation uses two sets of conventions, which he characterizes as follows.

Descriptive conventions correlating the words (sentences) with the *types* of situation, thing, event, etc. to be found in the world.

Demonstrative conventions correlating the words (statements) with the *historic* situation, etc. to be found in the world.

He then writes that a 'statement is said to be true when the historic state of affairs to which it is correlated by the demonstrative conventions (the one to which it 'refers') is of a type with which the sentence used in making it is correlated by the descriptive conventions'.[5]

The formulation and Austin's interpretation of it have several flaws. First, although it is not an explicit part of the dictum, Austin regards the above as an account of the *meaning* of 'true' or 'is true'. That not only makes the account vulnerable to the sorts of attacks reviewed in Chapter 2, section 7, but it may have motivated his heavy reliance on the role of *conventions* to elucidate truth; for no doubt meaning requires conventions at some level(s). These particular involvements of meaning and convention are weaknesses in the account. Second, the relevant connection between *statements* and states of affairs is not a matter of convention, demonstrative or otherwise, but of whether the statement is true or not. In making the statement one *uses* a sentence, and it is the sentence-as-used, rather than the statement, which is related in the appropriate way to a certain state of affairs. Finally, to say that a statement is true is not to say that certain semantic conventions are fulfilled. Strawson employed the last two weaknesses in Austin's dictum to argue that the latter had confused the conditions for a statement's identity with those for its truth. Each fault is eliminable, though it may be impossible to say whether after the overhaul we still have what is recognizably Austin's theory. What we can say is that the resulting view may continue to employ the distinctive devices brought to our attention by Austin's work.

Mackie amends the formula, avoiding to some extent the flaws mentioned, with the following restatement:

> We start with a speech-episode, which is the using a certain sentence in a certain way and in a certain context, and which thereby is also the making of a certain statement. The sentence, thus used, is correlated by what Austin calls demonstrative conventions with a certain historic situation or state of affairs. The sentence (irrespective of this particular context) is also correlated, separately, by what he calls descriptive conventions with a certain type of situation. And then to say that the statement is true is to say that this historic situation is of this type.[6]

The essence of both versions is that the truth of a statement is a matter of a particular situation belonging to a certain type. (To avoid possible misunderstanding we might add 'or being identical with that type'. For some statements are perfectly universal – for example, those made with some conceivable uses of the sentences 'Time passes' and 'Nothing is perfect' – and some are perfectly singular – such as statements made with eternal sentences, as we perhaps have with 'Jonathan E. Robertson eats (timelessly) dinner at 20:00 GMT, 15 June AD 1986 at location Y'. And it might be held that the correlative situation *types* do not permit instances.) Previous versions of Correspondence led friends and critics alike to query what it is about a particular statement – *qua* stated in a particular form of words – and situations that permitted the first to 'correspond' to the second. Suggestions ranged from the words naturally resembling the situation to the two having a structural correlation of elements. But none proved satisfactory.[7] However, correspondence as understood by Austin and Mackie needn't involve any isomorphism, or other sort of match, conventional or natural, by which elements of the sentence-as-used are correlated with those of the situation. We demand merely that a certain token be of a certain type. This eliminates much of the usual disquiet about how the pairings of the elements are to go. It also undermines one of the prime motives earlier in this century for seeking a theory of truth through a theory of meaning. For sentences need not be *pictures* of states of affairs in order for us to understand how they can be related to the world by ties of truth and falsity. Of course, we are still left with the question of the mechanisms by means of which the relevant type and token situations are isolated. (It *is* a legitimate question, but I shall shortly argue that it is not one that Correspondence need undertake to answer.) But even if these procedures stand in need of explanation, some of which we shall try to provide, the problems are much more manageable than those of fixing the way true statements do, and false ones do not, mirror the structure of the world.

In spite of Mackie's improvements, Austin's dictum could use more extensive refurbishing. For one thing, Mackie still employs sorts of *conventions*. Although this may turn out to be harmless, it is more provocative than the basic theory he wants to elucidate; and it is thus worth avoiding where possible. It is truistic that sentence-types which can be used to make statements are useful to us because they are appropriate to situations of certain types rather than others. Thus, a sentence such as 'Your dinner is on the table' *is associated with* or *isolates* one type of situation. However elusive the correct details of this point, its certitude should not be lost in squabbles over the kinds of conventions (if any) that may bring it off. Indeed, the notion of convention is itself moot.

Despite a few heroic attempts to harness it, it is still unclear whether we can attain a single account to cover very many of the uses to which philosophers have wanted to put it. But we should be able to avoid getting embroiled in these issues here; for we have no proprietary interest in meaning, and it is the sentence-situation association itself, not its mechanics, that concern Correspondence. Moreover, the mention of *historic* situations *may* restrict the formula to tensed sentences, and this is unnecessary at the present stage. Finally, although *what it is to say that a statement is true* could, in context, amount to no more than *the conditions constituting the statement's truth*, it is best to make explicit that it is the latter which is our quarry.

With those suggestions for changes in mind, let us reformulate Correspondence as follows:

> A statement made with sentence S is made true by *the specific state of affairs which S-as-used demonstrates being of a type discriminated by the type of S,* qua *sentence.*

This version preserves that part of Mackie's which says that a statement's truth is a matter of a certain situation (= state of affairs) belonging to a given type of situation (= state of affairs). Also the links of situations – specific or typal, conventional or otherwise – are with sentences, not statements. But this formulation also makes clear that it is *what* S and S-as-used do (that is, discriminate and demonstrate) and not *how* they do it, that concerns the theory of truth. If we can agree that sentences and sentences-as-used do this – and the evidence that they do is overwhelming – we can set aside questions of the mechanisms by means of which they do it. And this allows us to put to one side such questions as whether descriptive and demonstrative conventions are exclusive sets or whether they overlap, whether descriptive conventions determine the meanings of the sentences they cover, and whether the relations are conventional at all. Of course, not all issues disappear on the above view. We have already mentioned what we should do about situation-types without instances: namely, test the demonstratum for identity with the discriminatum. But we are left with the more important questions of *which* situation-types and situations are discriminated and demonstrated, respectively, by a certain sentence, and what is meant by a situation. With those provisos let us turn again to discrimination and demonstration.

4 DISCRIMINATION, DEMONSTRATION AND A STRAWSONIAN PUZZLE LAID TO REST

Not much can be said to elucidate further what it is for a sentence-type to discriminate a type of situation. The notion is intended to capture the elusive but unavoidable datum indicated earlier with the aid of terms such as 'associate' and 'isolate': namely, that a given sentence carves out one sort of circumstance for potential attention and neglects others. I do not know of anyone who rejects this – though, as we might expect, there are differences over the relation's extent and nature. Those who maintain that a semantic account of sentences requires that truth-conditions be given a central role rely upon discrimination. But also those who dispute this on the grounds that truth-conditions are occasionally verification-transcendent require, for their objection, that they can identify the situation which the sentence discriminates as a matter of its being verification-transcendent. Discriminated circumstances can be very broadly delineated, as in Strawson's example 'There have been wars before'. Nevertheless, the type of circumstance towards which this sentence directs attention is distinguished from that to which one is led by sentences such as 'There have been marriages before', 'There will be wars in the future' and 'There have never been wars'. The situation is, recall, a type, and thus needn't obtain.

The condition imposed by discrimination is rather modest. But one complication should be mentioned. It has been noted that a sentence is associated with more than one situation or state of affairs: that which its instances are used to deny as well as that which its instances are used to affirm. However, we should be able to distinguish these for purposes of understanding discrimination, since the connection with the type of state of affairs denied is only *by way of* the connection with the type affirmed. A handy rule of thumb is that we can say that 'x is F' can be used to deny that x is not F *because* it can be used to affirm that x is F, but we cannot say that it can be used to affirm that x is F *because* it can be used to deny that x is not F. One reason for this is that the denial in question can be coupled with the denial that x *is* F, if the intention is to say that no properties from the F-range are applicable to things such as x. But, more fundamentally, the converse 'because' relationship is simply regarded as erroneous. We would certainly admit that *if 'x is F' could not be* used to deny that x is not F, it *wouldn't be able* to be used to affirm that x is F. But this is, if anything, related to a contraposition of the *because* relationship we have insisted upon, and is certainly weaker than saying that the sentence can be used to affirm x is F because it denies that x is not F.

We now turn to *demonstration*. What is it for a sentence-as-used to demonstrate a specific situation? It cannot turn out the way a theory of reference must, although both demonstration and reference depend upon the same broadly referential devices of sentences-as-used to determine their connections. That is, both rely upon the singular terms, predicate expressions, common or general and abstract nouns (plus quantifiers), tenses and the like to determine their demonstrata and referents, respectively. However, demonstration is more like reference with mistakes and misapprehensions discounted. For example, suppose a speaker mistakes a grouse for a pheasant and says 'There's a pheasant in front of that bush'. Whatever she may have referred to, she demonstrated a situation of a grouse being in front of that bush. If she had hallucinated the fowl altogether, she may have demonstrated the situation of an empty patch of grass in front of the bush. Suppose another speaker mistook Algernon's voice for Ernest's, and was thus later prompted to recall 'Ernest was in the room'. On plausible accounts of reference he could have referred to Ernest, but the situation thereby demonstrated would be one in which Algernon was in the room. Thus, although demonstration must rely on the speaker's intention in, say, determining the location in which the relevant situation obtains (at least in the foregoing cases), some of the speaker's intentions may be ignored in order to arrive at the relevant situation which is tested for belonging or not belonging to a certain type.

It is important to realize that by 'a situation' we do not mean a concrete chunk of space and time, but *a featured circumstance*. Thus, a single slab of space-time, however finely sliced, could (perhaps always does) exemplify many situations. We can differentiate not only such widely disparate situations as Captain Cook's landing in Australia and my neighbour's dog burying his master's pyjamas; but also the runner's crossing the finish line and stumbling into the tape, though they occupy (roughly) the same location and time. As for subtler questions of identity, such as whether single situations are specifiable by non-synonymous descriptions, these turn on the same sorts of considerations that emerge in investigations of event- and act-identity.[8] Correspondence is compatible with either a liberal or a narrow interpretation of this kind of identity condition. That issue can be decided independently of the Austinian formulae. It is crucial only that there be at least one situation for each statement whose truth-value is determinable.

These remarks are relevant to a central objection which Strawson raised against the Austinian dictum. According to Strawson, 'The Austin–Warnock view is that one does not know exactly what statement is being made in any case unless one knows what particular historical situation is being referred to. So presumably it must be possible in principle in every case to specify this situation.'[9] For the sake of handy retrieval, we may officially phrase this as

(R1) One does not know which particular statement has been made unless one knows which situation has been referred to.

In our preferred idiom this requirement would be about demonstration rather than reference: to wit,

(D1) One does not know which particular statement has been made unless one knows which situation has been demonstrated.

Furthermore, these requirements gain whatever force they may have as epistemic reflections of requirements about statement-identity (and not merely our knowledge of it). Thus, each would be supported by:

(R2) A statement's identity depends upon the particular situation referred to.

(D2) A statement's identity depends upon the particular situation demonstrated.

Now, Strawson's observation certainly forebodes difficulty for the Austin–Warnock view, for if the situation mentioned in (R2) is the one whose relation to the sentence-as-used makes the statement true, then, read as intended, all identifiable statements, hence all statements, are true, and by (R1) we can know this just by virtue of knowing what statements are made. Strawson apparently accepts at least condition (R1) and perhaps (R2) as well. Thus, if we are to avoid this absurdity, we must scrap the other, truth relation defined in terms of that selfsame situation. Given the distinction between reference and demonstration, this dire consequence does not follow. But it prefigures a sufficiently similar one. For since the knowledge of the demonstrated situation is alleged to determine *both* our knowledge of the statement made, by (D1), *and* the truth-value of the statement, by the Austinian dictum, we could scarcely know what statement had been made without knowing whether or not it was true; absurdity enough to nullify any view implying it. Thus, even replacing reference by demonstration in our truth formula, there is enough potency in the Strawsonian objection to warrant serious concern.

Granting (D1) or (R1), it would appear that the only way to save the theory would be to find a more benign way to specify the situation it mentions. (We also must attach it by a relation other than the one we have dubbed 'demonstration', but we can ignore that complication.) Strawson searches unsuccessfully for a specification of a situation which both satisfies the (knowledge of) identity requirement while not thereby settling whether it belongs to the relevantly discriminated type. As might be expected, such attempts turn out to be thin descriptions, verging on vacuity in some instances, that bear little resemblance to anything we could acknowledge as obtaining. For example, for statement S made with the sentence 'Galileo formally recanted his opinions before the Inquisition on 12 June 1633', one might specify the situation, for (D1), of Galileo either recanting or not recanting. . . . But such choices drift so far from our grip on the notion of an actual situation that we are immediately confronted by embarrassing identity questions, for which it is difficult to see what basis there could be for a rational answer: questions such as whether this is the same situation as that of Galileo saying or not saying something. . . . We can see why Strawson quickly discovers that his search is doomed to fail. He concludes that attempts to salvage the Austinian dictum should be abandoned.

The way out of Strawson's quandary is simple: deny both (R1) and (D1). Although a statement states a situation to obtain, we need not know what situation actually obtains in order to know what statement has been made. Moreover, our version of Correspondence does not imply (D1) or (R1). In fact, neither does Austin's, however correct Strawson's ascription of (R1) to him may be. It is more plausible to hold either of the following:

(T1) A statement's identity is determined by its truth-conditions – that is, the conditions that *would* obtain were the statement true (and, perhaps, those that would obtain were it untrue).

(L1) The linguistic (or intentional) devices by virtue of which a sentence-as-used demonstrates a particular situation *are the same* as those by virtue of which the statement thereby made has its identity.

(T1) is, I believe, correct, and is defended in Chapter 7. But it does not require that anyone know of the *existence* of any actual situation. It says only that a certain situation *would occur* were the statement true. But (L1) is the more likely source of confusion here. Let us therefore turn to that.

In less stilted terms, (L1) says that it is because a statement has its particular identity that the sentence used in making it demonstrates the particular situation it does. Thus, it is a good candidate for the support of (D2). But it does not thereby lend credence to (D1). It is only an instance of the platitude that a thing exercises whatever capacities it has because of what it is. If it hadn't been that very thing, it wouldn't have been able to do just this. Our instance of the platitude does nothing to support the claim that we could not know what statement was made unless we knew the actual situation which, by virtue of its being that statement, it demonstrated. There is at least indirect evidence that Strawson conflates the questionable (R1) with the platitudinous (R2), and thereby the questionable (D1) with the platitudinous (D2); and that this may have been instrumental in his offering the exaggerated knowledge-of-identity requirement. For example, in alluding back to the problematic state of affairs created for Austin by knowledge of the statement's identity, he writes of 'an identified *existing* situation which it is a matter of the statement's identity that it refers to'.[10] Any existing situation a statement refers to (demonstrates), it does so by virtue of its being that statement. But the mere presence of the situation does not impose on our understanding a requirement that we first identify it in order to know what statement has been made. For the last remark yields no more than (L1) and hence no more than (R2) or (D2).

Nor does (L1) commit us to a demonstrated situation for every statement, and thus to a certain form of bivalence. Whether a certain statement demonstrates any situation at all can be left open. We need only insist that it must do so if it is to be true.

But perhaps it will be thought we have glossed over a legitimate source of uneasiness. For the restricted class of empirical judgments from which Strawson chooses his examples, it would be extraordinary if one understood the statements made while failing to have a certain level of knowledge about the situations they purportedly demonstrate. For example, could someone who did not know who Galileo is, what the Inquisition is, or anything about our calendar know what statement was made with S? However, the immediate problem with this appeal is that 'lack of understanding' here is a matter of degree, and it is not sharply distinguished from the sort involved in grasping the *sentence*. Surely we cannot demand total understanding if language users are ever to know what statements they make. Presumably the situation actually demonstrated involves happenings on that morning in the Convent of Santa Maria sopra Minerva in the heart of Rome. But it would be implausible to require that this be known. Must it even be known that it occurred in Galileo's vicinity on that morning? I think not. It would be surprising, but not impossible, to discover that Galileo employed a convention by means of which he signified his assent through *not* doing something at that time at a prearranged location some miles from his actual wherabouts. He may not have employed our routine means of stating. However, I do not wish to deny that something legitimate lies behind the uneasiness, but only to emphasize that it holds no promise for reviving (D1).

Consider also that although we believe that the statement is true, we might discover that it is an historical fabrication. Perhaps Galileo was spared the indignity by using a double to perform a mock recantation, while Galileo was miles from the enactment. In that case, the situation demonstrated *might be* different from the one we now believe demonstrated. In this unlikely state of affairs, it is difficult not to believe that the statement then made would be *the same one* we originally thought, though it turned out to be false. How then could knowledge of its identity hang upon that of the situation actually demonstrated?

Two minor clarifications. First, one may be able to tell from the sentence-as-used what *sort of* situation, if any, it will demonstrate. But if we allow this, we should distinguish the sort of situation demonstrated from *the type* the sentence-as-used discriminates. For some tokens of the type may not be instances of the sort, and obviously if the statement can be false instances of the sort will not all be tokens of the type. Second, if someone accepts S on the basis another's authority, then – assuming S is true – we must grant that she *knows* what situation has been demonstrated and knows it through knowing the statement that has been made. But she does not thereby know it just by virtue of understanding the statement. She must also believe it is authoritative. Thus, this is not an instance *per* (D1) in which one knows the statement only by virtue of knowing the situation demonstrated.

5 PARATACTIC UTTERANCES AND LIMITATIONS

How is our scheme applicable to sentences such as 'That's true', 'Yes', 'You're right', or 'It's just as she said'? These sentences are useless for discriminating the relevant states of affairs, since their conversationally pertinent content is nearly totally dependent on paratactic interpretation. But then we may simply recover the right type to be discriminated and instance to be demonstrated from the sentence used in the statement upon which the ones above are comments. This leads to varieties of uncertainty and indeterminacy that may at first seem a difficulty for our account. That is, in realistic discourse situations the statement upon which 'It's just as she said' is my comment may be made with a sentence such as, 'You can't pay all your debts'. And if this is directed to me, the relevant sentence in my words might be 'I can't pay all my debts', a different sentence from the one uttered. Moreover, her original words may be forgotten, and what I am commenting upon may be only her statement, which I would now put in rather different language. Alternatively, she may have said more than that, and it may be unclear, even in my own mind, just how much of it I am endorsing. For example, these uncertainties could emerge if I am queried about the possible interpretations or parts of what she said. What is the precise class of sentences whose utterances capture what I am agreeing to? Whether it includes a sentence I would use with 'G. V. can't pay all his debts' may depend on whether or not I believe those are my initials. Thus, there is both a measure of uncertainty and genuine indeterminacy in the decision about what sentence-as-used we choose for purposes of discrimination and determination in the case of the sentences now under consideration.

Should this be bothersome to a theorist? Not in most cases. We do not worry about the uncertainty and indeterminacy because, in the usual case, each of the candidate sentences that naturally come to mind will agree in truth-value. Further precision would be pointless. What of the case where the candidate sentences do not agree in truth-value? When this is realized we often ask further questions about what is meant; or where we are apprised of, say, ambiguity before speaking we may say, 'If she meant such-and-such, she's right'. But in some cases a crucial difference will not be resolvable by any such means; and here it is not important that we arrive at a definite answer, but only that our indeterminacy closely reflects that infecting our actual practice. Our practice also breaks down. And the claim of the present account of these essentially paratactic sentences is only that this inability to arrive at a definite answer is a reflection of an occasional inability in practice to discover what sentence(s) accurately interpret our utterance. This should be expected if our account is correct. Thus, an apparent problem with the account actually turns out to be one of its advantages.

It is still timely to issue a warning, as Austin[11] among others did earlier, against obsessions with the truth–falsity dichotomy. There are a number of other scales and distinctions of (what may be called for lack of a better label) *accuracy-success*, and they are often more to the point. Thus, a statement may fail not through outright falsity (untruth), but by being exaggerated, misleading, uninformative (secretive, concealing), out of place (for example, violating what Grice called a 'conversational maxim'),[12] vague, disproportionate or imprecise. For example, to suggest a bullet in the head as a cure for flu, where not a joke or sarcasm, is not proportionate to the discussion, but neither is it strictly false that this would cure one of the flu. Or if a scout says that the enemy has many troops behind the ridge, the commander may be more interested in whether they are enough to repel his attack than in the literal truth of the scout's report. Those of us for whom truth is an overwhelmingly important philosophical topic may easily contract the mistaken impression that it has a comparable authority in practical questions.

Moreover, even where 'true' and 'false' apply, they are not inflexible standards, oblivious to conversational context. In normal circumstances, to say that Iowa is flat is true – or, it is, as David Lewis puts it, true enough.[13] The statement is not falsified by any anthill or furrow that one happens upon. But if the conversational importance of precision is elevated, as in physics, this much flatness will no longer do. A similar phenomenon is illustrated by the use of various terms which, unlike terms such as 'caloric fluid' and 'ether', have outlived the rejection of the general theories with which they were originally associated. 'Mass' is one such expression. We would not accept everything a Newtonian says (or has said) about mass; but if it is said by a Newtonian that the mass of this object is between 2 and 3 grams, it would be pedantic to reject the saying's truth on the grounds that the object had to be moving slowly, and with respect to a certain frame of reference. We can assume what the intended frame of reference would have been, and that the object when weighed was moving slowly with respect to it. Whatever the underlying explanation for our accepting such claims – whether we need, as Hartry Field has suggested, notions of *partial denotation* and *partial significance* to account for the practice,[14] or whether we can manage the indeterminacy of the Newtonian conceptions in other ways – that collection of bits and pieces of background information we call 'conversational context' will be a determinant of how to apply our apparatus. Different cases may be accounted for in various ways. It may be a matter of the demonstratum, or the discriminatum, or their combination. But it is clear that room must be made for these adjustments if we are to allow any account of truth to approximate human practice with it.

6 LINGERING VEXATIOUS QUESTIONS

Certain vexed questions confront all versions of Correspondence. The following two highlight special sore points. Are there situations (/states of affairs/facts) for every one of the different kinds of truths, including counterfactuals and truths about social wholes? Shouldn't distinct truths demand distinct situations (and so on) making them true, thus leaving us with one situation per truth? Another vexed question can be raised about our version in particular: namely, since beliefs need not involve any sentences, how is our scheme of discrimination and demonstration applicable to this class of truth-bearers? I shall say a word about each of these questions.

First, using 'fact' to represent the world side of the truth-relation, I think it is correct that our intuitions about the kinds of facts there are and the kinds of truth there are diverge sharply. Intuitions restrict facts. Even if we allow other than fairly concrete items, we tend to quail at the notion of a conditional fact, much less a counterfactual one, and we do not feel comfortable about its being a fact that such-and-such is *possible* or that a chair *isn't* present. Moreover, can there be facts that nations do things, such as go to war, make treaties, raise taxes, as distinct from facts about what certain individuals do? It may be that the rejection of facts such as those mentioned is no more than a prejudice. But Correspondence, even the fact-based kind, also has other remedies. It is always possible to declare the statements of any of these various classes true not by virtue of their connection with facts of a like kind, but by virtue of their connection to statements of some other type, which in turn have connections with facts of the appropriate type. Thus, counterfactuals might be declared true or false on the basis of what actually has happened;[15] or the statement that the United States broke diplomatic relations with Libya might be understood in terms of the doings of certain individuals with recognized positions within each nation. The story need not go in either of these ways, but that it may show how nothing in Correspondence itself requires a realm of fact for every realm of statement.

Certainly the best tactic in this sort of dispute is to distinguish sharply between the interests of global and local realism. Global realism is represented here by our revised statement of Austinian

138

Correspondence; local realism, by the view that a certain fragment of language has truth-values founded in a distinctive sort of cognition-independent fact. (We must qualify this for realism about mental events, and must not construe 'distinctive' to rule out the possibility that this same set of facts may serve also as truth-constituter for another fragment of language if reductive analysis is successful.) This is not to concede local anti-realism for any or all of the areas we are not defending, but merely to insist that the issues needn't interlock. However, a consequence of this is that there is no guarantee, indeed no reason to believe, that there are different situations for every kind of truth. But that is wholly compatible with our procedure.

Next, consider true statements that are not reducible to or explicable in terms of other sorts of statements. Shouldn't different individual truths of this sort be made true by different situations? This seems a natural requisite, but it is doubtful that it can be satisfied. Imagine a true statement made with the sentence 'Jones, Smith and Robinson attended the banquet', and another, concerning the same banquet, made with the sentence 'At least two people attended the banquet'. The first is made true by (1) the situation of Jones, Smith and Robinson attending the banquet, and the second by (2) the situation of at least two people attending the banquet. Are (1) and (2) the same situation or not? The production of such cases and the baited question just posed contain an implied criticism of Correspondence. But the criticism contains a relatively superficial objection and a deeper one. Both need to be addressed.

In the superficial objection, it would be argued that this shows that there are no non-arbitrary identity-conditions for situations, and thus no sufficiently clear doctrine of Correspondence can be framed. The world is simply too messy for Correspondence. In reply to that I would answer as follows: (a) either answer to the question about the identity of (1) and (2) may be arbitrary; (b) this does not tend to show that all or more of the important questions about situation (/state of affairs/fact) identity have only arbitrary answers, and (c) the lack of a non-arbitrary answer is by itself no objection to Correspondence. For the point of the question, on this interpretation of the implied criticism, carries no suggestion that there aren't situations, but only suggests that we cannot tell whether we have specified one or two of them.

However, the absence of a razor-sharp principle of individuation is no more an objection to the existence of situations than our inability to decide whether we have two peaks or one with a deep saddle in it is to the existence or presence of mountains. Indeed, not only does our inability to answer the question non-arbitrarily *not show* that situations (or a situation) making each statement true fail to obtain, neither does it show that such situations are not genuine items in the world. At most, it discovers a borderline vagueness in the notion *situation* that prohibits us from answering the question. But a disputed border is not tantamount to anarchy.

But the deeper objection challenges the claim that situations are discoverable items. It uses (a) to argue that it is only through our contribution of principles of individuation that we may detect situations. Since situations require convention or whatever, which is our contribution, they do not belong to a cognition-independent world. This explains the lack of clear-cut identity and individuation principles governing them. The objection is a variant of the one we answered in Chapter 3, and we shall return to that answer presently. But first note that it is at least indirectly answered by remarks of the last paragraph. Such penumbral vagueness does not demonstrate chaos, and cannot be used to sponsor so ambitious a claim. For the condition of situations in this respect is no worse than that of many items whose credentials as cognition-independent cannot be challenged on this basis. Of course, one might employ the view of Chapter 3, section 5 to question the cognition-independence of anything that can be brought under concepts, such as crowns, trumpets and planets. But the conclusion does not follow from, and is not attempted on the basis of, the fact that for various circumstances we can imagine sticky individuation questions. However, aside from that point the objection fails because it simply ignores other explanations for the breakdown it cites.

Two other explanations, which complement each other rather than compete, are more persuasive than an appeal to our merely projecting situations on to the world. The first, again from Chapter 3, has to do with the unbounded luxuriance of reality. We can cross-classify parts of the world without foreseeable limit, and this prevents us from compiling a single, stable inventory of situations. But it provides us no reason for supposing that situations we extract from the world on one possible principle of classification are not in fact found there with cognition-independent boundaries. The homely moral of this exercise is just that the same pie can be divided in different ways. Second, we can harmlessly understand the crudity of our methods of discovery; for we need only be concerned with securing at least one situation per truth. (For the sake of exposition I assume there are no other reasons for including situations among our usable conceptual resources. Should this be otherwise, the point still holds, though it will require some irrelevant complication.) Where it is possible to make further distinctions between instantiated situations, but making them would not affect the assignment of truth-values, our unrefined (imperfect?) view of things need not and probably will not draw them. Indeed, we may suppose that some additional possible distinctions would complicate our method of identifying situations so as to make it more difficult to tell which of a certain class of situations was the one constituting the truth of a given statement. Since this would introduce an obstacle to assigning truth-values, it would be a reason for not adopting a method of specification that might be ontologically unobjectionable in itself. On the other hand, we need not answer the question whether (1) and (2) are identical so long as we can specify one or more situations sufficient to secure the truth of our two statements. Thus, it is understandable why such questions may be unanswerable even though situations exist mind-independently.

Finally, belief creates a problem. Our view requires both a sentence-type and an instance to determine the situation-type and actual situation that constitute truth or non-truth by the second belonging or not belonging to the first. But beliefs need not be embodied in sentences. They may be expressed by an action as non-verbal as opening one's umbrella. The predicament this presents for our view is no greater than it was for utterances such as 'You're right'. In so far as we ascribe a belief, the content of that belief will always be articulable in essentially the same way that a sentence is. Of course, if one merely opens an umbrella, this gives us much room for representing the belief expressed in a number of different sentences. This is allowable in practice because under ordinary conditions none of the myriad of distinct sentences with which the belief is representable will appear to result in different truth-values. And, as with our other similar problem, where representation does make a practical difference

141

to truth-value, we may undertake inquiries, such as querying the believer, to resolve the indeterminacy. On the other hand, when we are either deprived of the opportunity for doing this, or a further line of inquiry fails to resolve the issue, we do not question the notion of truth applied here, but the identity of the belief. Thus, difficulties in locating the relevant set of sentences to represent the belief – and which would give us within an acceptable margin of indeterminacy a basis for connecting the belief with a situation via discrimination and determination – are reflected in difficulties about the belief itself. If anything, this would seem to be a confirmation of our version of Correspondence rather than a problem for it. Given the large measure of indeterminacy infecting belief-ascription, we may still connect beliefs with classes of sentences. Where statements made with different sentences from the class threaten to diverge in truth-value, we seek further information to disambiguate the belief. Where this cannot be achieved, it is not our scheme for truth that becomes questionable, but the identity of the belief itself.

The foregoing has not answered all the questions one might have about global realism, but it has put both it and Correspondence on a firmer footing. It remains to take up the challenges presented by epistemologized doctrines of truth. Part II is devoted to that task.

PART II

VI

TRUTH EPISTEMOLOGIZED

1 A TAXONOMY OF NEO-ANTI-REALISM

Truth epistemologized is truth so fashioned that *its detection* is custom-fitted to our practices with it or to its available marks. Truth that can only be understood through conclusive justification, or through permissible moves within the language-related practices (for example, language-games) introducing it, or as the upshot of various styles of reasoning, or in terms of prevailing scientific theories can never transcend (=be independent of) the evidence for it, and is thereby epistemologized. On this conception, truth eluding us though we are in the most favourable position to capture it would be, *ex vi termini*, impossible. Correspondence and global realism clearly require a concept of truth that is *not* epistemologized. On the contrary, although it may turn out for unrelated reasons that no truth does in fact transcend our ability to gather the best possible evidence for it (on some conception of 'the best possible evidence'), the conjunction for a single proposition of best possible evidence and falsehood is not ruled out by anything essential to Correspondence. For the latter is characterized by way of a relation between our mental or linguistic products – the potential bearers of truth – and a world that may be independent of it, with no reference to our evidence-gathering capacities or to what we would consider knowledge or justification. Correspondence implies neither that truth need nor that it need not obtain given our best grounds for it. This is not to say that a definition or characterization of truth falls outside

145

the competence of epistemologists. As explained in Chapter 1, truth is still a prime concern of epistemology, if for no other reason than that so many of our other central epistemological notions cannot be adequately understood without reference to it. The main point on which the global realist departs from the epistemologizer of truth is over the matter of the fit between our powers of detection and the possession of truth by our beliefs and statements.

In the following chapters we shall examine three sources of support for cognition-dependent or epistemologized truth. They form what I deem to be the most serious remaining challenge to the global realism outlined and defended in Part I. The three doctrines to be examined were chosen for their philosophical prominence in the latter half of this century, in terms of both the following they have attracted and the concern they have aroused. The rest of the present chapter will be devoted to sketching and evaluating some generic views and tactics that have served epistemic truth concepts. But before turning to them, let us briefly introduce the views that will be our central concern in succeeding chapters. We might summarize them very briefly as justification-condition metaphysics-cum-semantics, language-game theories, and the incommensurability of competing theories. However, each deserves a further word.

The first view begins from the semantic claim that our understanding of assertoric sentences is grounded in our knowledge of the conditions which would justify their assertion or acceptance. From this it is inferred that our concept of a given sentence's truth can arise only from our grasp of its justification-conditions; thus truth cannot be a recognition-independent property of assertions. This view is most prominently associated with Michael Dummett, who has promoted it in a number of articles and in at least two hefty tomes. But the general view is also defended by, among many others, Crispin Wright, Peter Hacker and Gordon Baker. Its inspiration is no doubt Wittgenstein, in certain of his laconic dicta,[1] in (an interpretation of) his penchant for exploring meaning through use and in his constructivist hints concerning mathematical proof.

The second view is drawn from even more explicit pronouncements of Wittgenstein. Roughly, it is that all evaluation, including predications of truth and falsity, takes place *within* a network of

146

linguistically related practices termed a 'language-game'. Attempts to evaluate an entire language-game, or its elements, from outside that game are doomed. External critiques could only use a notion of truth (/falsity) founded on the standards of another language-game, and therefore would be, at a minimum, irrelevant. Since the possible moves within a language-game are always accessible to those participating in it, the circumstance constituting the truth of a proposition must be cognizable. Some Wittgensteinian commentators allow distinct language-games of the relevant kind, making possible relativism about truth, while others hold that all humans have their practice of truth-predicating confined to the same very capacious language-game, no others being conceivable. Both interpretations will be considered. Still other commentators maintain that Wittgenstein never held anything amounting to a theory of language-games, but used this 'family-resemblance' notion only to illuminate a number of unrelated concrete problems. Fidelity to Wittgenstein's ultimate intentions will not be as important to us as devising the most plausible version of the first two interpretations to see if they pose a threat to global realism.

A third view starts from Thomas Kuhn's thesis that the claims of scientists with competing dominant theories are always to some degree incommensurable. By itself this needn't engage global realism. If *theories* are neither true nor false, a view which Kuhn favours, that need only bear upon *local* realism. However, Kuhn's arguments also interdict common meanings and a shared perceptual world for the competing scientists. For Kuhn the meanings of our words and the world we inhabit are partial functions of our accepted scientific theories. Thus, there is no epistemically common ground for a theory of truth, such as Correspondence, to operate in. Theory-dependence, as understood here, is another form of cognition-dependence. Kuhn goes further. He claims that truth, like proof, is a strictly intra-theoretic predicate, applicable to beliefs or statements as interpreted in the light of particular theories, but not to a class of propositions not so interpreted.

Any of these currently popular views is a mortal threat to global realism. But it may be wondered why our exclusive concern is concentrated on such recent global anti-realism. Didn't we open this work by insisting on the conflict between these positions from the very outset of philosophy? The answer is that, while it is true that there is an important fund of historical anti-realist opposition, perhaps more pronounced in modern than ancient philosophy, what remains of it is either too cryptic, because partial, or wrongly focused to warrant the detailed treatment accorded more recent views. As for the ancient era, ignoring thin hints provided by the fragmentary remains of the pre-Socratic philosophers, the contributions of anti-realists have been obscured by the fact that the leading figures of the great age of philosophy were all dyed-in-the-wool realists. Thinkers such as Protagoras, who attempted to stem this tide, were very successfully relegated by Plato to the historical junk-heap as sophists. What remains of their views requires not so much interpretation as virtually total reconstruction. Protagoras' most famous dictum – that 'man is the measure of all things, of things that are that they are, of things that are not that they are not' – may be construed as radical relativism about truth. To that extent, our discussion of relativism in this chapter will be as much justice as we can render him. As for the so-called 'modern era', the epistemological turn initiated by Descartes in the seventeenth century has deflected anti-realists from a direct concern with truth to concerns about knowledge and certainty. Quite naturally, the anti-realist opposition has turned more to idealism and verificationism than to doctrines of truth. Of course, their treatments of epistemological topics were seen by them to have implications for a theory of truth, and to the extent that idealists had a preferred theory about it, it was Coherence. When verificationism eclipsed metaphysical idealism, Pragmatism was also selected. But the case against *global* realism and Correspondence was taken as, at most, a by-product of their critique of a mind-independent world. Our issue was seldom squarely addressed. We cannot launch a systematic investigation into idealism or verificationism; though, by way of indirect comment, we have raised objections to their favoured coherentist and pragmatic theories (Chapter 4). But this is no substitute for a full examination of them. Thus, for any particular edifice relying on such a theory of truth, we cannot tell by our earlier remarks alone whether it crumbles or merely totters. And there we must leave the matter.

In this chapter we shall be concerned with another general anti-realist theme: relativism. I shall try to state more clearly just what the position comes to, and offer a sketchily composed list of some of its serious difficulties. We shall also examine a more specific form of relativist ploy – associated with what is sometimes called 'historicism' – that I dub *inhibiting explanations of concepts* (to be contrasted with *enabling explanations of concepts*). This is not intended to imply that all anti-realists, or even anti-realists generally, would approve of the general or specific views displayed here. But the use of such typically relativist arguments and assumptions is more widely current among anti-realists than might at first be imagined. For example, we shall have occasion later to compare some of the points in Dummett, Wittgenstein and Kuhn with what is said about relativism below. In any case, it is useful to have before us, in clear terms, this method of radically rejecting global realism. For the charge, denial and repudiation of relativism is bandied about much in the sources we are discussing, but seldom clearly explained.

2 VERAMENTAL RELATIVISM: PATTERN (I) AND COMMENTARY

To begin with, what is relativism about truth? Relativist theses have been advanced for a number of subjects, including morality, aesthetics, culture, ideals and concepts. Even if we eliminate forms focusing on the more explicitly evaluative notions, we are still left with various kinds of doctrines that have gone under titles such as conceptual, cognitive and cultural relativism (and perhaps others). Our concern, of course, is only with relativism about truth-determinants, or what I shall call (I hope without creating further misunderstanding) standards for truth. But this sometimes arises as the consequence of a more direct argument for other sorts of relativism: say, about concepts, or standards of justification and rationality. I shall reserve the name 'conceptual relativism' for the doctrine that conceptual schemes are relative to particular groups, and the name 'cognitive relativism' for the corresponding doctrine about standards of justification or rationality. Relativism about truth itself I shall call 'veramental relativism'. To illustrate how the issues may intertwine, it may be argued that if some concepts can only be expressed within a certain group, then this limitation applies to any propositions employing those concepts. Thus, the truths expressed by some of those propositions can only be expressed relative to that setting. Similar arguments will be considered later. But here our primary concern will be with veramental relativism not arrived at through a different form.

Even the concept of relativism differs among discussants. Perhaps the most familiar type of characterization of relativism is that the relativist flags ascriptions. Thus, where the non-relativist would say something is X, the relativist requires that this be flagged (though perhaps only implicitly) by saying something is X *for A*, where A represents a group, culture, society, historical epoch, or perhaps even the human race. Although this is serviceable for many purposes, ultimately I believe we shall want to qualify it to exclude total subjectivism: for the latter may be more sceptical than relativistic. That is, for Xs in which A is always a particular person, to say that each individual has her own standards may be indistinguishable from saying that there are no standards for Xs at all. And although the relativist wants to emphasize that we cannot assume there are universal standards, it seems to me that relativism normally does this by stressing the intrinsic limitations on the standards that exist, not their total absence. But we needn't be further concerned with these problems, for I am more interested in the typical route to relativism than with the precise characterization of its final product. Thus, I want to examine relativist claims *via* the arguments used to establish them. And here it appears that there are two general patterns of relativist argument. Occasionally the patterns are combined (or confused) when defending a specific view; but our exposition can separate them. Concentrating now on veramental relativism, we can sum up the first pattern in the following three claims:

(I) 1 Under the authority of certain social norms (a civilization, a community, an historic period, a culture and so on) there are *objective* standards for the truth or falsity of statements.

2 Cutting across social norms, disagreements about the truth of particular statements arise from differences of standards in the divergent norms.

3 There is no universally obligatory standard of truth to determine which of the competing standards of evaluation is correct.

The claims in (I) are easily modified for other familiar forms of relativism. For example, by altering the form of evaluation for

150

statements and perhaps the relevant social units, we can generate moral, aesthetic, cognitive or cultural relativism. The thrust of the argument is that there are no higher standards to which to appeal than the local ones mentioned in 1.

For veramental relativism, notice that we do not require that the standard supposedly absent in 3 be available to the cognizer: there are no universally obligatory standards of any sort, accessible or otherwise. Since it is generally understood that the standards in 1 are cognitively accessible, this is a way of moving us from a non-epistemologized to an epistemologized conception of truth. (We shall return to this assumption below.) However, this does not prevent some versions of veramental relativism from begging the question elsewhere. That is, they may begin their argument by claiming that what is missing according to 3 are considerations that both parties would be predisposed to appeal to in settling their dispute: in other words, universally applicable justification-conditions. On this view a universal norm could be restricted to one that cognizers found readily usable in their practice. Those who proceed in this way may have begged the question in one or more ways. For example, they may already have in mind an epistemologized conception of truth, or they may have ignored the distinction of Chapter 2 between conditions of constitution and, say, the ways in which the words 'true' and 'false' are used in practice. In any event, if they could justify the assumptions which they bring to the argument, they would scarcely need (I) to refute Correspondence: that would have been accomplished by their earlier justification alone. Thus, we shall begin our inquiry by *not* assuming that the supposedly missing standard in 3 must fall within the compass of normal cognitive activities.

Before proceeding to the second pattern for veramental relativism, there are a number of comments to be made about the first one.

First, 2 might be deemed to require too much. Shouldn't the *mere possibility* that such disagreements may arise be sufficient to demonstrate that truth is dependent upon contingent human arrangements? But what sort of possibility is appropriate here? When other anti-realists speak of possibility in connection with verification, they typically envisage a strictly human possibility. Some might only rule out cognizers with superhuman powers. But others certainly want to rule out the possibility of any verification that was not available to us in our *current* epistemic situation. (Hence, talk of the human condition in the title of Chapter 7.) How restrictive one takes the notion of possibility to be will determine what weight a relativist sympathetic to this point is likely to place on the absence of any actual disagreements resulting from different standards for truth. But if there is any room whatever for a distinction between standards humans actually have and those they *might have* adopted, there is allowance for a relativist to hold that the mere potential for there being standards other than the ones we know of is all that is needed for 2 to have force. This would free veramental relativism from relying upon and having to interpret the available anthropological or historical data.

But, second, if one of the standards involved in the disagreement in 2 needs only be imaginary, the relativist's claim could be trivialized unless restated. For suppose that we all share one actual standard for truth. We can still concoct any number of arbitrary or wilful standards with which it conflicts, and simply declare by fiat that those who adhere to the merely invented standard need not acknowledge any other. This is a situation a non-relativist could countenance. How can it show that the current human standard is insular, non-universal, or lacking any of the other features that the most absolutistic view would want? To avoid this, and bring us closer to what relativists no doubt consider the nub of the issue, we might try to replace 3 with a tenet that says, in effect, that neither of the competing standards of truth can be shown to be *superior* to the other(s). But now we must elucidate this notion of superiority. The only plausible interpretation of that claim to my knowledge would be one to the effect that no competing standard could be shown to be *better justified*, or *more reasonable* or (*epistemically*) *more reliable* than its competitors. But, as we argued earlier, these notions from our reliability vocabulary (see Chapter 4, section 4) only appear intelligible in light of their relationship to truth. They are truth-linked, which is to say that a justified, reasonable or reliable view is one that has a certain enhanced likelihood or propensity toward truth.[2]

At this point a root-and-branch relativist might declare that all standards for determining truth-value are equally arbitrary; none is justified. Thus, any arbitrary challenger is good enough to establish relativism. But this position seems too extreme even for the most flat-footed transcription of relativism. We need go no further to answer this than to invoke the pragmatist insight that whatever else truth may be, it is valuable. Though this is not enough to yield a unique standard of truth, it does place a constraint on acceptable candidates. A truly arbitrary standard, one that need not be consistent with truth being of value, will not do. Thus, the veramental relativist still has the difficulty of unearthing a replacement for 3 to eliminate wholly arbitrary standards of truth.

Consequently, we shall consider the alternative course of requiring the conflicting standards in 2 to be *actual*, not merely potential. Of course, this flies in the face of whatever may have been plausible in the first comment. But it also requires that relativists discharge other polemical obligations about which they have been heretofore lax. To begin with, the claim that there are at least two different standards of truth requires clearer understanding of what makes standards really different. But, more importantly, it requires greater care in recording the relevant social and historical data. Up to now relativists generally have been content with noting differences in judgment and taking them with undue haste for differences of standard. But such claims need support from other sources. For example, there must first be a serious search to show the absence of any auxiliary assumptions which would serve as tacit premises in either of the parties' reasoning to make its difference from the other look more like a variance in opinion (say, about basic ontology) than in standards of evidence or truth.

To give one instance, Ian Hacking notes that those influenced by hermetic dogmas once reasoned that mercury is a cure for syphilis because it is signed by the planet Mercury, which signs the market-place where syphilis is contracted.[3] He takes this to be a different 'style of reasoning' from any, say, in classical mechanics, and thus a different standard for determining truth. There is certainly something disconcerting to a modern ear about this specimen, which seems to rely so heavily upon transitivities between signs and things signified. But Hacking's interpretation of it seems, to use perhaps an unhappy term for this example, rash. Wouldn't those who reasoned that way hold tacit beliefs or assumptions that would shift the strangeness from their modes of inference to the missing premises in this clearly enthymemic argument? For example, they might hold that the mysterious powers controlling things in the universe have pre-ordained an appropriateness between signifier and thing signified. Even without knowing much about the details of the actual case, it is difficult to believe that hermetic thinkers would have rejected the workings of causal influences behind these connections, though they may have been reluctant to specify their exact nature. Such superstitions are still found; but we should not expect to find a holder of one who *denied* the existence of causal powers behind the superstitious phenomenon which provided, say, the bad luck that ensued from having one's path crossed by a black cat or by shattering a mirror.[4] But if these are ultimately variations in general assumptions, and not standards for truth, they are not the right kind of evidence for veramental relativism. We would have to be selective in choosing the relevant assumptions; for if every novel general assumption about the construction of or causal forces in the cosmos generates a new style of reasoning, we shall proliferate such styles much too readily. But I can think of no principle for selection here. Eventually a relativist may wish to argue that fundamental differences about the constitution and the hidden forces in the universe constitute differences in truth itself or in the criteria for obtaining it. But this is not something that relativists can assume at the outset.

Fourth, veramental relativism is less common than cognitive relativism: that is, relativism about the justification or reliability of beliefs, or about the *criteria* for truth. With an eye towards pattern (I), we might state cognitive relativism as follows:

4 Under the authority of certain social norms and so on, there are objective standards for justifying beliefs (/statements).

5 Cutting across such norms, there are disagreements between members of distinct communities about (a) what counts as a justification, or (b) whether certain beliefs (/statements) are justified.

6 There is no universally obligatory standard of justification or rationality to settle disagreements of these sorts.

We are more likely to see 4–6 than 1–3 offered as a basis for veramental relativism; for the lack of a universally obligatory criterion of justification or rationality has been taken to preclude any standard of truth. Relativist expositions that begin with truth have a tendency to resolve their focus upon rationality or justification in the end. The trouble with this approach to our problem should be obvious by now: it only works on the assumption that truth is epistemologized. That is the only promising way to support the implied view that a discussion of *criteria* of truth exhausts what there is to be said about truth's determinants.

But showing this is not my central purpose in introducing 4–6 into a discussion of veramental relativism: rather, I wish to draw the reader's attention to the fact that 4–6 is not itself plausible without the support of veramental relativism. Once again, the culprit is the truth-linked nature of justification.

If, *pace* 3, there were a universally obligatory standard for truth, it could serve as the basis for constructing a universally obligatory standard for justification, and thus belie 6. On it a belief is non-relatively justified if it has a certain propensity (which may vary from context to context) for yielding truth. This basis needn't require that truth always be cognizable, but only that some non-relative truth is. For the claim is not that the universal standard will in fact resolve every disagreement. Evidence can always underdetermine an answer to a query about the reasonableness of a belief. What is sought is, rather, a way to avoid the consequence that there is a principled barrier to the non-relative resolution of any of the disagreements arising as in 5 (or, as in 2). And some humanly attainable non-relative truth will suffice to provide a measure for justification to avoid that consequence. Thus, anyone seeking to avoid the view that rejecting 3 overthrows 6 would have to maintain that non-relative truth *as such* – that is, all truth – is humanly unattainable.

We needn't deny that we are fallible graspers of truth, and must correct ourselves on occasion, or that some truth may be beyond human cognizability.[5] Neither admission would overturn our claim that a standard of non-relative justification could be grounded in one of non-relative truth. Moreover, we can admit that any standard of justification also will have aims other than yielding truth: in addition to minimizing falsehood, a preferred standard of justification should have, say, speed and power. But if these are not combined with the attainment of truth, it is difficult to see what is gained by a speedy and powerful form of justification.

The upshot is that cognitive relativism seems to presuppose, rather than serve as initial support for, veramental relativism.

That is a serious (possibly fatal) blow to those arguments that seek to get at veramental relativism through the cognitive variety.

Fifth, in fleshing out a set of local, objective standards, per 1, adherents inevitably seem to need reliance on the assumption that truth is epistemological or that it can be treated as such. If a person holds that a proposition is true, she certainly wouldn't concede that it stops being so at her cultural boundaries. What point would there be for her to hold that a proposition of physics was true if she did not intend it to remain so even should the intellectual climate replace physics with magic? Does she not also hold that the proposition is correct even among those who reject her standards? It appears that social limits on objective truth cannot be recognized as such by those employing the standard. And it is difficult to see how a standard could be really objective if its effectiveness requires that its adherents be ignorant of its true nature. To prepare a way out of this predicament, relativists are likely to choose for their limited standards what are in fact practical tests used by truth-seekers. But these are criteria of truth, means of telling that a statement is true. For example, Nelson Goodman has proposed one such local test – 'a version is taken to be true when it offends no unyielding beliefs and none of its own precepts'[6] – after declining to answer a more direct question about the constitution of truth (presumably because of its unanswerability). Of course, this approach destroys the attempt to use the argument to establish the cognition-dependence of truth; for its choice of local standard selects for treatment only what is already cognition-dependent about truth. But how could the situation be otherwise? What could relativism provide as a standard for truth that was both (a) objective, and (b) local, while being (c) cognition-independent? If we remind ourselves of the great obstacles to unearthing anything to satisfy (c) while it is also satisfies (a) and (b), we shall readily see why veramental relativism has trouble getting started unless it assumes at the outset that truth can only be treated in terms of its tests or criteria. But isn't this precisely what the defender of epistemologized truth is using veramental relativism to prove?

Sixth, some of the standards which veramental relativists will no doubt want to include in 1 will be examples that historically succeeded one another in what, from most historical perspectives, is considered a continuous culture or civilization. But it has always been a problem how people could simply come to adopt the new standards for truth without undergoing a severe mental disorder or brain surgery. What *reasons* could have struck them? If non-relativists have in the past been oblivious to the enormity of some changes in our intellectual habits – a charge that has substance – relativists have over-drawn such episodes from the other side to look like total discontinuities. This makes it difficult not only to see how the change may be prefigured in the old standards, which relativists may admit, but also to elucidate the change in any way whatever. Thus, relativists tend to retreat to descriptions that make the changes look cataclysmic – say, by describing the subjects as 'undergoing conversion experiences' or 'living in different worlds' – but which do nothing to explain why the new system arose from anything more than spontaneous generation. The excesses of previous non-relativist accounts scarcely excuse the new opposite ones. The embarrassments of such descriptions might be averted if we did not interpret the changes as radically as relativists do, as the adoption of a new concept of truth, but saw them as the rejection of some very general and widespread assumptions that came to be seen as unsupportable under certain continuously accepted standards. This enables us to appreciate both the radical nature of the departure and the continuities in our intellectual practices.

We have listed some leading difficulties with pattern (I) without raising the spectre, perhaps first explored in detail by Husserl, that veramental relativism faces either self-contradiction or must smuggle in some non-relative truth. This line has not been avoided because it is avoidable, but simply to impress the fact that the view must overcome a number of other major obstacles before it can be taken as a serious competitor. That somewhat obvious claim sometimes seems to have been lost in the exchanges over whether the position can be stated self-consistently. But all attempts I have seen to avert the charge of self-contradiction have done so – whether successfully or not I shall not say – by retreating to even less plausible or trivializing interpretations of veramental relativism: interpretations, say, that have denied the existence of truths where there were no judgers, although truth-constituters were still in place. For this reason, among others, we have omitted that dialectic in favour of arguing, straight off, that the original position has a number of implications that are either indefensible or badly in need of further support.

3 VERAMENTAL REALISM: PATTERN (II) AND COMMENTARY

Perhaps there is uneasiness about our original formulation of veramental relativism. It seems to lack a crucial factor: mutual misunderstanding between those who adhere to different standards. This brings us to a second pattern of the view. Outsiders must fail to grasp fully what insiders mean by their predications of truth. This makes the view more deeply conceptual. We might represent a version as follows.

(II) 7 Within, and *only* within, a certain set of norms and so on, it is possible to have concepts of truth and falsity.
8 Those who do not accept the norms in question cannot understand what the norm-relative concepts express.
9 Therefore, people with distinct norms and so on, have at best distinct concepts of truth and falsity, for which there can be no superior regulating concept.

As in 1–3, it is also assumed that differences in truth-concepts will lead to differences in evaluating particular statements, and that the absence of a sovereign conception prevents metaphysically satisfactory arbitration of these differences. But unlike 1–3 there is difficulty in seeing how holders of distinct norms can contemplate the same statement to generate a disagreement in the first place. For shouldn't all their concepts be treated like truth and falsehood? That aside, this pattern is useful because it emphasizes several chief features which we shall discuss in subsequent chapters – including the threat of misunderstanding claims made in an alien environment, the elucidation of the concepts of truth and falsity as embodied only within a certain language-game (Chapter 8), the need to 'go native' for full communication, and the incommensurability of claims made in different theoretical contexts (Chapter 9).

This form of veramental relativism does not escape every difficulty besetting the first form. For example, it too encounters the problem of finding a version of truth confined to a special group of believers but still a legitimate conception *of truth*. But it also has some problems peculiar to itself. We mentioned above the difficulty of construing a disagreement between people who seem incapable of framing the same propositions to disagree about. But even if this could be overcome, how could the application of truth on one conception to a certain proposition and the application of falsehood on a different conception to the same proposition result in incompatibility? Why is this alleged incompatibility any more problematic than saying that the temperature is 0° Centigrade but 32° Fahrenheit? Those who advocate this form of relativism may hold that the misunderstanding is only partial; and, while some of what the parties claim is incompatible, there is also a dose of a conceptual difference. It is unclear that the notion of distinct conceptual schemes required here makes sense.[7] But if it does, it is additionally unclear that the attempt to combine both genuine disagreement and a necessary absence of understanding is any more than an illicit mixture, due no doubt to confusion, of the two patterns of veramental relativism. For notice that on (I), step 2, nothing should prevent the disputants from being able to recognize that they have a genuine disagreement, even if not one with a genuine solution. Thus, the extent to which critical elements from the two patterns can be incorporated into a single consistent train of thought is obscure.

This barely scratches the surface of the issues surrounding (II). But it does give us some indication of the motivation behind a common form of relativism. And, as we shall have occasion to note, this pattern as well as the earlier one plays a role, if only a subterranean one, in the thinking of those whose views form the main topics of the succeeding chapters.

4 INHIBITING AND ENABLING EXPLANATIONS

Relativists and other sorts of anti-realists frequently turn the evidence in their favour by means of a manoeuvre I have called 'an inhibiting explanation', which contrasts with 'an enabling explanation'. Earlier we cited these as explanations of concepts generally, but more precisely they bear upon concept acquisition, and the concept whose acquisition is of immediate concern is truth. When we speak of acquisition we shall mean not only routines undergone in learning a concept (for example, the explicit teaching or training), but also the salient circumstances in which the learning takes place. An inhibiting explanation confines truth's legitimate application to the circumstances under which it is presumed it must have been learned. For example, perhaps it is held that we could only acquire our concept of truth through learning the justification-conditions for sentences. The inhibitist might conclude, though this is frequently not recognized as a further step, that truth is applicable only in circumstances in which its obtaining is specifiable in terms of the presence of conclusive justification-conditions (see Chapter 7). Or, it may be maintained that we first learn the concept truth by way of moves allowable with 'true' in language-games. The inhibitist once again may conclude that attempts to evaluate the underlying conditions of language-games as true or false – that is, from outside the language-games in which our first employments were learned – are senseless (see Chapter 8). Clearly, if either explanation is sound, truth can only be epistemic.

Although such explanations are frequently placed in the service of relativism, they need not be. For example, if there is only one way to justify sentences, or only one language-game, inhibiting explanations would still confine the application of truth within the boundaries of decidability, and thus still yield the desired consequence for epistemic conceptions. But the absence of conflicting standards of justification or language-games could prevent the relativist's reasoning from getting started. Nevertheless, because it is so commonly a factor in relativist polemics, this manoeuvre is an appropriate topic for the present setting.

We shouldn't lean too heavily on the word 'explanation' in this contrast. We do not require that an explanation be true, but only that it give some account, correct or otherwise, of the matter at hand. Accordingly, we can also talk indifferently of inhibiting and enabling *interpretations* or *accounts* of concept acquisition.

An enabling explanation does not dispute the inhibitist's contention that we come to acquire the concept of truth under such-and-such circumstances, but instead regards those circumstances as showing how we are *enabled* to frame our realistic concept. The circumstances under which the concept is learned are not regarded as freight, as it were, to be borne in all future applications; but more like an opportunity for introducing a fully objective concept whose status is not dependent on this particular setting. It is the circumstance that frees us to see what truth actually is, even if seeing this involves, among other things, truth's ability to be attached independently of these circumstances obtaining. Obviously, this explanation involves an extrapolation. The lesson we learn in the circumstances is more thinly described than the totality of the circumstance's manifest features, and it is the learner's task to subtract from the circumstances what is relevant to the concept.

The grin *sans* the Cheshire Cat is a reminder that extrapolations can land us in absurdities. But not all of them do. No one will deny that some of the attendant circumstances in which a concept is learned are irrelevant to its continued employment. For example, low levels of radiation and the presence of breathable atmosphere are considered irrelevant to most concepts learned under their omnipresence. Thus, extrapolations are always made, even by inhibitists. When are extrapolations licit? Efforts may be made to distinguish between permissible and impermissible extrapolations in terms of other distinctions, such as that between what is relevant to the content of learning and what is irrelevant, or between what *must be* involved in the learning and what *merely happens to be* involved. I shall not pursue such attempts because upon closer examinations none seems to yield a plausible account of permissible extrapolations. Perhaps there is no getting around judging candidates on a case-by-case basis.

If we cannot tell in general when an enabling explanation is permissible, can we at least decide where the burden of proof lies? Once again, I am loath to make too sweeping a claim; but in cases concerning truth it seems that the burden of proof lies, if only weakly, on the shoulders of the would-be inhibiting explanation. One reason for this is that in the anti-realist accounts we shall be examining, it supplies the original argument for the view. And we want to ask about any argument of this sort just why the learning of truth in such-and-such circumstances should be so critical in the case at hand that all applications of the concept in which similar circumstances are omitted should be thereby ruled out. But even without its singular role in the dispute, the question seems to be a quite sensible one to ask of any inhibiting explanation. There is an intelligibility gap between (a) how we come to understand a concept and (b) what it is we understand (by the concept): that is, between how we learn and the content learned.

Inhibiting explanations gloss over this distinction rather than demonstrating a capacity to overcome it. The gap is the basis for the so-called genetic fallacy. And though it may be too facile simply to dismiss, as commissions of that fallacy, all attempts to read features of (a) into (b), someone who attempts it owes his audience an explanation of why in this particular case it is an appropriate method for understanding the concept. The typal appeal 'But how can you imagine X without circumstance Y when X could only have been learned in Y?' is of no help. It sounds persuasive only for those examples where we are antecedently disposed to accept Y as a crucial element in the content of the concept X, and it is unconvincing in all other cases. But this is precisely what we wanted to find out about in the present case: namely, whether it should be a convincing appeal. Thus, unless we have antecedent intuitions that the Y *in this case* is an element without which we wouldn't understand the concept X, the appeal to X being learned (or needing to be learned) in circumstances Y will be of no avail.

Of course, this does not mean that enabling explanations should not also be scrutinized. However, some enabling explanations are appropriate for virtually every case in which we learn a concept for an open class of individuals on the basis of examples. For, from the examples learners are enabled to continue applying the concept to instances not previously encountered. Whether this is to be explained by innate similarity or quality spaces, templates for certain categories, or anything else is not of present concern. The point is rather that from certain cases learners *can go on*, and occasionally what they go on to bears only a faint resemblance to cases to which they had been previously exposed. The similarity between the issue dividing inhibiting and enabling explanations of the same concept, and issues such as projectability, the nature of learning and nativism is revealing. It shows just how familiar enabling accounts are. Thus, unless the alleged product of the sort of account in question departs radically from common sense, we regard the burden as falling upon the conflicting inhibiting explanation to show why we are restricted relatively narrowly to the conditions of learning in the particular case.

5 A CONCRETE INSTANCE

The inclination toward inhibiting explanations sometimes exercises an insidious influence on discussions of our topic. Perhaps it
will aid the exposition to have a concrete example. Thus, Richard
Rorty writes:

> To see relativism in every attempt to formulate conditions for
> truth . . . which does not attempt to provide uniquely
> individuating conditions we must adopt the 'Platonic' notion
> of the transcendental terms. . . . We must think of the true
> referent of [this] term . . . as conceivably having no connection
> whatever with the practices of justification which obtain
> among us. The dilemma created by the Platonic
> hypostatization is that, on the one hand, the philosopher
> must attempt to find criteria for picking out [this] unique
> referent, whereas, on the other hand, the only hints he has
> about what these criteria could be are provided by current
> practice (e.g., the best . . . scientific thought of the day).[8]

It will be evident that there is much in this passage with which I
would take issue. Relativism has been characterized by us quite
independently of any oversimplified contrast with Platonic hypo-
statization, and its defects are independently specifiable. Moreover, the truth-link upon which we have insisted shows that the
accounts of truth which Rorty criticises do have some connection
with our current practices, albeit one evincing a dependency that
is the reverse of the one Rorty evidently has in mind. But the
passage is of immediate interest for its last sentence. What could
be the dilemma? No doubt there is an innocent intepretation
upon which the only way we can arrive at any knowledge about
anything, including criteria for truth, is by way of our best
thoughts. But why should this generate a dilemma, and what
prompts the parochial emphasis on our best thoughts as '*current*
practice' and 'the best . . . scientific thought *of the day*'? The
emphasized phrases would be a distraction if Rorty only wanted
to say that we must use our rational faculties to the best of our
ability. I can find no other basis for a dilemma here, or an explanation of why Rorty uses these tendentious qualifications, than
that he intends an inhibiting interpretation of the acquisition of
truth: that is, the features which distinguish current practice from

163

other practices must be an important or critical determinant of the content, and in some way written into the content, of what is meant by truth or its criteria. This would ensure that the conception (or its criteria) was not transcendental. If this were not the case, would the fact that our conception of truth arose while we were exercising our current practice have any tendency to create a dilemma?

6 HISTORICISM

Inhibiting explanations are staples in theories that have been called 'historicist' in one of the many senses of that label. Though a number of other things have also gone under the title, the sort of historicism germane here is the type of view that *rejects* what Karl Mannheim calls 'the separability of the truth-content of a statement from the conditions of its origins'.[9] Karl Popper has entitled this view 'sociologism',[10] and it is taken by some as a defining article of the sociology of knowledge. On this version, a concept is fully understood once its historical and social circumstances are revealed; and opinions, including supposedly self-evident assumptions, are merely products of a peculiar set of social and historical situations. Perhaps no one has held that this is so for every concept and opinion. But it has been held by some as an appropriate way not only to analyse, but also to evaluate, significant concepts and views, often as a prelude to dismissing or qualifying them on those grounds. In place of the individual conditions of learning discussed earlier, historicists prefer social-historical circumstances. But their explanations are no less inhibiting. When considering historicism, the concepts explained should be taken broadly to include cultural norms, institutions and ideals, as well as concepts in the narrower sense. I shall refer to this assemblage as 'cultural values'.

This version of historicism, fuelled by inhibiting explanations of cultural values, rejects all trans-historical or ahistorical explanation. Since realism seems to imply an ahistorical justification of its subject-matter, historicism about truth-values would seem to imply anti-realism. In fact, the latter would be a species of relativism whose unit of local objectivity in (1) would be a socially or historically defined epoch.

The polemical outlook confronting historicist employments of inhibiting explanations are the same, *mutatis mutandis*, as those of the uses of this form of explanation discussed earlier. I shall not attempt a detailed account of its pros and cons, but instead confine myself to a discussion of one defence of historicist/relativist procedure to which the inhibiting–enabling distinction is specially pertinent.

Historicism might be advanced on the grounds that it is really no more than a determination to treat each social grouping equivalently. The explanation works better for cognitive than veramental relativism, but the gist of it is that, if there are social explanations for the standards of rationality (truth) in other societies and these explanations need make no reference to the credibility of those standards, we cannot consistently deny that the same sorts of social explanations can explain our own standards. This contention seems to me unimpeachable, but it is insufficient to support the present form of relativism. A social explanation may be inhibiting, enabling or neither. If it is *neither*, it holds simply that social conditions Y made possible, likely or inevitable the development of standard, belief or statement X. But given its exclusive concern with the conditions themselves, it needn't bear at all on the ahistorical credibility of X. However, not remarking on X's credibility is not a way of implying either that X is not credible or that there is no further legitimate question of X's credibility. To draw either conclusion is to suppose without licence that the social explanation must be an inhibiting one. Moreover, in addition to being inhibiting or neither, a social explanation may be enabling. It may describe the social conditions that are favourable to the flourishing of certain sorts of well-founded judgment.

If the X of an enabling condition is considered credible, it does not follow that the conditions under which it develops need be praiseworthy. For example, a certain tradition of scientific theorizing which is itself intellectually exemplary may have been made feasible by a culture in which slave labour under horrid conditions freed the time of a few scientists for idle contemplation. The standards of rationality developed under those conditions may be excellent ones despite the total unjustifiability of the social conditions. But this is not the main point to be made about enabling explanations. Rather, it is that an enabling explanation in this area will treat the social circumstances not as an explanation of limits on the nature of X, but as the situation which made it possible for a certain kind of productivity of its inhabitants' mental faculties. I have no wish to defend the various biases and creed bound outlooks with which this sort of comparative social investigation is often pursued. But *if* an investigator has an antecedent reason for thinking that the standards of society Z are superior to those of every other society, she may discharge the obligation to the postulate to treat societies equivalently by offering genetic explanations for the false views of societies A through Y, and an enabling one for society Z. Of course, this is not the only combination of explanations that may be offered. And it has no power *to show* that Z's views are superior. But we can clearly avoid the imputation of inconsistency in this regard while not denying the ahistorical credibility of certain standards, perhaps our own, simply by offering certain social explanations that are not inhibiting ones. This and this alone is all that is demanded by the claim that *all* thought has social conditions. Good advice about the dangers of ethnocentrism and the need for equitable treatment of beliefs will not extract more from the maxim.

7 THE TASK AHEAD

In the remaining chapters we shall come to grips with concrete instances of what we might call 'neo-anti-realism'. We shall see that its defenders occasionally flirt with relativism as we have described it in patterns (I) and (II), and that it is sometimes difficult to find any more to a particular line of reasoning than an inhibiting explanation of the acquisition of truth. But there is much more to each of the views we shall scrutinize than these naïve errors; and though we shall note these resemblances when they occur, the total views will not be rejected on those grounds alone.

The defence of this part will emphasize global realism more than Correspondence because the neo-anti-realist views do not focus upon the support of alternative truth theories. Rather, they insist upon the epistemic or cognitive status of truth in whatever theory it may appear. It just so happens that this adequacy condition precludes Correspondence. But it is also open to a neo-anti-realist to reject truth theories in general. Thus, the focus of this part is on the epistemic or non-epistemic character of truth.

This does not mean that our one previous form of non-epistemic anti-realism, Redundancy, will not reappear. It occurs in each of the next two chapters. But the neo-anti-realists favour it only for its deflationary implications; that is, it can be employed as a staging ground for objecting to Correspondence. The argument may go that if all that Correspondence can yield is contained in the Redundancy equivalences, or in the manoeuvre of disquotation in homophonic versions of Tarski's schema T, then answers to the question it addresses are uninformative or vacuous. From there the neo-anti-realist maintains that we must change the question if we are to obtain a *substantial* account of truth. And from this point the epistemic reconstruction of truth may proceed. Redundancy is used here only to clear the slate for the posing of different kinds of focal questions.

VII

MEANING, TRUTH AND THE HUMAN CONDITION

1 THE JUSTIFICATION-CONDITION CASE AGAINST COGNITION-INDEPENDENT TRUTH

As we mentioned in the last chapter, a group of thinkers influenced by insights of the later Wittgenstein have blended semantic and epistemological tenets into a heady anti-realist potion. We may begin with the supposition that a natural place to develop a semantics is with declarative sentences, or more precisely those sentences suitable for making *assertions* or *statements* (terms I shall use interchangeably). Whatever account of assertoric sentences is achieved may be subsequently extended either in the direction of subsentential elements or in that of non-assertoric sentences. But first we want an account of the *meaning* or *sense* (also used interchangeably here) of sentences. Expositions of anti-realism typically begin by limiting our practical choices between two sorts of account. The first, realist, account explains the meanings of sentences in terms of their truth-conditions. Since it is claimed that a theory of meaning is a theory of what it is that one who grasps the sentence *understands*, we could also say that on this account to understand sentence S is to understand its truth-conditions. (Some accounts may include falsity-conditions also, but I omit them here for simplicity.) The second, anti-realist, account renders the meaning of a sentence by way of the conditions under which it would be appropriate to assert it or to assent to an assertion of it. These conditions have been variously called 'justification-conditions', 'assertibility-conditions' and 'criteria', and, in addition to anti-realism, the view may also be known as criterialism or justification-condition semantics. For either of the views sketched, one's knowledge of the condition in question is ordinarily implicit, emerging more naturally from a speaker's practice than from her articulations of her understanding. But each view holds that its specific kind of condition is either identical with or the core of the sense of an assertoric sentence.

The anti-realist argument – or, rather, argument type, since this line of argument may embrace a number of diverse ways of filling in the details – can be divided into three stages:

1 reasons for preferring justification-condition semantics;
2 given 1, reasons why the justification-condition must displace any truth-conditional ingredients;
3 reasons why this shows that whatever coherent notion of truth we have must be the product of or relative to the justification-conditions that provide our understanding of sentences.[1]

The start of the argument for 1 is frequently the appeal to the Wittgensteinian notion, as Dummett puts it, that 'meaning depends, ultimately and exhaustively, on use'.[2] This cries out for elaboration. The general idea, before further refinement, is that the circumstances manifesting our ability to use an assertoric sentence are those in which we may correctly apply it; that is, those in which we are *justified* in doing so. It might seem at this early stage that the circumstances could also be described as those in which an assertion of the sentence would be true, but 2 is intended to show why this description is inadequate.

According to the anti-realist, some assertoric sentences are *decidable*, their truth-conditions are *recognizable*, or they are *conclusively verifiable*. These are several of the more popular ways in which anti-realists describe cases where the circumstances for a justified application of the sentence may coincide with what the sentence, as asserted, intuitively appears to assert. Thus, I may be justified[3] in asserting 'the bed is spongy' when I feel the sponginess of the bed. But in addition to being a condition for justifying my use of the sentence, it is also the condition whose truth the sentence is used to state. In such cases justification- and truth-conditions coincide. The problem arises in other cases, in which the conditions that standardly justify affirming a sentence 'fall short' of those that, on classical grounds, we conceive of as making it true. Examples regularly cited by anti-realists include the following classes of statements: unrestricted universal quantifications, those about the (remote?) past, counterfactuals, ascriptions of sensations to others, scientific theories and laws. For such 'undecidable', 'unrecognizable' or 'verification-transcendent' instances, the justification-conditions which account for our understanding of them cannot be identical with their classical truth-conditions. Since justification-conditions must play the same role in these instances that they play elsewhere, it is concluded that it can be only incidental to our understanding that truth-conditions are recognizable in other cases. It is through reasoning such as this that anti-realism concludes, in 2, that we must choose between a justification- and truth-condition semantics: we cannot combine them.

Stage 3 is the most puzzling. Competition between truth-conditional and criterial accounts seems at first to have strictly semantic significance. Let us indicate that it is the semantic accounts we are concerned with by labelling them 'realism$_s$' and 'anti-realism$_s$', respectively. The contention of stage 3 is then that anti-realism$_s$ permits us to reject realism$_n$ (m = metaphysical and/or global).

The argument at stage 3 is none too clear. One possibility is that since all other expressions acquire their senses by way of the conditions under which we are justified in recognizing their instances, the situation is no different for 'true'. Thus, we must also come to understand that expression by way of decidable or recognizable circumstances.[4] Another might be the view that our conception of truth is obtained only through the role of truth- (or falsity-) conditions in semantic accounts. Given that it is dislodged in those accounts, we must replace our notion of truth which one derived from our notion of a justification-condition.[5] Yet another possibility would be to see the connection between sense and use as an inducement to transform global realism into the doctrine that sentences always have determinate truth-conditions, which is then understood as the view that they are always either determinately true or determinately false, regardless of our ability to detect which. This associates global realism, or at least its core, with the Principle of Bivalence, or PB. Anti-realism$_s$, together with the

170

verification-transcendence of some truth-conditions, is then taken as an argument against PB; or at least as a challenge not met by global realism. Each of these ways of finishing the argument contains at least one controversial tenet; namely, that a concept such as truth can only be acquired *via* circumstances in which its obtaining is recognizable, that we have not enough data to justify possession of this concept other than through its role in semantic accounts, that realism for a given class of sentences can be reformulated as the view that bivalence holds. We shall examine these tenets in the course of our discussion. For now they simply serve to make a bit more accessible a perplexing leap from anti-realism$_s$ to anti-realism$_m$.

One more terminological matter: for anti-realists$_m$ our notion of a truth-condition *derives* from that of an assertibility-condition. I shall therefore speak about underived and derived truth-conditions or truth throughout this narrative as interchangeable with realist and anti-realist truth-conditions (/truth), respectively.

Although it is mainly stage 3 that will occupy our attention, additional comments about the first two stages are in order. The argument for anti-realism$_s$ connects our understanding of a sentence with recognizable situations. But, as noted by Colin McGinn,[6] the type of connection envisaged typically takes one of two forms in criterialist writings. First, *the acquisition argument* holds that we could come to learn a sentence only by connecting it with recognizable situations of a certain sort. Thus, how we arrived at an understanding of a sentence places restrictions on what that understanding consists in. Second, *the manifestation argument* holds that one can ascribe language-mastery only to those who are capable of displaying it, and only circumstances in which the sentence one accepts or asserts manifests what is affirmed can count as a sufficient display for ascribing mastery. Because the argument on behalf of anti-realism$_s$ has these complementary strands, and transfers its results to its attack upon realism$_m$, any challenge to criterialism is charged with showing *both* how we could come to acquire a non-epistemic notion of truth *and* what in our practice manifests our doing so.

A word about conclusive verification is also in order. To say that we have conclusively verified a statement is not to imply that our judgment is infallible. It allows room for mistake. But possible mistakes must be of a restricted sort: roughly, they consist in our misrecognition of the scene we thought we were confronted with. Beyond this clarification, in practice the notion of conclusive verification (/recognizability/decidability) has fluctuated between two interpretations: namely,

> (a) having the *strongest* available evidence (completeness of justification)

and

> (b) having the *most direct* available evidence (finality of verification)

Truth-conditions are verification-transcendent by lacking *directness*, feature (b). But this needn't entail that our claims about truth-conditions in such circumstances are epistemically inferior *unless* indirect justification always fails to be complete: that is, unless the highest degree of justifiability were only available when in the presence of what we claim to obtain or when a direct proof is at hand. Certainly, if we could be *fully* justified in affirming that such-and-such truth-conditions hold on the basis of 'indirect' evidence, this would take some of the sting out of the charge that the conditions were verification-transcendent. And not infrequently the verification-transcendence of truth-conditions is represented by anti-realists and their commentators as if the central problem created were a lack of *knowledge* or *certainty* that such conditions hold in this instance.[7] For empirical claims, directly confronting a situation normally betokens stronger evidence than anything else, but it needn't. It is an empirical matter whether my seeing a colour patch is a more reliable indicator that it is mauve than a read-out from a mechanism measuring the patch's absorption of light-waves. Of course, if construals (a) and (b) should come apart, this needn't prove fatal to the line of argument. For, if criterialism places its chief emphasis on the acquisition of meaning rather than on gaining the strongest evidence, the situation in which the evidence is directly discernible can remain most favoured. Nevertheless, the argument has occasionally been guilty of trading on an ambiguity between (a) and (b). And, more importantly, the argument may draw much of its appeal from a combination of these factors. If verification-transcendence cannot be shown to put the case for a truth-condition at an epistemic disadvantage, it is more difficult to see why the global realist is in a quandary.

In a curious passage Dummett writes that 'it is misleading to concentrate too heavily, as I have usually done, on a form of anti-realist theory of meaning in which the meaning of a statement is given in terms of what conclusively verifies it; often such conclusive verification is not to be had'.[8] The last clause only admits what anti-realists elsewhere insist: namely, that truth-conditions are occasionally verification-transcendent. But the first part suggests the concession that *it is wrong to insist* that we must have conclusive verification. If by conclusive verification Dummett means (b), then this is just the objection to the anti-realist$_s$ argument which we have been contemplating, and we must now wonder how the case against global realism is to be restored. But could Dummett mean by conclusive verification (a), or the combination of (a) and (b)? It is difficult to see how Dummett could mean that the strongest possible evidence was not to be had in certain cases, for he persistently argues that the only possibilities that we can find coherent are set by the limits of human capacities in our current situation. Thus, the only possibility we need consider is what is currently available to us, and on this interpretation he would end up saying something like 'the strongest *available* evidence isn't available for certain cases'. Of course, again, he could mean that the combination of (a) and (b) is not to be had; but for reasons just noted this could not be, by Dummett's own lights, for want of the strongest possible evidence in cases of this type.

In sum, this is the kind of argument, together with its assorted unclarities, which we must now appraise. The foregoing outline may have omitted some of its additional virtues or interesting nuances, but I believe it suffices to provide a basis upon which to discuss fairly its central impulse.

2 TRACKING THE ARGUMENT

Let's begin our inquiry by scrutinizing the way in which the argument gets started. It takes us at a dizzying pace from the announcement of its programme to give an account of sentence mastery to the introduction of recognizable (/verifiable) truth-conditions. Even those reluctant to accept criterialism seldom question this near-automatic transition. We shall anatomize it here.

Justification-condition semantics is animated by the thought that for a language-user to understand a sentence is for her to be able to use it. As mentioned earlier, this ability to use gets glossed in various ways. For example, it is for the language-user to be able to apply it, or to know the conditions under which it would be apt to assent to it or assert it (and, perhaps, to dissent from it or deny it, though we can ignore these for simplicity). *Prima-facie*, this skill knowledge might seem to incorporate other more specific capacities. I pick out the following two for their relevance to the point I wish to argue:

(a) the capacity to recognize the circumstances stated to obtain (by assertions of the sentence in question);

(b) the capacity to recognize *good and uncontested evidence* for the circumstances stated to obtain (by assertions of the sentence in question).

It might seem that (b) is the more general capacity, of which (a) would be a special case. But for now I am interested in an interpretation in which (b) neither collapses into (a) nor includes (a): that is, an interpretation including cases of (b) falling outside what anti-realists$_s$ would call conclusive verification. Both specifications seem to be potential explications of the animating thought behind the argument, for both involve capacities to spot justified employments of an assertoric sentence. However, given the way anti-realist$_s$ expositions proceed, one wouldn't guess it. Typically, (a) is taken as the only way to meet the vague *use* requirement on sentence sense, and the fact that (b) alone is available in certain cases is taken to be problematic.[9] The data are complicated somewhat by acknowledgements, such as the one just noted in Dummett, that anti-realism$_s$ should not emphasize (a) to the exclusion of (b). The problem with such acknowledgements, as I shall argue below, is that if they are written into the anti-realist$_s$ procedure at this early stage, it is difficult to see what basis there is for using the account to attack realism$_m$. Since the qualification cannot be sensibly integrated into customary anti-realist$_s$ procedure, I ignore this afterthought in the exposition.

The question of realism aside, it is puzzling why criterialists have not made more of (b). For even with sentences in which truth might be said by them to be decidable, language-users regularly find themselves in situations with good and uncontested grounds for truth which fall short of conclusive verification. It is arguable on principles to which they should be sympathetic that anyone who failed to appreciate such evidence would not only have committed an ordinary oversight, but would also fail to a measurable extent to have grasped what the sentence asserts, and thereby would fail to understand the sentence. However, this problem aside, we must still query what in the insight from which this approach to semantics begins allows us to take (a) as a sufficient test of grasping the sentence, but permits us to ignore (b) or to deny outright its adequacy.

My answer is, 'Nothing that I can discover!' As mentioned, I have only found criterialist expositions that begin by glossing what it is to grasp a sentence with (a) and simply omitting mention of (b). In such instances the argument against (b) seems to amount to no more than an unimaginative survey of the possibilities for elucidating knowledge of sentence application. Readers may confirm that harsh judgment for themselves by consulting the texts. For example, in the specimen just cited from Crispin Wright, after identifying the having of criteria with (a), he simply declares that many types of situation on the standard conception of truth-conditions fail to meet it.[10] And this is offered to explain why realism$_m$ encounters difficulties for anyone who takes *use* as his polestar. But if (b) is included among the ways in which we may exercise our ability to use a sentence, no such difficulties ensue. For, taking prime examples from anti-realism$_s$'s class of disputed statements, we can have good and uncontested evidence (though not conclusive verification) for an unrestricted generalization, for another's having a sensation, for an event's having occurred in the remote past, or for a counterfactual claim (that such-and-such would have occurred if things had been different in specific ways).

It should be emphasized that this has not been a defence of the identification of understanding and use, but merely an exploration of the most natural way to give substance to its guiding but crepuscular insight. What we have discovered is that the appeal to use delivers much less than anti-realism$_s$ wishes to draw from it. Capacity (a) stands to sentences as the recognition of instances stands to concepts. In sentences for which justification-conditions and truth-conditions may be said to coincide, as in the simplest examples of empirical concepts, recognizing instances may be an important part of use. Even here (a) and (b) are distinct, but because there are instances to be recognized, and failure to do so counts against possession of the sentence (/concept), those differences are unlikely to obtrude as issues. However, this is not because of the direct significance of (a) to the explanation of use in general, but because of the centrality of justification and the fact that *where there are truth-conditions or instances to be recognized* such recognition plays a role in our justificatory procedures. But in the disputed cases, or with heavily theory-laden concepts, where one could not be accused of any sort of semantic blindness by failing to note the truth-conditions (/instances) obtaining, (b) seems quite sufficient to secure our ability to use the sentence (/concept). The key to this gloss on 'ability to use' is perhaps already augured in the choice of vocabulary of criterialism such as 'assertibility' and 'justification' to describe the vital condition. It is the knowledge that we are entitled to *assert* the sentence, or that we are *justified* in doing so that is crucial to the ability to use it. Where this incorporates (a), that is an appropriate element in our skill. But the shift in emphasis to (b) – on a broader interpretation that may include (a), but needn't do so on all occasions – requires that elucidating what it is to use a sentence should not be tailored to the decidable cases. Dropping that demand forfeits anti-realism₅'s method for showing that the non-decidable cases look problematic. As long as conditions that appropriately allow us to manifest that (b) can occur, we can supply an acceptable account of the ability to use the so-called verification-transcendent sentences.

3 THE PRINCIPLE OF BIVALENCE

A crucial factor in Dummett's version is his claim that '[w]e may . . . characterize realism concerning a given class of statements as the assumption that each statement of that class is determinately either true or false'.[11] This is the Principle of Bivalence, or PB. Elsewhere Dummett calls it 'a touchstone for a realistic interpretation of statements of some given class'.[12] (We needn't be concerned here with Dummett's insistence upon distinguishing PB from both the Law of Excluded Middle (LEM) and *tertium non datur*.) The rejection of global realism is closely associated with the rejection of PB for sentences generally.

It is not always clear whether the rejection of PB is intended to support or to be supported by the remainder of anti-realist doctrines. A rejection of PB opens the possibility that undecidable statements don't have truth-values, thereby removing one potential challenge to the adequacy of justification-condition semantics. The mere falsity of PB, much less its vulnerability, would not imply that the exceptions to it are the cases which criterialists call undecidable, or that they would be exceptions *just because* they were undecidable. But challenges to PB may have been used to clear the ground for rivals to justification-condition semantic accounts. On the other hand, if certain criterialist semantic claims are used to show that in some instances truth-conditions would be unrecognizable, or that statements would not be true or false in virtue of something, this might be used as a basis from which to criticize PB. Thus, the rejection of PB may appear both in a supporting and supported role. Which of these intended and the further details of each sort of argument are topics for further study. But I shall sidestep such queries and provisionally grant for the sake of argument that the rejection of PB is, as anti-realists claim, vital to the case against global realism. What I propose we concentrate on is the claim that we can adequately characterize global realism by PB, or that PB, relativized or not to a class of statements, is the nerve or 'touchstone' of global realism.

One way to see the peculiarity of this association is to ponder the distinction between the notions of a truth-value and a truth-condition. To say that a statement has a determinate sense, even if we choose to understand that sense in terms of truth-*conditions*, is not to say, *pace* Baker, that it 'must be definitely true or definitely false in any possible world'.[13] Its truth-conditions may lay down specific circumstances in which it would be true, others in which it would be false, and yet others may not be captured by the distinction and thus not classifiable. Dummett, early in his concerns about this issue, considered that possibility, and ruled against it. He concluded that the point of having a true–false distinction dictated that any sentence which failed to win (= be true) must have lost (= been false). But the only challenge to this he considers is Strawsonian presupposition, which he believes does not make the same sort of principled distinction made by the true–false distinction. However, there are various more mundane reasons, unrelated to issues dividing global realism and anti-realism, for the failure here of an exhaustive dichotomy.

One way this may happen is through our choice of characterizations for truth and falsity. As with philosophical distinctions generally, we can characterize one side of a purported dichotomy positively, say as the Xs, and the other side in terms of its non-satisfaction of the first characterization, as the non-Xs. Thus, if we choose to delineate falsehood as the value attaching to any statement that is not true, then assuming the truth-making condition is always definitely present or not, we shall have guaranteed that every statement is either true or false. This is all that can be done by way of characterization of the distinction alone – that is, without raising the issue of definite presence – to insure PB. Let us call such a characterization an *exhaustive* one. However, for a second method we may choose instead to give a characterization of *both* values in terms of features that their bearers possess and which do not require characterization in terms of failure to satisfy the other set of features. Even with the proviso in one characterization that the statement should not possess the features of the other half of the distinction, the addition of features that are not simply the converses of those of the other class opens the possibility for bearers that possess neither; that is, that fail to satisfy the characterization for truth and for falsity. In fact, on this sort of characterization it would appear that the likelihood that statements will fall through the cracks is heightened if we consider the relative importance of requirements for framing the distinction.

Two sorts of embarrassing cases could plague anyone's formulation: those in which a single statement has both properties (is true *and* false), and those in which it has neither. Avoiding the first is obviously of utmost concern, and to insure against it it is important to remove any areas of overlap between the characterizations. However, providing areas that may overlap for some cases is the most obvious insurance against the second, lesser, type of embarrassment arising in others. Thus, work designed to avoid contradiction will impair efforts to obtain a characterization of the second type that classifies every case. But the characterizations of truth-conditions on either method may be just as definite and determinate. Nevertheless, we see how the second method can threaten to violate PB.

A central aspect of this scenario is that the adoption of the second characterization has no foreseeable consequences for arguments over global realism. The method makes it easy for PB to fail, but doesn't seem to make truth, where discovered, any less determinate or to favour anti-realism. Indeed, we may be confronted by different conceptions of what determinateness consists in, which may in turn help explain the reigning confusion over this issue. On one conception a determinate notion is a relatively detailed or informative one; it is less bland and thus tells us more about instances exemplifying it. Here the second characterization may allow both truth and falsity to be as determinate as they would be on the exhaustive characterization. Their determinateness would be imparted to sentences whose sense they elucidated: that is, it would be determinate what the given sentence's truth or falsity consists in. Moreover, whether an assertion of the sentence was true, false or neither would be as rigorously determined by such truth-conditions as it would be were PB in force. Finally, if the assertion were true, there is no less reason for supposing that its truth is a matter of the state of the world independently of our cognitive practices than if PB had governed our sentences. On the second conception of determinateness, truth-conditions presumably would only be determinate if they were sufficiently broad to ensure that every candidate item had one of the two truth-values in any circumstance. This variety is determinate only in the sense of yielding a definite (/unqualified) decision for each instance, not in the detail of the answers it yields. But I have stressed all along that it is not a question of *whether* a statement is true or false, but what accounts for its truth or falsity, that distinguishes global realism (and Correspondence) from its competition. Thus, this second form of determinateness could not be the focus of our attention, whether or not the first sort proves relevant.

If we recall that it is primarily truth-*conditions*, not truth-*values* that could figure in semantic accounts of sentences (or statements), it may be easier to see why the emphasis on this second sort of determinateness is misplaced. Of course, the features of the particular account of truth-conditions are important for deciding whether these truth-conditions are sufficiently determinate. But it is difficult to see what special importance resides in whether the truth-conditions yield an unqualified true-or-false answer for every conceivable circumstance.

Using somewhat similar reasoning, John Locke, in his celebrated doctrine of nominal essences, held that our ordinary classificatory vocabulary does not capture distinctions exemplified in mind-independent reality. For Locke, a chief reason that classificatory expressions such a 'man' are not 'Nature's Workmanship' is that the classification is not perfectly sharp: we can be embarrassed by cases that are neither definitely men nor definitely non-men.[14] But the reasoning seems just as misconceived here as it does for PB. The embarrassment could be nature's not ours. Reality may be messy. Perhaps Locke's theological views kept him from countenancing this possibility; if so, I can only admit that they seem to me weak grounds for arguing against a *tertium quid* in nature.

We needn't rely heavily on the particular case used. PB may be violated in various ways not bearing upon realism, of which that was only one. For example, Dummett offhandedly cites vagueness as a negligible source of failure; but vagueness has convered such a wide variety of complaints in the philosophical literature that on some interpretations exceptions to PB could reach epidemic proportions. For example, is a sentence such as 'This is red' vague because it might be uttered while ostending a patch falling in the penumbra between red and orange? (I am assuming that the statement made is thereby not definitely true nor definitely false.) If it is the sort of vagueness that defies PB, it is scarcely negligible. Indeed, very likely it infects most empirical discourse. Of course, such cases do not impeach the determinate and mind-independent truth of other statements made with the same sentence: say, if 'this' referred to a (British) pillar box. Thus, it is difficult to see what such failures of PB imply about realism.

Again, consider the pair of sentences

(1) Everything Weinberger says about strategic defence is false.
(2) Everything Smith says about strategic defence is true.

Prima-facie, neither is self-contradictory and they are mutually compatible. Though highly improbable, they are used to make

straightforward empirical claims. But let us imagine one of Weinberger's strategic defence-related utterances is (2) and that everything else he says about it is false, while Smith's only such utterance is (1). Then both (1) and (2) are true if and only if they are
false.[15] The case cannot be handled, as in some treatments of the
liar paradox, by a hierarchy or charges of illegitimate totalities.
But for the occurrence of certain empirical contingencies, each
might have had a consistent truth-value. On a perfectly natural
reading of PB these two statements violate it. They cannot be
given definite truth-values. But, once again, what effect could this
have upon global realism?

To reiterate, the central issue dividing global realists and anti-
realists is the proper account of statements having whatever truth-
values they do have, *not* whether every statement has (a classical)
one. It is the nature of truth, not its extension, that matters.
Certain anti-realists may have had in mind collateral doctrines
that would have seemed to make PB more focal: for example, the
view that the only prospect for showing that any verification-
transcendent statement is true is to show that all statements (of a
given class) had to have truth-values. It is perhaps this sort of
argument that takes Dummett from the innocently interpretable,
though equivocal, remark,

> Realism I characterise as the belief that statements of the
> disputed class possess an objective truth-value, independently
> of our means of knowing it; they are either true or false in
> virtue of a reality existing independently of us[16]

to the clearly committed

> [A realistic interpretation of statements of some given class]
> is, essentially, the belief that we possess a notion of truth for
> statements of that class under which every statement is
> determined either true or not true, independently of our
> knowledge or our capacity for knowledge.[17]

But enough has been said to show that he is not entitled to take
PB as a proxy for global realism.

It might help to see the issues more clearly if we examine
Dummett's reasons for this way of viewing the issue. He gives an
elegant account of his motives in the Preface to *Truth and Other
Enigmas*. Suppose we begin with a dispute between Platonists

and intuitionists in mathematics; not as an inductive basis for generalizing to other areas, but as a paradigm, displaying micro-cosmically the operation of maxims that turn up in a number of philosophical divisions.[18] The positions give us two pictures: that of the Platonist in which the mathematician *discovers* pre-existing abstract structures, and that of the intuitionist in which a reality *is created* by our practice. Dummett finds each inadequate. Not only do they fail separately to capture the whole of our practice, but both are so useless in directing mathematical inquiry that, no matter which we adopt, precisely the same sorts of reasoning will have to be undertuken. For example, supposing we want to quan-tify over elements of class M, commitments to one or the other of these views cannot tell us whether we can construct a totality of elements closed under the impredicative comprehension axiom. We must either 'construct' or 'specify' the domains over which our variables range. This will involve the same operation, the only difference being that our commitment to intuitionism or Platonism will cause us to describe what we are doing in one of these two different ways.[19]

Since one's ontological commitments do not seem to settle the issue, Dummett suggests that the dependencies may go in the other direction: namely, by seeing the sense we ascribe to assertoric sentences, we can tell whether a determinate truth-value applies to statements of this range. Redirecting the dispute from a question of the mind-independent existence of entities to the determinateness of truth-conditions for a range of sentences is seen by Dummett as an advance. But, most importantly, he does not view it as a change of topic. The difference that originally failed to determine our practices is the same one that is supposed to be settled by the requirements of the best semantic account. The only change is the abandonment of a particularly arid way to frame the original dispute in favour of a more promising *programme*.

However, it should emerge from my summary that Dummett's reconstruction couldn't do so. For, if the earlier presentation was incapable of deciding the question by a difference of semantic accounts, any reconstruction purporting to preserve it must be equally so. This is because, if *s* is a semantic claim and *o* is an ontological one, then it is only reasonable to suppose that not-*s* and not-*o* are respectively, semantic and ontological claims. But, if *s* entails *o*, not-*o* entails not-*s*. However, the latter entailment is just the sort of semantic consequence which Dummett has claimed that ontological doctrines do not have. One way to square the denial with the result is to concede that the *o* (/not-*o*) related to *s* (/not-*s*) in the reconstruction does not embody the original ontological differences, but is rather a kind of neo-ontology that has been declared to be internally related to semantic practice. No doubt, the reconstruction may yield a less amorphous controversy; but why should we count it as a natural successor to the original one?

This is not an argument that differences between realism and anti-realism do not show up in our linguistically related practices. On the contrary, I shall presently argue, *pace* Dummett, that a commitment to underived truth-conditions is made manifest in recognizable conditions. Thus, commitment to one or another position is not always idle, whatever the outcome in the special case of quantifying over a limited domain. The problem is with the demand that different ontological commitments should affect our practice in a specific way, so as to yield one of two rather definite semantic accounts of declarative sentences. I agree with Dummett that a prior commitment to global realism or anti-realism will not decide between the semantic doctrines. But I emphatically dissent from his resolution to have our chosen semantic doctrine determine our realist or anti-realist commitments (for given classes of sentences). It seems to accomplish the appearance of doing this by trimming the original commitments in such a way that they only masquerade as non-semantic. And now I hope it is evident how the shift of focus to PB has disguised semantic consequences merely to appear as if they were the legitimate distillates of the old ontological positions.

That behind us, let us seek out the differences which underived truth-conditions could make to our linguistic abilities.

4 DEFEASIBILITY

Not only are justification-conditions sometimes defeasible, occasionally only such defeasible conditions can be associated with a sentence. This has been generally conceded, but its full significance seems to have eluded anti-realists. It weakens their view in the following ways. First, truth-conditions, like truth itself, cannot be defeasible without violating their fundamental tenets. How, then, can the criterialist project of fashioning truth-conditions out of only justification-conditions succeed? Second, the inability of criterialism to account for the phenomenon of defeasibility demonstrates the need for a regulatory notion, a role for which underived truth seems well suited, to explain the character of this evidence. This comprises two sub-points. (a) It provides an illustration of how a notion may be introduced into our practice, and thus have a use, other than by figuring as a recognizable condition. Thus, our practice admits concepts other than through paths to which criterialist arguments restrict us. (b) Whatever is required to explain defeasibility matches perfectly the desiderata one could reasonably expect from the realist conception of truth.

These matters will be explored in greater detail. But first let us have a fuller sketch of defeasibility.

The notion was introduced into contemporary philosophy through H. L. A. Hart's discussion of legal reasoning.[20] Roughly, a defeasible condition is one that forms a *reasonably sufficient* ground for something, but which can be overridden by further evidence favouring a contrary judgment. Though defeasible evidence *e* may be normally sufficient to justify statement S, we can imagine additional counter-evidence *c*, which, if present, would make it justifiable to withhold acceptance from or to reject S. It is crucial to this notion that the defeat of *e* need not be a reason to change one's belief that *e* has obtained, or even to declare that *e* is not normally evidence for S. To allow, at the outset, that one might have been wrong about the evidence itself is to declare that one is fallible, but that is not yet defeasibility.

One reason for keen interest in defeasibility is that it lays claim to a variety of perfectly adequate sufficiency which is less than logically strict. That is, it transgresses the requirement

$$(p \rightarrow q) \rightarrow [(p \mathbin{\&} r) \rightarrow q],$$

for, where *p* expresses the defeasible condition normally sufficient for *q*, its hallmark is that the addition of further evidence *r* will not always preserve its sufficiency. Some have found this unpalatable and tried to avoid it – say, by discerning a tacit qualification always attaching to *p*, such as 'providing nothing untoward happens'. However, as accounts of our actual practice with evidence, these haven't had much to recommend them. In any case, interest in defeasibility has flourished despite such proposals.

We should also note that defeating condition *c* above may itself be defeasible. Indeed, this always will be the situation in the relevant verification-transcendent cases. Thus, Smith's moaning while clutching his abdomen may be a defeasible justification-condition for a statement made with 'Smith is in agony', but one which is defeated when the behaviour takes place during a stage performance. However, the latter may be in turn defeated by knowledge that the behaviour deviates sharply from both the script and the direction, thereby re-establishing the case for the original statement. But, again, if we also know that Smith planned to spice up his dull role for a movie mogul in the audience, this may be used to defeat all previous evidence for Smith's agony, and so on. Such chains of defeasible conditions will interest us later.

Verification-transcendent sentences are marked by defeasible assertibility-conditions. When criterialists list cases – ascriptions of sensations to others, statements about the remote past, unrestricted generalizations, subjunctive conditionals, scientific theories – they emphasize that whatever assertibility-condition we have can be overcome by further evidence. This makes statemental verification inconclusive. It is not conversely true that every case of defeasibility concerns a statement with recognition-transcendent truth-conditions. For example, while observable characteristics may justify the claim that something is a dollar bill (diamond bracelet, Picasso painting, Hitler diary), the claim may be defeated by further information which is not itself defeasible. Thus, we cannot regard defeasibility as a sinecure for cases from our embattled class.

The first problem we raised for criterialism was that, while justification-conditions may be defeasible, this is never so for truth-conditions. If *t* makes S true, there is no further condition *t'* whose addition to *t* can render S untrue. This is both a self-evident and a fundamental feature of truth. One might set out to revise the concept, but what point could such a fundamental reform have? Does it serve any purpose other than the relief of a beleaguered anti-realist attempt to construct truth-conditions out of justification-conditions? Indeed, how does it differ from a proposal to abandon truth altogether and replace it with assert-ibility? Any attempt to introduce defeasible truth-conditions would, it appears, preserve only a name, not its substance. Better to forsake all such subterfuge.

Of course, the problem occurs because of the anti-realist claim to be able to account for truth-conditions in terms of assertibility-conditions. As I hope to show, if this cannot be done in the cases in which assertibility-conditions are uniformly defeasible, it cannot be done in any cases. But in each of the disputed cases, as we have just seen, assertibility-conditions are defeasible. Confining ourselves to them, how are we to generate non-defeasible truth-conditions? The gap between defeasible grounds and truth-conditions seems unbridgeable. I cannot even imagine the outlines of a rationale that would permit us to use only defeasible conditions and get out of them a set of truth-conditions. In lieu of one, the project cannot get started.

Dummett makes it perfectly clear that for anti-realism 'the truth of the statement can consist only in the existence of . . . evidence [for its assertion]'.[21] One might take remarks of this sort not as implying that assertibility-conditions always yield truth-conditions, but only as implying that if they cannot, the sentence can have no truth-conditions. This might even seem to conform more closely to Dummett's misgivings about PB for certain classes of sentences. I shall explore that interpretation shortly. But first it should be noted that this understanding of his dicta isn't always available. Responding to the suggestion that an account of meaning in terms of justified assertion makes understanding in terms of truth-conditions superfluous, he remarks,

> Rather, from such a standpoint one would say that the only legitimate notion of truth is one that is to be explained in terms of what justifies an assertion: a sentence is true if an assertion made by means of it would be justified.[22]

The clear implication of the last clause is that assertibility-conditions are sufficient for truth-conditions, and that lack of truth-conditions in an account of understanding is not an option. No exception is made for verification-transcendent sentences, though they are clearly in the forefront in the discussion.

There is more than a single account of these matters in Dummett's writings. Another account existing side by side, though incompatible, with the one above is that in which he approvingly reports Wittgenstein's treatment of other-ascriptions of pain.[23] He holds that the truth-conditions for, say, 'John is in pain' are given by Redundancy; thus, though independent of assertibility-conditions they are trivial, and the core of our understanding must be derived from the conditions under which we would be justified in asserting it. We can dismiss this account here for a few reasons: for one, we have dealt elsewhere with Redundancy (Chapter 4, sections 7–8); for another, the account clearly concedes that truth-conditions are not a function of assertibility-conditions. But in addition, there is a peculiarity about the argument that should not escape our notice. The *triviality* here would appear not to belong to truth-conditions themselves, but to how they are formulated or specified. I do not know what a trivial truth-condition, or for that matter a non-trivial one, would be. And it is certainly not obvious how triviality could effect the *genuineness* of truth-conditions. But if we omit the charge of triviality, what would the account be saying other than that a statement's truth-conditions and the core of its semantic account, in terms of assertibility-conditions, are separate matters? And that is simply one way of rejecting the criterialist argument.

But the point of current interest is contained in those passages in which Dummett unmistakably implies that justification-conditions are sufficient to account for truth-condition. Crispin Wright manifests the same tendency in his discussion of other-ascriptions of sensation. Moreover, he is wonderfully forthcoming about the defeasibility of justification-conditions in such cases. To wit:

> the inaccessibility of others states of feeling may be viewed as an expression of the essential defeasibility of other-ascriptions of sensation, the fact that any state of information which warrants such an ascription can always coherently be envisaged as being added to in such a way that the resulting state of information no longer does so.[24]

He then offers an anti-realist treatment of such utterances – again, attributed to Wittgenstein, but proferred as a plausible view with which he cannot find serious error – in which the sentence's truth-conditions are reductively explained 'in terms of the practical skills regarded by [the criterialist] as constitutive of understanding that sentence'.[25] Indeed, Wright re-emphasizes the point, with regard to this very defeasible situation, when he says that ' "grasping the truth-conditions" is . . . constituted by possession of a complex discriminatory skill exercised in response to public circumstances'.[26]

But defeasibility remains an insuperable obstacle to giving the content of a truth-condition from justification-conditions. In some contexts, though not those just cited, anti-realists have made remarks admitting as much,[27] but I know of no place where they have made even an attempt to overcome it. Perhaps anti-realism$_s$ would fare better simply by denying truth-values to sentences all of whose assertibility-conditions were defeasible. On this account 'Smith is in agony' may be justified, while a simple yes-or-no answer to the further question 'But is it true that he is in agony?', would be rejected. This position might even appear to conform better to anti-realist$_s$ apprehensions about PB.

Although the proposal avoids the difficulty of fashioning truth-conditions from defeasible materials, and is technically feasible, it encounters other serious difficulties. For one thing, the equivalence of 'p' and 'p is true', which we have seen that various anti-realists$_s$ depend upon elsewhere, fails; but not for the expected reasons. In our discussion of Redundnacy we saw how it would come to grief if we were allowed undefined values. However, in the present case we may be fully justified in putting forward that p while being unjustified in putting forward that p is true; and this is puzzling. Nevertheless, my more fundamental reason for rejecting the proposal is that it requires us to select from among the set of justification-conditions, in a way that must be arbitrary for an anti-realist$_s$, some items which have special powers not given to all. Non-defeasible justification-conditions, despite the fact that they play no different role in sentence mastery, are afforded the capacity to construct justification-conditions, while others are deemed to lack it. Realists$_s$ could explain this difference; anti-realists$_s$ cannot.

In order to reinforce this point, consider mixed cases, in which a sentence has both defeasible and non-defeasible grounds for assertion. In many of these cases the defeasible conditions are the more accessible and common grounds for judgment, while the non-defeasible (final) tests are the authoritative grounds primarily used only to settle the odd dispute or questions. 'This is a dollar bill' has for its ordinary justification-conditions general appearances, which are defeasible grounds, but may yield in cases of special importance to chemical or microscopic tests, or even to witnessing the printing process. This is not an atypical pattern: ordinary masters of a sentence, and even experts in most moments, rely upon defeasible grounds, deferring to experts and specialist techniques, which it would be useless for most masters to conduct, for conclusive results. In such cases defeasible conditions are more important for mastery than non-defeasible ones. And it is solely from an account of sentence-mastery that the anti-realist$_s$ professes to generate the account of truth-conditions. Nevertheless, on the proposal before us, it is only the non-defeasible conditions which can be used to generate truth-conditions. I do not question the prudence of not allowing the defeasible conditions to serve in this capacity, but I do question the entitlement of anti-realism$_s$ to make this distinction. What, within its description of our semantic resources of assertibility-conditions and the connection of sentence meaning with use, enables it to determine which assertibility-conditions are suitable as materials out of which to construct truth-conditions?

No doubt, in some cases the very thing specified as a justification-condition will serve as a truth-condition. But if the foregoing is correct, even in those cases a condition's determining what counts as truth for a sentence *will not be a function of* its determining what counts as justification. That is, even in the cases in which defeasible evidence is not considered, justification-conditions have no priority. For, if defeasible justification-conditions cannot determine truth-conditions, nothing about non-defeasible ones places them in a better position to do so. Both sorts of justification-condition have the same mandate in a criterialist account, and the distinction we have drawn between them is nothing which those accounts are in a position to use.

5 TRUTH MANIFEST: THE REGULATION OF JUSTIFICATION

The second weakness which we claimed defeasibility introduces into criterialist accounts rests on the fact that this phenomenon cries out for explanation. One aspect of this criticism suggests a way in which truth may yet be seen to play a role in our practice. We may approach the issues by posing a pair of pointed questions for the criterialist.

(Q1) Why should we countenance additional evidence to override an assertibility-condition that has not itself been invalidated?

(Q2) Given that we do hold some conditions to be defeasible, why should a claim of defeasible conditions (such as those illustrated with 'John is in agony') take one direction rather than another?

Rephrasing (Q2), we might ask what determines that a bit of evidence, e', is relevant to overturning e. Why shouldn't wildly different evidence be relevant to e instead? Anti-realism$_s$ seems to lack the means for answering either question. It collects assertibility-conditions to associate with sentences and, once done, its task is accomplished. Let us allow it the right to define its charge this narrowly. But if it appeals to the limits of its proper task to relieve it of any duty to answer (Q1) and (Q2), this leaves it without the authority to pronounce that underived truth-conditions cannot be manifested in the use of sentences. For the only canvass it can take is from an insular perspective. And this is scarcely a basis for so sweeping an appraisal.

Two points help clarify the force of the objections.

First, just as anti-realism$_s$ has professed to be able to understand truth-conditions solely in terms of justification-conditions, so realism has always worked in the opposite direction. That is, starting with truth-conditions, it has supposed that it can thereby explain why certain things count as evidence while others do not. This is what we have repeatedly referred to as the truth-linked criteria of justifiability.[28] It is part of the traditional lore of realism, but not always kept in perspective. For, whatever the details of the role of truth in these proceedings, it means that realism and anti-realism do not confront (Q1) and (Q2) on an equal footing. The questions pose a problem for anti-realism; not because anti-realism is deemed incapable from the outset of answering them (though this may be so), but because nothing in the anti-realist construction even acknowledges the existence of something in need of this sort of explanation. Realism, on the other hand, with its hegemony of truth, which is supposed to guide and limit conditions under which a sentence may be justifiably asserted, is designed so that defeasible cases do not create a new or special problem. If the realist conception of truth can be made out in other respects, and it can be shown how truth on this conception controls relevant justification, the defeasible cases are as manageable as any other. However, even granting criterialism's other claims, (Q1) and (Q2) still stand in need of new answers. This is critical. Since anti-realism$_s$ claims to rectify flaws in underived truth-conditions, it is obliged either to account for its achievements as well in some other way, or to show that they were not real achievements. For the latter, anti-realism$_s$ would need to establish that (Q1) and (Q2) do not issue from legitimate demands. And there is no hint in the anti-realist corpus that they believe this, much less an attempt to show it. Ultimately, realist answers to the two questions will not need to claim as much as realism characteristically allots to truth: we do not need to know that the justification-conditions are absolutely reliable, but only that our conception of truth reckons them so. But it is a part of this standard function of truth, on realist views, to account for the relevance of evidence, that permits us to invoke truth in answering (Q1) and (Q2).

Second, it is worth noting that whatever factor answers (Q1) and (Q2) is given a place in our behaviour *without requiring that it also form a recognizable condition*. Let us call any such factor, in a neutral voice, 'verisimilitude'. Perhaps anti-realism$_m$ has some other basis for claiming that verisimilitude, or anything that is to be counted a part of our practice, must be specifiable as a recognizable condition. If so, this would limit the *bona fide* aspirants for verisimilitude. But the reason for the limit has nothing to do with the nature of our questions. Answering (Q1) and (Q2) suffices to give something a role in our linguistic practice (assuming justification-conditions have such a role) by virtue of the fact that it regulates relations between bits of evidence and accounts for the character of certain kinds of evidence. In the absence of an additional anti-realist$_s$ argument to restrict the sorts of things that may do this, underived truth-conditions are candidates for verisimilitude.

Although nothing in verisimilitude's office shows it to be restricted by the conditions for cognizing it, anti-realism$_s$ demands such a limitation. But if we are in search of a condition that

191

governs recognizable conditions, what prospect is there that this condition will itself be recognizable? The problem here is not that a recognizable regulator would confront us with an infinite regress or a self-regulating condition, either of which may boggle the mind. For there may be ways to avoid the dilemma altogether since the only conditions which have been shown to need regulation are defeasible. Rather, the problem is that a recognizable condition that sufficed would have to take over the total role formerly ascribed to truth. A suggestion for a truth surrogate is needed and our choice is rather meagre. For example, we might advert to a verifiable 'leading' process, of the kind earlier scouted for Pragmatism. But three difficulties come to mind with that or any other suggestion like it.

First, it is not easy to see how leading will give us the right sort of knowledge (which is what we need) of which evidence is relevantly defeated by which other evidence. It is not merely this particular proposal, but any other of which I can think, that raises this difficulty. Thus, if the *coherence* of our evidence is appealed to, it is equally difficult to see how this begins to work in answering (Q1) or (Q2).

Second, it is unclear that criterialists would want to go so far. It is more in character for them to stop with their anti-realism$_s$, and not even raise the possibility that they must be committed to anything on the scale of traditional Pragmatism in order to defeat global realism. The commitment to an alternative traditional theory of truth may, by lumbering, them with an unappealing theory, be enough to destroy much of their impetus. Thus, we shall be disappointed if we look to them for helpful suggestions to avoid the present predicament.

Third, and most importantly, we have already seen in Chapter 4, section 4, the difficulty, yet to be resolved, of using any reliability-vocabulary (of which 'justification-condition' and 'assertibility-condition' are prime examples) without linking it to truth. And that is precisely the task in which this alternative must be engaged. Till we have some notion how a condition can be a justification or evidence without reference to any propensity to deliver truth, we are unlikely to get any account not linked to truth of how one piece of evidence can be relevantly replaced by another.

This may seem a far cry from a defence of underived truth. For even should anti-realism$_s$ fail in this regard, it might be asked how we know that verisimilitude amounts in this case to the sort of truth found in the Correspondence Theory. The misgiving is a natural one, but is beside the point given the prescribed limits of our task. We are not now seeking a reason to adopt global realism, but an answer to a particular form of anti-realist$_s$ objection to it. That objection would work equally against *any* conception, including but not confined to realist truth, which was *transcendent* in the anti-realist$_s$ sense: that is, which did not enter our ken as a recognizable condition. Showing how any transcendent conception, as it were, may yet make a difference to our practice is enough to explode the anti-realist$_s$ case against underived truth. It shows that eliminating truth from being a verifiable condition – in the situation in which all justification-conditions are defeasible – does not preclude it from all discernibility in our practice. Thus, all we require is that truth, or truth-conditions, *could* supply answers to (Q1) and (Q2). But I also believe enough has been said, including the hopelessness of finding a recognizable condition to serve as versimilitude, to go further: even to promote the candidacy of realist truth. For, since the argument for truth-conditions *depending upon* justification-conditions, even in cases in which both are recognizable and the conditions coincide, also relies upon verifiability being the only way a condition could come to our notice, new avenues opened by the need for answers to (Q1) and (Q2) supply yet a further reason for rejecting the argument for *any* dependence of truth-conditions upon justification-conditions.

However, it is not merely that underived truth-conditions are one among several well-developed candidates for verisimilitude: they are the natural option. Defeasibility supplies a paradigm of the sort of situation in which our knowledge of truth-conditions allows a language user to modify acceptance of an assertion in the face of conflicting assertibility-conditions. Thus, a behavioural manifestation of realist truth would be a case in which one may sensibly affirm, for any disputed statement S and full set of assertibility-conditions $a_1, a_2, \ldots, a_n$, 'S may not be true although $a_1, a_2, \ldots, a_n$.' This is precisely the case in which one is relying on the acknowledgement of the epistemic independence of truth-conditions. It is such an acknowledgement that makes it possible for lecturers to display scepticism for students as a *palpable* view. Of course, criterialists as a group hold scepticism to be a refutable theory, but I am uncertain that any would be so bold as to venture that it is in the simplest way *unintelligible*; which is what would be needed if one were to disallow the above manifestation.

What I have attempted to show is how, in the case of sentences from the disputed class, our language use and behaviour distinguish between cognition-dependent and cognition-independent conditions. This is what criterialism denies that we can do, or at least challenges global realism to do. We could set up the case schematically as follows. What we must show is that every finite class of defeasible conditions is distinguishable from any truth-condition. Let us begin with a propositional function:

'*x* might be (have been) the case although *y* is not (had not been)'.

It takes ordered pairs of arguments whose first member is a condition, truth- or justification-, and whose second member is a possible state of affairs denoted by a nominalized sentence. We confine ourselves to cases from the disputed class – cases in which any finite collection of justification-conditions is defeasible. For this range of values, any instance in which the value of *x* is a class of defeasible justification-conditions and the substituend of '*y*' is the appropriate nominalization of the sentence for which *x* is a set of justification-conditions, the value of the whole sentence will be *true*. While for any pair of arguments in which the value of *x* is a truth-condition and the value of *y* is the state of affairs denoted by the appropriate nominalization of the sentence for which *x* is the truth-condition, the value of the resulting sentence will always be false. Indeed, given those values, any competent language user will realize in the first case not only that the sentence is true, but that it couldn't be otherwise. In whatever way affirming obviously necessary falsehoods is nonsensical, she will realize that she cannot sensibly deny this utterance. On the other hand, she will realize that she can never sensibly accept it when she realizes that the value of *x* is the appropriate truth-condition. Why shouldn't this count as a fitting behavioural manifestation of a transcendent conception of truth? We must not make too refined a skill out of what transpires here. It is very close to the surface of our justificatory practice. For we are only describing a circumstance in which one knows not only that something is a justification-condition, but knows as well in the broadest terms with what force that justification-condition is to be taken. It is very doubtful that one could properly be said to have the former knowledge without being in possession of the latter.

A final rejoinder for anti-realism might be to declare that we have not eliminated every conceivable candidate other than truth for the role of verisimilitude; therefore, we cannot use the above as an indisputable behavioural manifestation of transcendent truth. So long as there are other potential explanations for this combination of admitting evidence while denying the statement, we are still in search of the unmistakable manifestation demanded by the original anti-realist$_s$ argument.

If the basis of the concern is just the general fear that behaviour underdetermines a realist explanation of it, the nature of the requirement has shifted. There are well-known arguments in the literature purporting to show that *all* explanation is underdetermined by the evidence for it. Thus, it is as applicable to the situations in which criterialists select their justification-conditions, from among the welter of accompaniments of our assertions, as it is to the explanation of our grasp of defeasibility. If this perfectly general point is adduced as an argument against our purported manifestation of truth-conditions, the consequence will be scepticism, not anti-realism$_s$. On the other hand, we can show that realist truth-conditions can be manifested in our behaviour *up to the point where evidence underdetermines explanation*, and that the work it does there has not been accomplished by anti-realist$_s$ versions of verisimilitude. Thus, in so far as we are willing to accept *any* explanation, which will always be marked by underdetermination, truth regulating evidence is superior to anything which criterialism has found to replace it.

Before ending this stage of the discussion, it behoves us to distinguish the role accorded truth in ordering our defeasible justification-conditions from certain more popular doctrines assigning to truth superficially similar roles. For example, truth has been invoked to explain the 'success' or reliability of our beliefs. In an earlier realist incarnation, Hilary Putnam, comparing truth in an account of understanding with the use of a tool, writes that a 'number of tools have this feature: that the instructions for use of the tool do not mention something that explains the successful use of the tool'.[29] This does not prevent that something from in fact explaining successful use. These words do not sound unlike what has been said in defence of truth's part in explaining how our defeasible conditions can have this feature and can be related to their potential defeaters. But there are important differences.

What Putnam seeks is a kind of *external* success gained through our use of truth. Our practices are deemed reliable or well-founded by it. Similarly, others have claimed that mind-independent truth accounts for the convergence of our theories, the utility of induction, or the satisfaction of our expectations. However, plausible such views may be, they should not be confused with the present defence. Our account requires nothing so strong. The appeal to truth-conditions, by way of the potential truth of sentences, does not guarantee that our evidential practices are well founded, that they meet any external standards for success. Truth-conditions account for our readiness to count on ordinarily sufficient justification for a statement as overwhelmed when confronted with conflicting evidence of certain sorts. But no goal other than the gathering of evidence need be appealed to. For all we have said, external standards might rate our practice of gathering evidence to be altogether delusive or otherwise harmful to our cognitive well-being. Nevertheless, the practice is an orderly one, and implies a guided operation. The success insured by truth-conditions is *internal*; it is contrasted not with the unreliability of our justificatory procedures, but with chaos and randomness. This is worth remarking so that critics do not wrongly suppose that attacking claims of external success made by some forms of realism allows them to dismiss the problems with which (Q1) and (Q2) confront them.

6 STATEMENT-IDENTITY

(I) *Statements T and T' are identical if and only if they have the same truth-conditions.*

This is a generally received account: the identity of statements rests upon that of truth-conditions. If there are serious competitors to it, as opposed to refinements of it, they are not conspicuous. Although it seems as if the thesis could be accepted by global realists *and* criterialists, it is of interest to us because, as I shall argue, it is in reality the source of grave difficulties for criterialism.

I shall begin by using (I), without defending it, to state those difficulties. Later we shall look at various attempts to undermine (I). In the discussion I shall concentrate on statements about the past, since there is handy a recent back-log of realist and anti-realist charges and counter-charges about the identity conditions of such statements and the past-tense sentences with which they are made.

It should be clear at the outset that one anti-realist tactic is of no avail here: namely, dispensing altogether with truth-conditions in cases where their account in terms of assertibility-conditions fails. Given (I), this would require forgoing statements in those cases, and that makes it difficult to see what an account of assertibility-conditions could be for. Thus, the view eliminates any forms of anti-realism that would deprive 'statements' of the disputed class of their truth-conditions while at the same time seeking to understand the sentences used to make them via assertibility-conditions. But this is not the criterialist's only recourse. He may seek derived truth-conditions for sentences.

We may begin with an objection to anti-realism first proposed by P. F. Strawson.[30] His version is framed as an objection to anti-realist treatments of *sentences* rather than *statements*, and Crispin Wright has replied to it in that form. Later I shall take up the original objection and Wright's reply. But first let us rephrase Strawson's example as if it were about statements. Although I shall argue that it contributes a worthwhile observation in either guise, the formulation I am giving it first highlights the difficulty of squaring anti-realism$_s$ with (I).

Consider the following *sentence* about the distant past:

(C) Charles Stuart walked bareheaded to his place of execution.

The King's valet will have had one set of grounds for asserting it, a modern scholar a very different one. Those of the former might have included remembering having witnessed the event, remarks of others present, or later finding a hat hanging on the royal hat-rack, while those of the latter no doubt are largely confined to written accounts and remarks based upon them, none of which may trace back to current eyewitness accounts of the episode. Despite this it would be absurd to say that these were tokens of sentences of different types, or that the two utterances of it *had different meanings.* Of course, changes may have come about in the meanings of some of the words, so that we do have sentences with different meanings in the straightforward way in which such distinctions are duly recorded by grammarians. However, on the anti-realist account, such vast differences in assertibility-conditions alone should suffice to create a major difference in the meanings of the two utterances of (C).

But whatever one says about sentence meaning, isn't there a strong presumption that the valet and scholar made the same statement with their utterances of (C)? Both attempted to 'say the same thing' about the same person, and with what appear to be the very same expressions. But how can the criterialist accept this result? Given the massive differences in their grounds, the criteria for their utterances must have been very different. Truth-conditions are a function of criteria. How is it possible to have the same truth-conditions emerging from two such divergent sets of criteria? This is not to deny that there may be some overlap as well. And the less specifically the evidence is characterized, the greater the likelihood of overlap. But that would be the kind and amount of overlap we should expect to determine distinct statements. Indeed, it is not merely that anti-realism$_s$ lacks any reason for allowing two very divergent sets of justification-conditions to determine a single truth-condition; rather, the problem is that, given that justification-conditions are the *only* materials it supplies for elucidating truth-conditions, anti-realism$_s$ has its best available reason for saying that the truth-conditions for the valet's and scholar's statements are not identical.

We would fare better at showing that both sets of criteria determine a unique (set of) truth-condition(s) if we were entitled to some designative notions, which would enable us to claim that the justification-conditions converge on a certain state of affairs. But if we had identifiable states of affairs *before* constructing them from justification-conditions, we would have had what is needed for *underived* truth-conditions: namely, T and T' are identical if and only if they state the same state of affairs to obtain. Once again, it is not only that anti-realism lacks these resources, but given the nature of the total resources it proclaims sufficient, it is difficult to see how it could fail to produce answers that seem to be at odds with any promising solution.

Let us now turn to various counter-objections which anti-realism might raise to this line of argument.

First, it might be argued that there are other possible accounts of statement-identity. For example, we might say that T and T' are the same statement when (a) they share all relevant entailment relations, or when (b) they can be used to perform all the same illocutionary acts (in Fregean terms, when they have the same force). These or similar alternatives give us statement-identity without underived truth-conditions.

The sketchiness of the proposals counts against them. It is not so much that we cannot judge their plausibility without more detail – let us assume that they are plausible; but without elaboration we have little idea whether their plausibility derives from their relying upon realist truth-conditions. Alternatives (a) and (b) are not distinctively anti-realists proposals and, where they have been offered, our current dispute has not been a looming issue. Accordingly, those who offered them may have viewed them as refinements of (I) instead of as alternatives to it.

To illustrate, how might we decide if a statement made with the sentences 'The father of James II trod hatless to the executioner's block' has the same illocutionary force as one made with (C)? There may be a number of things to consider here, but surely the fact that the subject referred to is the same man is one of them. But the realist referential determination required for this is as much an anathema to the criterialist as underived truth-conditions. Turning to (a), shared entailment relations, similar questions arise. If any such scheme is to be promising outside formal disciplines, the notion of an entailment relation will have been broadened at least enough to include principles of co-referentiality, thereby allowing us to extend the entailments with one expression to utterances with co-referential expressions. For example, to begin with, it is plausible to suppose that a statement made with 'Lenin is entombed in Red Square' could be made with 'Vladimir Ulyanov is entombed in Red Square'. But if the first then entails 'Lenin is entombed', then on (a) so must the second. This would be blocked without that part of the realist account of truth-conditions, its account of reference, which a criterialist must reject as unearned if he is to be entitled to reject anything.

This is not to claim that (a) or (b) *cannot* get along without realist notions. The anti-realist may produce alternative conceptions with which to replace them. There are perhaps grounds for suspicion that if anti-realism employs its distinctive notion of an evidential condition to elucidate reference as he has truth, the same problems will reappear in another form. (For example, the valet and scholar refer to Charles Stuart by way of distinct information, and thus identity of reference will be a problem.) But the chief point is that the mere allusion to alternative accounts of statement-identity found in the literature is no basis for a hope of avoiding the present difficulty. On natural readings these accounts draw freely upon our understanding of truth-conditions, and we have yet to be given any reason to believe that they are capable of doing otherwise.

A second objection might try to exclude all consideration of statements from an account of sentence mastery. It may be admitted that an account of statement-identity is a legitimate subject for further inquiry, but is beyond the problems of sentence meaning addressed by criterial semantics.

This objection seems futile as long as semantic theory is supposed to disclose anything about truth-conditions; for, although meaning may be a feature entering at the level of sentences, truth and falsity are features of statements if anything is. But, in addition, as Dummett himself remarks, 'the sense of a sentence is not given in advance of our going in for the activity of asserting'.[31] Realism$_s$ and anti-realism$_s$ both begin from statement-making uses of sentences, and proceed by abstracting elements from them for the sentences they treat. Both truth- and justification-conditions for 'the canary is out of its cage' vary with the canary and cage in question. Thus, what are obtained are not truth- or justification-conditions for sentences *per se*, but for their real or imagined assertions.

This does not mean that once a condition is abstracted from a potential statement-making use of a sentence there remains a need to interject the statement in the formulation of an account of the resulting sentence-mastery. The statement's role may have been exhausted in making the characterization of sentence-mastery possible, without itself forming a part of it. But even thus narrowly construed, a semantic theory cannot disclaim that it has implications for accounts of statements. If those implications prove unsatisfactory, they certainly redound to the discredit of the theory having them.

Nor should it be supposed that the points raised here depend upon the adoption of a philosophically moot notion of 'statement' that could in principle be scrapped. I have said very little about 'statements' or 'stating', terms I have used interchangeably with 'assertion' and 'asserting', because there is nothing of particular philosophical concern about the use being made of them. A thinker who chooses to replace mention of statements with, say, that of ordered triples consisting of sentences, speakers and times must be queried about the same sets of distinctions and identifications. Of course, in speaking of statements we are concerned with 'what is stated' (and, on one interpretation of the more equivocal phrase, with 'what is said') rather than 'the stating (saying) of it'. But beyond that distinction nothing critical turns on speaking of statements here. To see this more clearly, let us suppose that what are normally called 'statements' are replaced in a purified language by what Quine has called 'eternal sentences'. For such sentences indexicality, tense and perhaps even normal ambiguity are eliminated through explicit formulation within the sentence itself, thus evading certain stock objections to sentences as truth-bearers. All that is needed to create the same problems for the anti-realist$_s$ within this framework are things, classes, features or whatever, with more than one way of designating them. Thus, if we suppose for exposition's sake that 'Mark Twain is the author of *Pudd'nhead Wilson*' is eternal, then so is 'Samuel Clemens is the author of the book Peregrine Worsthorne mentions at t', where we may assume the aforementioned book is *Pudd'nhead Wilson*. Now, without the vocabulary of statements we cannot articulate the question, 'Do these sentences make the same statement?' But we might ask, 'Do they say the same thing?', on our preferred interpretation of 'say'. And, in any event, the point of a question should not disappear just because of a vocabulary too impoverished to formulate it.

A final, but central, issue remains. We have assumed throughout the discussion that the scholar and valet have made the same statement. But we might examine the fortunes of denying this just on the grounds that the statements were made under widely disparate evidential circumstances. An anti-realist of this stripe could proceed to embrace further consequences of this view, such as that a layman can never make the same statement on a subject that an authority can make. This threatens to undermine the whole basis of our intuitive judgments about statements, but perhaps it can be brought off.

Though I am unfamiliar with so bold and direct a challenge to our statemental intuitions, Dummett[32] supplies the materials for one in rejecting a realist appeal to a 'truth-value link' (as distinct from our truth-link) between statements made at different times. The truth-value link is exemplified by the claims that the truth of a certain present-tense statement, A, can entail that a certain past-tense statement, B, will be true when uttered at a future time, independently of the evidence available for B when it is made. Thus, A might be a statement made with 'The road is being paved', while B would be the statement made one year hence with 'The road was paved'. At most, Dummett is claiming that the global anti-realist is not forced into incoherence, for he can reinterpret the realist's words into his own patois to preserve literal adherence to a truth-value link. (For example, evidence in the past means for him evidence now available for there having been evidence in the past.) Strawson's example revised for *statements* allows us to see the nub of the realist complaint without appraising the technical adequacy of Dummett's reinterpretations. In reply to the problem stated as whether the valet and scholar made the same statement with (C), it appears that the appeal of last resort for Dummett's global anti-realist is to emphasize our 'immersion in time'.[33] This requires us to realize that our statements are subject to change over time (though we might wonder why that should be a problem for us if we translate it into the anti-realist's own preferred way of viewing things), and that we cannot 'stand in thought outside the whole process and describe the world from a point which has no temporal position at all'.[34] Our impression of B's truth may change from the time at which A is uttered to the (now) future time at which B is envisaged as uttered. Although Dummett does not mention statement-identity, the reasons he gives for the realist's inability to convict the anti-realist of incoherence would also show that statements being made over extended intervals could not have identical truth-conditions, and thus could not be the same statement on (I). The 'immersion in time' of valet and scholar thwarts our effort to maintain that they made the same statement.

But even if the anti-realist cannot be shown to be fatally inconsistent, his position may suffer from less spectacular faults still amounting to a full refutation of the view.[35] For if divergent grounds are enough to change the identity of the statement, we should be led thereby to deny that a lawyer may state to a jury what an eyewitness has stated (unless the lawyer was also an eyewitness), or that anyone can state the same thing on the credit of another's authority. Perhaps these unwanted consequences could be avoided in letter, if not in spirit, by an anti-realist reconstrual of the phrase 'stating the same thing'. But the following explains why I take this to be unsatisfactory.

If each side can agree, as I believe it would, that distinct spatial location is insufficient to prohibit speakers from making identical statements, we can agree that the account of what 'the same statement' amounts to here need not differ from anti-realist$_s$ to realist$_s$, though they may disagree about *why* the statement is the same. We may suppose that the statement of each speaker is based on the same evidence and truth-conditions and that they utter the same sentence. In both cases, the identity claimed could be labelled by us 'strict' or 'unqualified'. (Mightn't we ask, impertinently, aren't we immersed in space?) Now it does not seem to me that when we say that the valet and scholar made the same statement we take sameness any less strictly. But the identity for the spatial case would be an identity ascribable from *either* position, while that of (C) changes systematically with viewpoint. Whatever the differences between space and time, they do not bear on the way or sense in which statements may be said to be the same. Dummett's anti-realist seems committed to claiming otherwise.

What then are we to make of the admonition to take 'seriously the fact that we are immersed in time'? Presumably Dummett finds it easier than I do to know what it enjoins and what limitations it places on our practices. But if it affects anything, it would seem to be with regard to *what we can know* rather than *what our sentences can mean*. Then is Dummett presupposing that our sentences can mean only what we can (in a favoured way) know? This is what the original objection has called into question. Thus, we would need an independent way of showing it. I do not firmly grasp the intended significance of Dummett's dictum. But in what I can understand of it there seems nothing to save anti-realism$_s$ from the earlier objection that does not already presuppose the view under attack.

7 CRITERIALISM AND SENTENCES

Quite apart from statements, Strawson's original objection has gloomy consequences for anti-realism$_s$'s treatment of sentences. Let us briefly return to that issue. According to Strawson's case, the anti-realist$_s$ should hold that sentence (C) has a different meaning for the valet and the scholar, for each attaches it to a markedly different set of assertibility-conditions. Crispin Wright[36] offers the following two-part rejoinder. First, multiplicity of criteria is compatible with a sentence's having a single meaning. Second, multiplicity of criteria is a feature even of realist$_s$ accounts; thus, it should not be regarded as a peculiar difficulty of any one theory. Let us examine these points in order.

The first remark seems unexceptionable. One assertibility-condition for the truth of 'Cynthia despises Joseph' might be her impassioned denunciation of him, another might be her ignoring him when he is present. But the commonplace nature of this situation shouldn't deter us from inquiring whether it is to be expected from criterialism, or even whether it is everywhere compatible with it. What in the criterialist canon provides a method for discovering unity in a multiplicity of criteria, other than criterialism's determination to take our justification-conditions as they are found in common speech? And the lack of a way in which to unify multiplicity may lead to problems. To illustrate, we trot out the following absurdity. Suppose we take all the assertibility-conditions we can muster for (C) and combine them into a single group with those for 'The cat has mange'. Then (C), it would appear, must also mean what 'The cat has mange' does (though the converse may not be true). What in criterialism prevents this absurdity while allowing the combination underlying (C) or underlying 'Cynthia despises Joseph'? Assertibility-conditions by themselves do not disclose what constitutes an acceptable or an unacceptable bundle; and if something else in criterialism's view does, without surreptitiously appealing to a realist understanding, no indication of it has thus far emerged.

Wright has said elsewhere that it is 'far from clear' that a criterialist must 'make intelligible' the multiplicity of assertibility-conditions. 'His task is to characterize what a master of the object-language knows.'[37] But construed as a rejoinder to the foregoing criticism this is inadequate. If questions of identity and difference of sentence are decidable at all, what other than semantic theory could decide them? Isn't this knowledge part of the very same package the master of the object language has that enables her to pair sentences with assertibility-conditions?

However, pursuing a harsher line, a case could be made that criterialism is not even compatible with having a multiplicity of criteria underlie a single sentence. For assertibility-conditions paired with a sentence supply the central part of the criterialist's account of the sentence's meaning. It appears that there could be no better criterialist reason for sentence tokens A and B to differ in meaning than that their assertibility-conditions do not coincide. Thus, the presence of distinct and independent assertibility-conditions should be prime evidence for ambiguity in the sentence. If we discount this sort of key in interpreting criterialism, we make it an enigma how assertibility-conditions can nevertheless play their role in the determination of sense.

The other part of Wright's rejoinder is that, since any semantic account can allow multiple conditions for a single sense, the problem is not peculiar to justification-condition semantics. Wright's example clarifies his intention. He imagines an utterance of 'Strawson once visited the University of Warwick', construed presumably as the denial of an unrestricted generalization. That sentence could be used to make the same true statement if Strawson visited at time t1, t2, . . . tn (where t1 $\neq$ t2, t2 $\neq$ tn, . . ., t1 $\neq$ tn). Thus, we have a multiplicity of temporally indexed truth-conditions for a single statement. This is an odd way to count truth-conditions, since it is obtained only by dividing a single more generic truth-condition into a (possibly infinite) disjunctive set of conditions. But its singularity needn't detain us.

The chief difficulty with Wright's reply lies elsewhere: namely, in its assumption that because other semantic accounts are able to divide the motley of conditions into non-arbitrary sets, we ought to assume that criterialism can do so. But the present point is that we are able to do this with underived truth-conditions just because we avail ourselves of the realist notion of an epistemically independent state of affairs to provide us with a way of deciding non-arbitrarily which truth-conditions go into a single collection and which do not. It is precisely this sort of appeal to an external standard that anti-realism$_s$ attacks; and the latter's renunciation of any such standard is its present undoing. It does not allow us, in Plato's terms, to carve reality at the joints; for it denies that there are any joints prior to our training in the use of sentences. Thus, although Wright insists upon the birthright of criterialism to multiply assertibility-conditions for single sentences, he neither explains what gets it started nor why its practice does not go off the rails.

8 ACQUIRING TRUTH-CONDITIONS

Even if the errors of criterialism undo it, there remains its challenge to global realism to provide an account of how the latter's verification-transcendent truth-conditions can be *manifested in our practice* and *learned*. If this cannot be met, the victory, it might be claimed, is to agnosticism rather than realism. We have gone some way toward meeting the challenge by showing how such truth-conditions enter the operation of defeasible evidence and are used to secure statement-identity. But this only addressed that part of the challenge concerning manifestation. Could we explain how we may come to acquire such a notion, other than by feebly speculating that it may be innate? Given the anti-realist$_s$'s own account of sentence learning, an inability to answer may appear a glaring deficiency in our account. Of course, for all that the notion may be innate. But let us accept the appearance of deficiency and try to remedy it here.

The answer I propose may be disappointingly obvious: namely, beginning with the same linguistic practice that the anti-realist$_s$ describes, we may come upon what he calls verification-transcendent truth-conditions through extrapolation from the uncontroversial cases. The extrapolation is made possible only because the learner must realize that the feature of *recognizability* in the learning process is not crucial to a truth-condition's status as such. This simple point deserves fleshing out. However, before supplying the details, I shall make a qualification.

The unfolding of events I am about to describe is a bit of armchair psychology, no less mythic or a priori, say, then Hobbes's state of nature and original Covenant. I chose it only because it suits the criterialist's equally armchair account of language acquisition: that is, it begins from the same cases and with the same materials. The purpose of injecting it here is to give the story a twist upon retelling which introduces a possibility of verification-transcendent truth-conditions omitted in the criterialist's earlier narration. What better way to take up the anti-realist$_s$ challenge?

Suppose, then, that we begin only with the so-called conclusively verifiable sentences. Truth- and assertibility-conditions may coincide in them: that is, confrontation with roughly the same physical stimulus is a circumstance in which both may be recognized. But even in these cases there is ground for distinguishing the two sorts of conditions, since *not all* assertibility-conditions will count as truth-conditions. This is to reiterate the earlier point that we could scarcely be credited with a mastery of a sentence if we did not also recognize some justifications of its assertion which would not be final or decisive verfications. Wittgenstein has aptly remarked on the fluctuation of criteria and symptoms in our language.[38] But it is not the vacillating boundaries between these categories which prompt this observation. Rather, the point is that if *all* a language user could do for a given sentence was to assert it, or assent to its assertion, when confronted with the situation that could be described as its truth-condition, but had no comprehension of the varying probabilities of its truth in other situations, he might be a remarkable organic detection device, but certainly would be less than a master of the sentence. Moreover, logical distinctions between assertibility- and truth-conditions emerging from the previous discussion (that is, that only the former may be defeasible) impress the same sort of distinction. Thus, even without verification-transcendent sentences, a conceptual distinction between assertibility- and truth-conditions is forced upon our attention.

The criterialist may respond that this is only grounds for distinguishing two sorts of assertibility-condition. However, the present significance of the distinction is not that it immediately introduces verification-transcendent truth but that, in order to make it, we must be able to ignore certain features of the total situation for one of the distinguished items (inconclusive justification) which are vital to the other (conclusive justification, truth). Even the anti-realist will want to discount a number of constant accompaniments as not figuring in or limiting the content of the condition – such as taking place on the face of the planet, or with ambient background noise. Thus, not every constant in the learning situation is part of the lesson or limits it. Anti-realism treats the feature of *being recognizable* differently. We can see the plausibility of doing so in the case of assertibility-conditions. For their whole role in his theory is to supply graspable cues to the language user for assertion or assent. But there is no similar inducement for reading *being recognizable* as part of the content or limit of truth-conditions, though it is, *ex hypothesi*, present in each learning instance. I do not deny that the learner may be aware, in each instance, of both the fact that such-and-such are truth-conditions for S and that he recognizes them as such. I only insist that they are different lessons learned.

What is the alternative? We are imagining a simple case in which it is argued that, *because* recognizability accompanies the learning of truth-conditions, it places limits upon or is part of the content of what is learned. If this is so, it must be because of a broader principle. But the most natural generalization – that any constant accompaniment has a similar role with respect to concepts learned with it – is patently implausible. To see that we need not look further than the illustrations of the last paragraph.

If, as I have argued, recognizability is not or need not be a limitation on an acquired concept of truth-conditions, nothing in the initial stages prohibits the learner from extrapolating from those instances to the disputed cases. Thus, we can acquire an understanding of truth-conditions, and truth, even when not in a position to recognize its having obtained. This instantiates a quite general precept. Normally, that a concept, say C, is grasped *via* a practical ability to recognize instances of C does not imply that any part of *what* is grasped is that there is such a practical ability. We shall examine below additional reasons for rejecting the extrapolation in the particular case of truth-conditions. But here the crucial point is that it is not prohibited just by our having acquired it through non-disputed cases. We might even venture that the extrapolation is prefigured in the learning situation, if, as I have described it, we have no reason to expect learners to feel compelled to restrict truth-conditions for the reasons that they restrict assertibility-conditions.

Anti-realism$_s$ may also offer other grounds to prohibit an extrapolation. These may take the form of completely general considerations or of specific grounds against the particular instance of truth-conditions and recognizability. Let us investigate each sort of objection in turn.

We begin with our earlier distinctions between *inhibiting* and *enabling* explanations of concepts (Chapter 6, section 4). As applied here, an inhibiting explanation of truth would hold that the circumstances under which we are capable of acquiring the notion places limits on what sense the notion can make. One circumstance which is essential to our acquisition is that the truth instanced be recognizable. But this would ban all extrapolation, at least from circumstances that *always* accompanied acquisition. We needn't make the view this rigid. Rather, we can regard it as a propensity to ban all extrapolation from contexts in which the concept is learned *without positive reasons for accepting it.* Thus, it attempts to place the onus upon the extrapolation to disprove its guilt. An enabling explanation, in accord with our earlier description of it, would be to regard differently the same set of circumstances which the inhibitist takes as placing restrictions on truth. Rather, the enablist views the learning situation as the opportunity we are given to introduce us to a concept that need not at all be understood in terms of the peculiar circumstances of its introduction. In other words, the circumstances (in this case, recognizability) are necessary for *the introduction* or *the acqui-sition* of the concept, not for *the concept introduced* or *acquired.* This is a propensity to see the extrapolation of truth as innocent until proved guilty by further argument.

The confrontation looks like a stand-off. This would be unfavourable to criterialism since we have been seeking decisive reasons on its behalf for rejecting global realism. Moreover, the anti-realist position here is, as it freely admits, revisionary. Thus, whatever force attaches to the fact that the concept of truth we actually possess is not confined to justification-conditions works against an inhibiting interpretation that seems to imply that we *can't* have it. But I believe we can do better than settle for this stand-off. We can discharge the obligation, at least weakly, to inhibiting explanations by giving a reason for not confining truth or truth-conditions to recognizable circumstances. Recall that in describing the extrapolation it was explained in terms of recog-nition not forming a part of the lesson when we learn what a truth-condition is. Recognizability attaches to the opportunity for acquiring the concept, but past that has nothing to contribute to the nature of truth. This is precisely the critical difference between truth- and justification-conditions. For as its very title indicates, *justification* is the sort of thing that cognizers have (such as for propositions, conclusions, projects, actions). There is no clear sense to the supposition that something counts as a justification though its obtaining is beyond our powers to discern it. (This is not to deny that something indiscernible in principle might be a justification were it possible to obtain it, whatever sense may be made of this subjunctive.)

But what of answering the challenge to enabling interpretations? This would be to show that there are *no* grounds, other than a general inhibitist cast of mind, preventing the particular extrapolation. This takes us from the general issue to the specific one. The question we must now ask is whether there are particular reasons, not emanating from a proclivity for inhibiting explanations, for banning *this* extrapolation.

Specific objections may begin from the familiar Wittgensteinian caveat that we cannot explain what it is to be 5 o'clock on the sun just by invoking its *similarity* with what it is to be 5 o'clock here.[39] But if this is not to rule out extrapolation without exception, we must have special reasons for thinking it applicable to the particular case, and those reasons must not presuppose the anti-realism which the objection seeks to support. How would we apply it here?

The charge must be that once we have learned truth-conditions in circumstances in which we can recognize that they have obtained, we could only extend them to circumstances in which they cannot be recognized by way of forming a misleading picture. It might go like this. We imaginatively project ourselves into a situation in which we suppose truth-conditions to be uncognizable, but, by virtue of imagining such a situation, we at the same time try to reap the benefits, to which we are not entitled, of having cognized them. The argument has an unconvincing ring to it. Perhaps we can put our finger on the difficulty by comparing it with the case for which Wittgenstein originally intended his remark: namely, by grasping what it is for another to feel a sensation by abstracting the sensation from my feeling of it. If we take our experience as the starting point, which is just what Wittgenstein wanted to deny, special problems may be created by the attempt to divide feeling something from *my* feeling it. If I learn sensation R by experiencing it in my own case, when I extrapolate to other cases I must extrapolate not only R but *also* an experience of it. The thought of an instance of a sensation without its being experienced doesn't make sense. But then what we must transfer to another is not simply R, but its experience. However, this must not be the experience of anyone in particular, for it is the thing that we are supposed to be able to transfer from one subject to another. Consequently, what we must suppose is not only that we can separate R from a particular person who has it, but also the experience of R from any particular person. This 'disembodied' experience of R is certainly stranger than anything we started with, and it is at least doubtful that it is intelligible. Because it flows from the initial step, we cannot even begin to extrapolate.

I am not suggesting that the worry just described is ultimately well-founded; but we can appreciate the force it seems to have in that case. However, its force depends on treating the phrase 'experiencing R' very differently from the way that even anti-realists want to treat 'recognizing truth-conditions'. For it is doubtful that *two separate things* are mentioned in the former phrase, the experience and R. Despite its status as quasi-grammatical object, there is grave doubt that there are things such as R independently of their being experienced. Thus, if it weren't for some particular experience, the particular R never would have existed. And this is the basis for the complaint about the extrapolation. But, for all their insistence on the recogniz*ability* of truth-conditions, few anti-realists to my knowledge believe that the very same truth-conditions which are in fact recognized wouldn't have been exemplified had it not been for the fact of their actual recognition. Indeed, anti-realists will permit even this much independence from the contingency of actual recognition for justification-conditions.

Hence, despite some attempts at blinkered applications to our issue of the Wittgensteinian slogan, there is no obvious transfer from the case of sensations to that of truth-conditions. To accuse global realists on no more justification than this of being captivated by a picture seems presumptuous. So far as I can tell, we have yet to be presented with a serious problem that must be addressed.

9 PALPABILITY AND VERIFICATION: COUNTERFACTUALS AS A TEST CASE

However, let us not rest content with the failure of the Wittgensteinian analogy to apply clearly to our attempted extrapolation. For there are particular cases that may bear more interesting analogies to our own case. One such might be Dummett's cautionary against an extrapolation argument for elucidating counterfactuals.[40] Of course, any treatment of counterfactuals could be compatible with global realism, since the issue is itself a local one. But counterfactuals may be a test case for the larger issue. For, since they are among the least attractive instances from the disputed class for a realist$_s$ treatment – unlike, say, statements about the past or others' sensations – if an anti-realist$_s$ account doesn't persuade us here, it is unlikely to be compelling elsewhere.

Dummett begins his challenge by highlighting a principle, which we may call P:

If a statement is true, it is true *in virtue of something*.

This requirement is easily met by statements that can be *barely true*; but counterfactuals are not among them. If they are true, they must be true in virtue of something else. But what is a counterfactual true in virtue of? We cannot put ourselves in a position to recognize the situations constituting their truth, or even describe one. And, for various reasons that we may accept, they are not reducible to other sorts of statements. Realists may advert to descriptions of beings with superhuman powers, but Dummett rejects this because '[w]e could not . . . explain that a being who had insight into counterfactual reality would be able to determine by direct observation the truth or falsity of any counterfactual conditional, because the expression "a direct insight into counterfactual reality" provides no picture of what these powers consist in'.[41]

However, instead of a being with superhuman powers, let us imagine a being with human powers who may be in, and thus observe in, *a possible world other than our own*; one in which the antecedent obtains and which is in other relevant respects closer to the actual world than any other merely possible world. No doubt Dummett may protest just as vigorously to this scheme.

212

Nevertheless, the change this forces upon his available replies is revealing.

P is *not* about the way in which we can learn or manifest counterfactuals, but about *palpability*. To make it palpable that a statement is true realistically, and not true because it satisfies Redundancy's equivalence, we must be able to imagine something in virtue of which it is true. It cannot just be true *sans phrase* and that be the end of the matter. But on that score alone, my alternative answer seems to satisfy all that one could require for a large number of counterfactuals. The cognizers are not superhuman observers, but beings with our powers; and we need only imagine that they observe the antecedent fulfilled. They are then in a position to observe whether the consequent is fulfilled. What could be more ordinary and commonplace? If this doesn't provide a picture of what these powers consist in, it is difficult to see what Dummett could be requiring.

If the scene is to be deemed unintelligible, Dummett must then be objecting to the notion of *possibility* it requires. (No doubt he could object also to the notion of a possible world being the relevantly closest one; but that objection, whatever its merits, seems to be of a different order. It is usually not the sensicalness of the notion that is attacked, for the sorts of counterexamples presented to it indicate that its critics find it readily intelligible. It is the choosing a standard for proximity to the actual world which would not be arbitrary that baffles critics.) But what sort of complaint could be lodged against this variety of possibility? Judging from the line which Dummett takes with statements about the remote past, it would be natural for him to say that my description of the case provides no directions to show how we, situated as we are, may put ourselves in a position to make such an observation. Thus, it can be no part of our practical ability in recognizing truth.

I ascribe this reply to Dummett only because I can find nothing else in the offing. But on it the objection shifts again from a question about the *palpability* of a circumstance to one about *how we might come to know that a situation arises*; that is, to recognizability. Palpability alone does not cause us to question how we came to be in that situation so long as the situation is unexceptionable from a logical point of view and its internal description contains nothing extraordinary. But with the new turn in the objection, the only problem is that given physical laws we couldn't in fact ever be in a position to recognize it. This will not do, for it is the recognizability requirement itself that Dummett's case against counterfactuals has been commandeered to defend. Thus, to argue that this 'provides no picture of what these powers consist in' *because* we couldn't from our actual place be that cognizer is reasoning in a circle. Of course, we have directed Dummett's remarks in ways in which he may never have intended them to be taken. But this has been done only in the cause of tapping whatever means anti-realism$_s$ might have to avoid the fatal consequence. What appears to be the case in the long run is that the view is held together by a rather tight knot of preconceptions, which offer mutual support only where they are not questioned from outside.

Put otherwise, questions of palpability, such as those raised by P, evoke thought-experiments. Dummett is no doubt correct that there are limitations on permissible thought-experiments. For example, we cannot cavalierly suppose that we are dealing with superhuman observers. But the limit P imposes is rather specific. It is an antidote to a particular failure to make our suggestions palpable. We cannot suppose without further argument that palpability, and thereby permissible thought-experiment, is also governed by the condition that we could *here and now* place ourselves in the position occupied by us (or someone else) in the thought-experiment situation. What is question-begging is this indiscriminate admixture of considerations of palpability and practical recognizability.

This is not the only chink in Dummett's armour. His argument seems to proceed on the supposition that P may be satisfied by counterfactuals only if they are either reducible to another kind of statement or barely true. It is intuitively obvious that they are not barely true, and there are various requirements of reduction – for example, that the sentences be meaning equivalents, that they form a lower layer in a well-defined semantical hierarchy – preventing them from being reducible. But Robert Stalnaker has pointed out that counterfactuals which have truth-value (and not all do) have specifiable circumstances, though perhaps not ones generalizable for counterfactuals as such, by virtue of which they would be true.[42] And these pertain to would-be actual situations, not just to what is perceived in another possible world. Thus, P may be satisfied by specifications that for various reasons will not meet the more stringest desiderata of reductions. The point seems to me well-taken. But the one I wish to stress, which seems characteristic of the general anti-realist$_s$ methodology, is that recognizability is not demonstrated to be necessary, but assumed all along. It has already been integrated into the operation of the requirement, P, that our account of truth be palpable. If we do not accept that conflation, we are unlikely to accept not only anti-realism's concern about counterfactuals, but also those it generates about the past, other-ascriptions of sensations and so on.

10 SUMMARY

Let us take stock. Although anti-realism's attack on global realism was itself attacked, no attempt was made to evaluate in any systematic way the purely semantic thesis of anti-realists that declarative sentence meaning could be adequately explained in terms of assertibility-conditions. However, we did deny that the semantic claims could be made fully intelligible without the supplementation of realistic truth-conditions. This connection needn't be written into the formulation of the purely semantic theses; but its looming presence makes it possible for us to take some assertibility-conditions as defeasible and to settle questions of identity and difference for statements and even for sentences.

Moreover, we scrutinized the forms of typical anti-realist arguments, and concluded that, first, the Principle of Bivalence does not build a bridge between the semantic claims and global anti-realism; second, the exclusive emphasis of the arguments, from their onset, upon recognizable conditions is unwarranted; and, finally, the reasons given for requiring that truth-conditions be recognizable are inadequate. This should be more than sufficient to ward off attacks on global realism from that quarter. But just over the crest of the hill is another wave of dissent inspired by Wittgenstein: the view that each of our utterances belongs to a language-game. Since, as this view develops, language-games are the final court of appeal for any utterance, there can be no higher authority, such as reality, to sanction our beliefs and statements. For this reason truth can be no more cognition-independent than language-games. We now turn our attention to this new challenge.

VIII

LANGUAGE-GAMES AND ANTI-REALISM

1 INTERPRETING WITTGENSTEIN?

The later work of Wittgenstein, (namely, that after 1930) is a well of inspiration for anti-realism. A network of notions – most notably language-games, forms of life, explanation and rules – are given twists that seem to discourage so much as raising traditional questions about the relationship(s) of language to reality. But there are serious obstacles to locating with passable precision Wittgenstein's contribution to this issue. As elsewhere in his writings, we must first assemble his epigrammatic observations into sustained and coherent lines of attack. For example, there are two prominent anti-realist construals of Wittgenstein's remarks on language-games and forms of life. One is a relativist interpretation; on the other Wittgenstein, though not a relativist, is a transcendental idealist and still an ardent anti-realist. Both challenge global realism, and we shall treat them in turn in this chapter.

These are not the only possible interpretations of Wittgenstein's texts. Some commentators have maintained that he never intended to provide a general theory of language or language-games; that he used language-games only to illuminate a number of diverse puzzles, and that those uses do not lend themselves to a feasible or useful systematic thesis about language-games as such.[1] On another view, Wittgenstein has retained his earlier realism, but it is whole language-games rather than elementary propositions that get linked to and tested by cognition-independent reality.[2] On yet a third interpretation, compatible with realism, it is not so much that the connections towards which global realism gestures are straightforwardly mistaken, but there can be no account of them. Such connections may be *shown*, but there can be no super-scientific accounts of the relations between language and reality.[3] These alternative views are not being swept aside. But suggestions of anti-realist interpretations in other passages raise threats to global realism, and thereby warrant our attention even if they are not faithful to Wittgenstein's ultimate intentions. Unquestionably they have spawned considerable success among his sympathetic commentators. Thus, without wading deeper into these very muddy exegetical waters, we shall concentrate on the two anti-realist interpretations mentioned above. If the reader wishes, she may regard us as having turned poor Wittgenstein into an eponym for the possibly fictitious philosopher concocted from an assortment of textual clues.

2 A PROFILE OF LANGUAGE-GAMES

Before turning to the aforementioned anti-realist arguments, we must sketch more fully the crucial notion about which they revolve: *language-games*. While *forms of life* may also seem crucial, Wittgenstein has much less to say about them, and our investigation doesn't turn on their specifics. In fact, forms of life are elucidated in terms of languages [PI, para. 19][4] and languages are elucidated in terms of language-games. Thus, the most basic notion in understanding Wittgensteinian reasons for rejecting realism is that of a language-game. It is worth noting that when Wittgenstein first explicitly introduces this notion, he connects it with issues dear to global realism. He writes in the *Blue Book*:

> The study of language-games is the study of primitive forms of language or primitive languages. If we want to study the problems of truth and falsehood, of the agreement or disagreement of propositions with reality, of the nature of assertion, assumption and question, we shall with great advantage look at primitive forms of language in which these forms of thinking appear without the confusing background of highly complicated processes of thought. (BB, p. 17)

Unfortunately he does not develop the notion further in that work, though he uses it again in the *Brown Book*. Greatly over-simplifying, I shall assume that the notion introduced in these works remains constant throughout Wittgenstein's later writings; or, at least, if there are changes, that they do not alter the general picture we shall draw.

What are language-games? Primarily, they are primitive or simplified contexts in which a relatively homogeneous fragment of language-related activity occurs. Wittgenstein also remarks that the whole language may be called '*the* language-game' (PI, para. 7), but ordinarily language-games are simpler: either simplified fragments of an advanced language or the whole of primitive languages, in each case introduced to eliminate the confusing complexity of a developed language [PI, para. 5]. Wittgenstein's few specimen lists of language-games (such as PI, para. 23) are confusing, containing items that seem cross-classified just where we want illumination. But we can infer from his examples that language-games may be of two general types: artificial and natural. Artificial language-games, such as that of the builders (PI, para. 2), are devised to highlight ways of taking expressions that could, or do, occur in larger languages. Natural language-games are parts or aspects of our natural languages that have been isolated for the same reason; but because they are extracted from a broader context, they raise unavoidable questions about individuation. Since natural language is supposed to consist of a myriad of such criss-crossing and overlapping games (PI, para. 18), it is much more difficult not only to say where one begins or ends, or that it forms a self-contained and complete game, but even to supply reliable guides for such decisions.[5] Nevertheless, artificial and natural language-games must share basic features if either is to be of use, for both demand constant comparison in vital respects. We may sum up those basic features in the following list.[6]

  i Language-games are sufficiently single-tracked to allow the point or purpose of an expression to emerge with clarity and ease. (PI, paras 5, 122, 130)
  ii They make manifest and concrete what counts as a *justification* of a use of an expression and in what contexts evaluation is permissible. By placing forms of expression back into their natural, larger context, we can see the

proper limits of evaluation, and why certain attempts to criticize forms of language may be precluded (e.g., illegitimate, nonsense). (PI, paras 10, 17, 21, 261; Z, paras 114, 313–15; OC, paras 110, 229, 247–8)

iii We learn to participate in a language-game through training, imitation, example. We are not, *ab initio*, taught rules, nor could we proceed by grasping them; but only reflect in ways leading to their formulation after attaining mastery of the game (namely, becoming full-fledged members of the language-community). Though not guided by such rules, our behaviour may be describable in their terms, as formulated, say, by philosophers, linguists or logicians. (PI, paras 5–6; Z, para. 419; OC, paras 95, 283, 534, 543)

iv *Explanations* are concrete, given by instances, examples, ostensions and so on. They are not incomplete when in this form, and not underwritten by a *general* unarticulated rule towards which they are inadequate gestures. No hidden rules or intrinsically interpretable mental episodes make them work. The particular precedes the general in language-mastery. (PI, paras 37, 71, 208)

v Language-games are *complete* or *autonomous*. They may subsist without having a larger purpose. Thus, they do not allow a method of evaluation (/justification) or comparison (say, for effectiveness) with other language-games. Any criteria for their evaluation must emerge from within the game itself, and be made possible by aspects of the game that include a role for self-criticism. (PI, paras 18, 47, 217; OC, paras 103, 204–5, 253–4, 284, 559; Z, paras 314, 320, 331)

vi There are normal conditions which make a language-game possible (*boundary conditions*). These are usually general features of nature, and their obtaining need not be expressed by traditionally conceived necessary truths. They may consist, for example, of the general rigidity of rods, or of our having certain interests in common. Though they make a language-game possible, they are not ingredients of it, and thus may be inaccessible to any epistemic attitude within it. Although in the background, they may not be able to be brought to the foreground without change of game. (PI, para. 242, p. 230; Z, paras 351, 540–1; OC, paras 83, 98, 103–5, 162, 308, 341–4, 375, 401, 509, 617)

I again emphasize that Wittgenstein may have never intended his scattered employments to form a generalizable doctrine. 'The work of the philosopher', he believed, 'consists in assembling reminders for a particular purpose' (PI, para. 127). Thus, for example, his most prominent purposes may have been served by stressing that a language-game *can be* autonomous. But, this account would continue, it would be a mistake to infer from those instances and his silence on others that Wittgenstein believed all, or even most, language-games were autonomous. But against this it may be urged that some passages in which autonomy is not explicitly discussed suggest that it must nevertheless be present *just because* we are dealing with language-games. However, I do not wish to arbitrate this interpretational dispute. Suffice it to say that these articles, including (v), form a widely received interpretation that is of particular interest to global realism and which can be traced to certain of the things Wittgenstein wrote.

It is (vi) in particular that underwrites the first, relativist interpretation of Wittgensteinian anti-realism. Recall that patterns (I) and (II) of veramental relativism in Chapter 6 each required at least the possibility of 'conflicting' standards: in this case, conflicting language-games or forms of life. For practical purposes, that means at least one language-game and so on different from our own. Item (vi) shows how that may be intelligible. Though we may have to adopt a certain frame of mind, (vi) allows us to imagine a situation in which boundary conditions of our language-games are not met, or are at least generally believed not to be met. For it is perfectly understandable that these boundary conditions *might not have* obtained. Then (v), the autonomy of language-games, assures us that there is no objective external standard, no sovereign language-game, which would resolve conflicts that might arise from such divergent linguistic practices.

Let us now look more carefully at this relativist line of attack. Some of the details to be spelled out and the objections raised to it are as applicable to the second, transcendental idealist, interpretation as to this one. None the less, the interpretations are separated because, as we shall see in section 10, the second one creates new possibilities for the global anti-realist. With that, let us begin with some preliminary elucidations.

3 ANTI-REALIST IMPLICATIONS

It is said that Wittgenstein rejected all *explanation* in philosophy. But I wish to broaden 'explanation' to cover any sort of philosophical account of a given subject. On that liberal construal we can say that language-games are frequently introduced to contrast *horizontal* with *vertical explanations*, and that Wittgenstein invariably prefers the former to the latter. Vertical explanations are characteristic of traditional philosophizing. They get their title from the sorts of the connections with which they render explanations of semantic phenomena. They proceed *from* the level of language or its use *to* another level; say, that of mental episodes or referential ties to language-independent reality. Thus, a typical vertical explanation would be that the meanings of expressions are constituted by their relations to self-interpreting thoughts or mental images, or that the truth of a proposition is constituted by its relation of agreement with a fact, or the justification of a proposition by its vertical relation to certain evidential conditions. Language-games are often presented to show that the meanings or justifications of a game's elements are determined by the role of those elements in the larger game. On the anti-realist view under consideration, this is the case for truth as well. We come to understand truth by way of understanding how we develop criteria for it, and those are determined by the horizontal relations of (true) statements generally to the language-games to which they belong.

A realist may be tempted to reply initially by insisting upon the distinction between the general structure of our criteria for truth and *what makes* a proposition true. As Wittgenstein presents them, language-games yield insight into such matters as how we satisfy ourselves that something is true, what believing in the truth of a proposition commits us to, and various ways in which we are licensed to react to truth challenges. But these do not show, the reply may continue, that what constitutes the truth of our propositions is similarly subject to the linguistic practices we adopt. The Wittgensteinian rejoinder must be that exempting truth's constitution in this way from our practical tests for it violates the requirement that language-games be autonomous. For, in effect, it tells us that there is a standard, though perhaps inaccessible to us, for externally evaluating language-games based on the way in which the propositions justified in them compare with reality. To this the global realist may respond that it was just such a prohibition, imposed by the autonomy condition, that was being called into question.

What can the language-game anti-realist use to fend off this riposte? Perhaps he will reply that this is to treat a language-game as if it were no more than a collection of propositions, a sort of tacit theory embedded in the totality of the commonsense beliefs of its participants. But a language-game conveys a form of life, and, whatever is to be made of that elusive notion, a form of life is more than a kind of theory, however global. '[I]t is not a kind of seeing on our part; it is *acting*, which lies at the bottom of the language-game' [OC, para. 204]. Thus, justification can only take place inside a language-game, thesis (ii). To the realist, this may look more like a restatement of the view than a defence. But, for the nonce we shall simply allow that Wittgenstein's many scrupulous descriptions of concrete practices are capable of showing how such reorientations of traditional assumptions can ring true. Ultimately we shall have to say more about the nature of the persuasive descriptions. But for now we can concede that there is substance to the popular view that Wittgenstein's aseptic descriptions break the hold on us of certain traditional philosophical conundrums, that they are as therapeutic as polemical. Thus, perhaps enough high-quality description simply brings us to see that the whole network of our beliefs is grounded in action rather than reflection

4 A RELATIVIST VERSION

Nothing in this preliminary exposition distinguishes the relativist from the idealist strand in language-game anti-realism. But we said earlier that (vi) makes relativism a promising interpretation because it opens the possibility of there being, in some sense, conceivable 'forms of life' other than our own. For it does not beggar the imagination that the boundary conditions of our current language-games should have been otherwise, or be thought to be otherwise. In 1950 Wittgenstein penned a stunning example of this in his comment on an hypothesis that one had been to the moon.

> If we are thinking within our system, then it is certain no one has even been on the moon. Not merely is nothing of the sort ever seriously reported to us by reasonable people, but our whole system of physics forbids us to believe it. (OC, para. 108).

In response to someone who admits that we do not know how gravity would be overcome, or how we would create an artificial atmosphere, but nevertheless claims, 'We don't know *how* one gets to the moon, but those who get there know at once that they are there; and even you can't explain everything,' Wittgenstein replies, 'We should feel ourselves intellectually very distant from someone who said this' (*Ibid.*).

Of course, the example is not very convincing, and not just because manned space-flight projects were put into operation about a decade after Wittgenstein wrote this. Rather, the more fundamental problem is that, though Wittgenstein does not rule out all extraordinary reporting, he seems to set a very low limit on acceptable (/sensical) reporting of the extraordinary. We generally believe we are much better prepared to contemplate the possibility of things (and thus to find them sensible) at least as extraordinary as Wittgenstein found space travel. But, that aside, if this is an example of the expected threshold of boundary conditions for language-games, it seems rather easy to imagine conflicting forms of life. We need only compare Europeans of 1950 with those of 1970.

In another passage Wittgenstein writes:

> Supposing we met people who did not regard [a proposition of physics] as a telling reason. Now, how do we imagine this? Instead of the physicist, they consult an oracle. . . . Is it wrong for them to consult an oracle and be guided by it? – If we call this 'wrong' aren't we using our language-game as a base from which to combat theirs? (OC, para. 609)

Of course, as pattern (I) of Chapter 6 illustrates, it is not sufficient for relativism merely to note actual or possible differences of

223

opinion. If those differences were sufficient for relativism, the many such ordinary differences daily encountered in the market-place would be a good argument for it. But Wittgenstein's notion of a language-game gives us a principled ground for denying that the differences in question could be resolved the right way. Any standard we employed would have to be justified by some langu-age-game or other (the superiority of horizontal explanation), and thus we could do no better than impose the standards of one language-game on those of another. Even without the evidence for potential conflicts, the inability to devise standards for constituting truth that transcend any language-game places global realism in an untenable position. The combination of the contingency of the boundary-conditions of language-games with the restriction of justification to single language-games poses even more starkly the difficulty of realist appeals to a cognition-independent reality.

5 RELATED ARGUMENTS

Before starting objections, we should note that the pattern of argument we have been surveying does not exhaust attacks of Wittgensteinian vintage against global realism. Two other promi-nent objections traceable to remarks in Wittgenstein might be mentioned here, if only to excuse ourselves for ignoring them in this chapter.

First, Wittgenstein accepts the deflationary view of truth encap-sulated in Redundancy [PI, para. 136; RFM, Pt. I, App. I, section 6]. This could be a separate argument, but it also might be a stage in his canvass on behalf of language-game autonomy. For example, it seems to be Redundancy or some of its sub-theses that teach us that 'the idea of "agreement with reality" has no clear application' (OC, para. 215) or goes round in circles (OC, para. 191). And this in turn shows us that talk of 'agreeing' and 'tallying' can only be elucidated through the expressions' role in language-games:'What does this agreement consist in, if not in the fact that what is evidence in these language-games speaks for our proposition?' (OC, para. 303) Whether as an independent argument or as supplementing claims of language-game autonomy, we can set aside these remarks to the extent that they are repetitions of the Redundancy Thesis sufficiently anatomized in Chapters 2 and 4. It is conceivable that Wittgenstein is concerned exclusively with a thesis about the *use* of truth-predicates. But he seems to take this as a direct reflection on traditional theories of truth, and some commentators agree that in supporting the equivalence theses Wittgenstein believes that he is acknowledging all that can be said on behalf of Correspondence.[7]

Second, the tenor of Wittgenstein's writings may suggest that the understanding of truth cannot be severed from the understanding of *criteria* for its determination (for example, Z, para. 437). But instead of holding this for language-game reasons, it might be maintained on the grounds that the way we acquire concepts and manifest our use of them in property ascriptions prevents truth from being totally separable from justification. The line of argument being suggested is thus far similar to the one discussed in Chapter 7, but is less developed to this point. In the version now under consideration we need not deny that we can be fully justified in believing something that is not so (OC, para. 195). Nor need we be infallible about the things constituting boundary conditions of our language-game (OC, para. 425). Indeed, some propositions for which we have little or no justification may yet be true. But on the current line of argument all such cases *necessarily* will be exceptions if there is to be a conception of truth. Since our understanding begins with ways in which we determine truth, those methods are forever bound to our concept of truth. Radically non-epistemic theories such as Correspondence are thereby precluded.

If we accept the loosely adumbrated view about the order in which concepts *must be* acquired, and even accept that this places limitations on acceptable views of truth, there are still various ways to regard these principles. One way to satisfy the implicit requirement would be simply to exclude any accounts of truth that, by their articles, *were incompatible with* things happening in this sequence. On this construal there is no need to proceed to read the details of acquisition or justification into *the nature* of truth, and then the dire consequences do not flow for Correspondence. But that might be considered too weak to capture the present insight, and thus another interpretation might be offered in which our methods of justification were factored into, and not merely causally antecedent to, our concept of truth. However, stating it baldly like this invites bewilderment, not to say charges of the genetic fallacy; for there is an understanding gap between the way in which we acquire a concept and the nature of the concept thereby acquired. To bridge this gap we would need intermediary premises, such as a distinctively semantic thesis to place limits on what is meaningful. This would bring us to a full-fledged version of the sort of criterialism discredited in Chapter 7. But nothing we have said since about language-games introduces novel support or otherwise provides grounds for reopening the case for that view.

However, there is one curiosity concerning the criterialism of Chapter 7 and the present view that is worth an additional remark. On a credible anti-realist account of language-games there is an incongruity between the views. Criterialism clearly intends its justification-conditions to be in the main language-independent circumstances in the world. This is in no way impaired by the insistence that they also be epistemically accessible. But on a certain view of language-games emphasizing horizontal explanations, nothing in a language-game, including objects ostended in ostensive explanations, is anything more than another 'instrument of the language' (PI, para. 16). Tables and chairs, in so far as they figure in a language-game, are just special kinds of symbols, and not something wholly non-symbolic.[8] Otherwise, we would have to introduce vertical connections to explain the introduction of some elements of the language-game. Thus, elucidations never get beyond signs or what is infected by signs. Perhaps there is a way to square all the Wittgensteinian dicta on these two subjects. But it is worth noting just how different the spirit of the present anti-realism is from the views considered in the last chapter.

6 LANGUAGE-GAME AUTONOMY AND IDENTITY

A first problem besetting the relativist argument is that of obtaining even approximate identity and individuation conditions for natural language-games. As we have seen, we are presented with scenes of actual or possible striking differences in attitude from ours, of the sorts to which standard forms of anthropological relativism might appeal, and are told that these display irreducibly different notions of evidence or truth *because* the subjects of this behaviour are engaged in a different language-game. But if this mention of a language-game is to have explanatory weight, we must know at least broadly what counts as a different one. Otherwise, we are not debarred from contemplating the possibility that the others do in fact subject themselves to *our* notions of evidence and truth, but that at least one of us misemploys them. This too would account for the differences. How could we tell that in condemning them we are indeed imposing an alien standard on them? How can we tell that certain conditions are boundary conditions for a language-game rather than just general assumptions *within* a larger game? Once doubts about identity and individuation are raised, they are hard to dispel. For it becomes clear at once that questions about, say, identity-conditions cannot be answered in terms of anything other than language-games themselves, for anything else would violate the prohibition on vertical explanations. Language-games would be explicable *via* an external standard.

That brings us to the closely related issue of language-game autonomy. For natural languages, individual language-games must fit together into a single language. Shouldn't this imply constraints on combinations of language-games? Of course, part of what Wittgenstein contended was that we must abandon the traditional supposition that language has a systematic unity which would permit sharply focused theses about it such as verificationism and theories of logical form. But surely, if there is to be a single language, even a jerry-built one (PI, para. 18), rather than a hopeless chaos, we should require at least that none of its language-games be allowed to nullify possibilities and prospects opened up by others. But then what are we to make of autonomy? If we take it at face value it seems we should allow that *any* possible language-game can be added to *any* language without incongruity, much less paradox. To the extent that we see magical explanations as *incompatible with* those from physics, demonic possession as *incompatible with* modern medicine, or panpsychism as *incompatible with* mechanics, we reintroduce for the autonomy of language-games a difficulty parallel to the one the earlier Tractarian Wittgenstein encountered with the notion of the logical independence of elementary propositions.

Many of the uses to which Wittgenstein wished to put language-games do not need the doctrine of language-game autonomy or any answers to questions about identity and individuation. (Indeed, many uses do not need *natural*, as opposed to *artificial*, language-games.) But it may be well to remind those who employ language-games as a nostrum for all ills that not every traditional issue is responsive to so makeshift a notion. Nevertheless, we need not rest the defence of global realism on such infirmities in its critique. For a more fundamental criticism of the relativist line is that a close examination of instances of language-games discloses no argument against global realism. Language-games may tell against various collateral doctrines that Correspondence theorists often covet, but they simply do not make points against Correspondence itself. So that we may turn to that point I shall assume that we have a sufficiently definite conception of language-games with which to proceed.

7 THE ELUSIVENESS OF ANTI-REALIST CONSEQUENCES

To reiterate, the foremost complaint about the anti-realist language-game strategy is that once the genuine virtues of language-games are sorted out, no grounds for rejecting global realism will be found among them. Taking language-games to preclude realism requires that one smuggle in further assumptions, and the sorts of assumptions that look promising here are those that we have already rejected elsewhere.

We may begin with a consideration of the most celebrated example of a language-game: that in which a builder uses the vocabulary of 'block', 'pillar', 'slab' and 'beam' to elicit an action from an assistant (PI, para. 2). Though an artificial language-game, it is arguable that it shows each of the following: that we cannot identify these expressions with the similar-sounding ones in our language; that the meanings we or they ascribe to such expressions cannot be determined by mental accompaniments of the terms' utterances, but are set by the roles of the expressions in their respective language-games (PI, para. 20); that the builder's language-game is not *incomplete* just because it has no place for some of our distinctions (PI, para. 18); that a lack of syntax or compositionality need not detract from the use of the builder's expressions being functionally equivalent to what we call commands (PI, paras 18–19). More to the point, it is arguable that the example shows that we must consult the relevant language-game to see whether an embedded form has the role of designating, naming, referring to, denoting (and so on) blocks and the like in the way that our phonetically similar expressions designate, (and so forth). Thus, even the possibility of word–world connection depends upon a word's language-game role. But this has no tendency to drive out all vertical explanations. That an expression's designative (and so on) capability be determined by whether its role in a language-game is compatible with its actual designation being a vertical connection between an element in a language-game and a fact or object in the non-linguistic world. The descriptions of cases do not add up to support for the claim that the actual connections between a determinate sentence and a state of affairs making it true or false is an intra-linguistic as the connections which determine the identity of the sentence. I have no doubt that, when put this way, those who support the view under attack would tend to agree.But I have been unable to discover any better grounding for their view.

In fact, for those who believe that the builder's utterance 'block' is *the same command* as our 'Bring me a block', there had better be other than intra-language-game connections for determining the identity of illocutionary acts. For these 'commands' occur in two different language-games. And if the only relevant semantic determinants were those between a language-game and its elements, we would have no footing on which to judge that semantic similarities between elements of different language-games occur.

Let us look again at the example in which the builder gives one of the four instructions to an assistant and the latter obeys. While we believe that, say, *our* term 'slab' can be used as a name for an object or a type of object, Wittgenstein would argue that this is not so for the builder's similar vocable. Furthermore, this is shown by the horizontal tactic:

> Now what do the words of this language *signify*? – What is supposed to show that they signify, if not the kind of use they have [PI, para. 10]. . . . When we say: 'Every word in language signifies something' we have so far said *nothing*

whatever unless we have explained exactly *what* distinction we wish to make. (PI, para. 13)

Thus, we see that the builder's 'slab' *is not* a name by seeing its role in that language-game. Accordingly, we determine that our word 'slab' *is* a name by seeing its role in our language-game. But this shows at most *how it is established* that a term is a name, and perhaps even to a certain extent what it can name. It does not show that when it actually names, the only connections it can have are with other elements inside the language-game. This would be to confuse the basis for setting up the relation with what has been set up by it.

This is an amicable resolution of the dispute. We can concede for the sake of argument valuable insights to language-games and agree that Wittgenstein thereby rectifies fundamental mistakes of his predecessors. We may allow, for example, that the meanings of linguistic elements cannot be determined in isolation, and that the particular conscious state of the speaker at the time of utterance is not a determinant of word-meaning. But we have also left room for global realism: for connections between linguistic or language-use elements and facts or things that are independent of our linguistic practices. However, this will be unacceptable to some. For example, Wittgenstein says of aesthetic judgments that 'they form a very complicated role, but a very definite role, in what we call the culture of their period. To describe their use . . . you have to describe a culture' (LA, I, para. 23). A typical anti-realist gloss on passages such as this is that they claim that aesthetic notions (such as appreciation, beauty or art) are not 'independent of social change and history, but rather . . . products of human culture and history which could have been otherwise'.[9] Notice that the author of the comment is not maintaining that their *discovery* is a product of human culture and so forth – a claim consistent with realism about judgments concerning them – but that the notions themselves are cultural/historical products. Since this conclusion is intended to turn merely on a comparison of different language-games [LA, I, para. 26], there seems nothing special about the particular subject-matter: aesthetics. If the view works, it can be applied to any non-aesthetic notion showing a similar dependence on a language-game.

This interpretation may seem especially impressive for aesthetic notions. Normative concepts generally have been, for whatever reason, preferred sources for non-cognitivist claims. Perhaps it is not only due to the fact that there is disagreement on these judgments, but also that the disagreement is perceived to be widespread or pervasive. Thus, we seem readier to accept the view that, say, standards of appreciation are cultural products even independently of the prospect of diverse language-games. (Notice that this particular sort of language-game is not an independently identifiable phenomenon but is individuated by cultural and historical epochs, or changes of fashion.) But nothing about language-games alone, as opposed to the usual historical and anthropological categories, carries the conviction that these notions are purely cultural products. Indeed, if it were otherwise, it is difficult to see why the point does not emerge for 'block' and so on in the builder's game, since we have there a supposedly complete and autonomous language-game.

Wittgenstein describes several more cases in which participants in language-games embodying very diverse outlooks confront each other. There are instances of scientific versus oracular or magical societies, and of religiously devotional versus secular communities. In each case Wittgenstein's emphasis is upon the difficulties of understanding and the hazards of the easy assumptions that the alien community is in the same line of business as the familiar one. He emphasizes that the confrontations are often more akin in important respects to attempts at conversion than to straightforward argument and counterargument. He may be right about the dangers of misunderstanding. If that is the whole of the point, global realists could agree. But they may still maintain that if our own line of business is fact-stating, that participants in another game may be doing otherwise has no tendency to show that the alleged vertical connections of our referring phrases and statements must be limited or reinterpreted consistently with anti-realism. By itself this does not provide evidence *for* global realism, but it helps to show that the latter is untouched by the introduction of a language-game analogy for understanding language.

8 VERTICAL AND HORIZONTAL CONNECTIONS

With great oversimplification, here is an *Übersicht* of the difficulty. Imagine our viewing the original situation as comprising the following levels, the first and third of which may be initially conceived as essentially non-linguistic.

(1) Mental occurrences: M_1, M_2, M_3, . . ., M_n
(2) Language (sounds or marks): L_1, L_2, L_3, . . ., L_n
(3) Reality (entities, states of affairs, etc.): R_1, R_2, R_3, R_n.

Possibilities for relevant vertical connections would be between (1) and (2) (meaning, grasping of a linguistically manifested rule) and between (2) and (3) (reference, truth). Language-games, such as the builder's or shopkeeper's (PI, para. 1), are designed to show, negatively, that M items do not elucidate the uses of linguistic units L, and, positively, that horizontal connections concerning the role of L items at level (2) are sufficient to reveal whatever we could legitimately seek to know about those uses. One important respect in which this oversimplifies is that the adequacy of the horizontal connections is obtained, in part, by replacing a very strict conception of what belongs to language itself with the enriched notion of a language-game. A language-game incorporates not only utterances, but also many of the activities and things that we would intuitively classify under (3). For example, the normal responses to utterances (obeying commands, being put into a certain situation by having made a promise) are parts of the game, as are hoping, expecting and intending. As we mentioned earlier, on one interpretation even the samples which are appropriate subjects for ostensive teaching are treated as signs belonging to the language-game. Thus, horizontal adequacy is effected through an enlarged view of what belongs at level (2). But the first concerns, and the ones emphasized in this paragraph, have been with the employment of language-games to rule out connections between (1) and (2) to elucidate understanding of language or skill at following a rule.

Up till now not much has been said about the connections that concern global realism: namely, those between (2) and (3). But with the success of the preceding endeavour, perhaps it is then inferred that the conception of an ampler language now found at

(2) is self-sufficient (/complete/autonomous), meaning by this that it does not need explanations of its constituents from another source. From this it is easy to slip into an extension of the self-sufficiency claim to preclude connections with other levels as explanatory of any facet of language. Once recognized, the progress thus far is an added inducement to epistemologizing the relata at level (3) so that they may join the enriched class of linguistic constituents at (2). Though qualifications are appropriate, in the end I can find no better argument grounded strictly in language-games – as opposed, say, to classical anti-realist considerations – for using these notions to sever all connections (interpreted as in realism) between (2) and (3). Thus, with trepidation, my diagnosis is that a conclusion reached because of the alleged inadequacies of mentalistic accounts of meaning and rule-following has been extended beyond the applications justified by its premises.

A qualification should be entered. Critics may be quick to point out that the referential theory of meaning implied in Wittgenstein's *Tractatus* and suggested in the passage from St Augustine's *Confessions* that opens the *Philosophical Investigations* shows that reference is not an innocent bystander in just the sorts of vertical explanations of linguistic understanding attacked in Wittgenstein's concrete language-games. The point is well taken. And, in so far as the connection between an expression and its referent is supposed to explain linguistic understandings or meaning, we may grant for the sake of argument that it fails. But at most this impugns a use to which it has been put, not the connection itself. Surely realist accounts of reference and truth are not hostage to referential theories of meaning. Thus, I see no reason to retreat from the view, at least on this basis, that the anti-realist uses to which language-games have been put are over-zealous extensions of more pertinent applications.

9 THE ROLE OF INHIBITING EXPLANATIONS

We cannot overlook the possibility that *an inhibiting explanation* of truth may have also been influential here. Recall that when the distinction between inhibiting and enabling explanations was first introduced (in Chapter 6), the former were said to confine future applications of a concept to the precincts marked out by the situation in which they are acquired. We have granted for argument's sake that 'true' and 'false' are learned *via* the roles they play in language-games, and these roles are in turn defined by certain moves in those games in which we have learned that those epithets are appropriate. Moreover, that a linguistic unit counts as an assertion, and is thus an appropriate bearer of truth or falsity, may be determined by its role in its language-games. From considerations such as these, and aided by a disposition to interpret the concept of truth inhibitingly, it may be concluded that the only conditions allowable for the *accurate* application of truth or falsity are steps of one sort or another within a language-game; that is, steps within a particular sort of human cognitive practice. This simply leaves no place on the conceptual landscape for the cognition-independent standard of accuracy supported by global realism.

Arguments incorporating undefended applications of inhibiting stories are at best inconclusive. For example, they require the supposition that a learner is a rather unimaginative *tabula rasa* with respect to the particular item of knowledge under consideration. For, in effect, what it leads us to suppose is that the lesson learned must have written into its specification the entirety of the empirical panoply in which it occurs (with a qualification for the level of prominence, of course). The learner cannot come equipped with any sort of innate resources – ideas, dispositions, quality spaces, salience gradients and so on – that would permit her to zero in on certain of the elements as the real lesson, while seeing at the same time the irrelevance or dispensability of the remainder. At least, if she employs such equipment it is assumed that she must have mislearned. However, all this is mere presumption at the present level; it stands in need of further warrant.

This does not show that an enabling assumption would fare any better: but if we recall that the limited reason for raising the issue is to evaluate an objection which incorporates an inhibiting explanation against global realism, it will be clear why we need not show this. The reasons for global realism were contained in Part I, and consisted in a large part in removing misconceptions about Correspondence as well as eliminating competitors. At present we are only interested in discovering whether considerations introduced by neo-anti-realists provide grounds for over-turning the earlier conclusion. Nevertheless, over and above what the realist needs, there does seem to be a reason for *favouring* an enabling interpretation of the facts here: namely, very similar abilities to extend our notions beyond the previous conditions of practice seem to be portended by the nature of the language-game analogy. An under-emphasized but not altogether neglected feature of language-games is their flexibility. Within them are various potentialities for change, extension, adaptation.[10] As Wittgenstein puts it, languages 'seem . . . in a certain sense to have led beyond themselves, for I am now able to construct new language, e.g., to invent words' (Z, para. 325). We are not required to describe each modification as the realization of a totally new language-game, and more frequently than not it is not even reasonable to do so. Many changes clearly seem prefigured in the earlier practice. Capacities for change needn't be exercised. But when they are exercised the situation confronting us must be given a description of the enabling kind: that is, the exercise of a new concept and so on issuing from, but not wholly capturable in terms of, materials made manifest in earlier forms. In other words, these changes always take us 'beyond' the conditions of previous practice.

What alternative descriptions of such changes are available if we choose to try to avoid enabling explanations? Perhaps something fitting the following characterization: We may regard languages and language-games as very short-lived and static phenomena, rapidly succeeded by new ones that cannot be eluci-dated in terms of their predecessors. Although this proposal may be coherent, it is unsatisfying. It has a close analogy to a view of a person as a rapid succession of temporal slices, no further explanatory connections subsisting between neighbouring slabs. Both descriptions seem contrived, and leave no allowance for even the most minimal accounting of one phase in terms of preceding ones. Its bare possibility, granted for the sake of argu-ment, should not disguise the fact that it is out of sympathy with the animating spirit of the language-game analogy to give 'aseptic descriptions' of concrete practices. Rather, in the present context it could only be motivated by a desire to deny one plain fact of our linguistically related practice, that of its protean forms, in the interest of inhibiting accounts of it.

235

If this general point is allowed, is there any barrier of principle to taking our notions of truth and falsity, assumed learned *via* devices for making plausible moves within a language-game, to have set up a standard for correctness that is logically independent of our practices? Some of the fears working against this suggestion were already allayed in Chapter 3. For example, this does not imply that at most one set of descriptions (from one language-game) can be correct, nor does it imply that anyone's descriptions are neutral. It is difficult to see that language-game considerations alone prohibit such a cognition-independent notion of truth. But this is not the only significant consequence of the present discussion. Not only has it been argued that the adherence to the language-game analogy needn't prevent global realism; but it has also been shown that an inhibiting interpretation of our truth-related practices is not a necessary condition for the adoption of a language-game analogy. Thus, global realism need have nothing to fear from claims of language-game theory to provide insights about our uses of truth.

10 A TRANSCENDENTAL IDEALIST VERSION

Taking a different tack, let us consider what I have called the transcendental idealist version of language-game anti-realism. We begin by scrapping (vi): boundary conditions for language-games are no longer capable of being regarded as potentially dispensable. Appropriating and perhaps slightly disfiguring a useful expression from Jonathan Lear,[11] let us speak of our collection of language-games (or form of life) as our having a certain *mindedness*. This includes not only those language-games in which you and I actively participate but also those we can make sense of, which are recognizable possibilities. Occasionally it may seem as if there are other ways of being minded, ways that might have evolved instead of our own. But on the current interpretation this is not the case. Our mindedness (form of life?) contains various unrealized potentialities; and this makes it possible within a single form to recognize many kinds of *étrange* language-games, and even to come to understand, without acquiring a different mindedness, future developments – say, in science and art – that we could not now imagine ourselves comprehending. In fact, the boundaries of our mindedness are the limits of what does and will make sense. Wittgenstein sometimes confronts his readers with seemingly alien language-games (for example, PI, para. 185; RFM, I, para. 3; OC, paras 609–12; Z, paras 338–40). But, as Bernard Williams suggests, we are not to take this as another kind of mindedness.

> Seen in this light, the alternatives are not the sort of socially actual alternatives, relativistically inaccessible or not, which we have been discussing; nor are they offered as possible objects of any kind of explanation. Rather the business of considering them is part of finding our way around inside our own view, feeling our way to the points at which we begin to lose our hold on it (or it, its hold on us), and things begin to be hopelessly strange to us.[12]

We cannot make sense of another kind of mindedness: but as a justification of ours this claim would be a futile gesture. That should not in turn lead us to suppose that there must be a more rarefied, description-defying sense in which another kind of mindedness *is possible* for us, thereby returning us to relativism by a crooked route. The non-existence of an ultimate justification has to do *not* with the lack of a sufficiently neutral standpoint from which to describe our mindedness, but with the lack of any sensical standpoint at all outside our mindedness. Thus, to take a notorious example, to give a graspable general recipe that by itself guaranteed that we could continue to follow a rule in one way rather than some other (barring mistakes) would require something that directed the way we were minded without itself being subject to it. And that makes no sense.

In its broad outlines, this view is similar to one Donald Davidson arrives at as a result of his attack upon the notion of a conceptual scheme.[13] We might call it the Wittgenstein–Davidson view. According to Davidson, suppose we begin, as seems promising, by identifying *our* conceptual scheme with the set of languages translatable into it. Thus, an alternative scheme would have to be a set of languages that were largely untranslatable into ours. (Translation, of sentences *and* whole languages, is a matter of degree, subject to a multitude of vagaries. Davidson allows us to discount various local untranslatabilities. For exposition's sake, we may speak as if a language is either translatable into ours or not, *tout court*.) But though we can imagine various ways in which another language fails to fit precisely into ours – for example, 'a language may contain simple predicates whose extensions are matched by no simple predicates . . . in another language'[14] – Davidson finds unintelligible the dualism between *scheme* and *content* that would make distinct conceptual schemes a realizable proposal. Since alternatives are not intelligible, talk of ours is otiose. We are left with the boundary of what is intelligible or sensical, and nothing more.

Returning to Wittgenstein, we might explain his view in terms of distinct levels at which explanation could be expected. The first is the empirical level, at which we find scientific explanations from zoology, astronomy and so on. Some have believed that there is a second level at which philosophical or conceptual explanations are rendered; but Wittgenstein officially rejects all such explanations. A modified Wittgenstein view might reclassify some of them as empirical, amplifying that category considerably. But what is significant for Wittgenstein is that he denies that explanations are possible at the deepest level: that at which we find our form of life, mindedness or conceptual scheme. This was also true for the earlier language-game view; but there it seemed to depend upon the capacity of language-games to replace all the legitimate explanatory potency of traditional philosophy. Here the inability to explain is founded on the fact that our 'form of life' already encompasses everything that could be used in an explanation or justification. Though we can explore potentialities on a vast scale from within it, we can conceive of no other. The best we can do is to mark its edges with the use of a limitation vocabulary including expressions such as 'unintelligible', 'unthinkable', 'nonsensical', 'impossible', 'incomprehensible' and 'inconceivable'.

To understand better the threat to global realism contained herein, we may see this view as a kind of *idealism*. But, if idealism, it is certainly *transcendental* rather than *empirical*. The empirical idealist regards cognizers as among the empirical objects in the world, and allows that reality, including ourselves and whatever depends upon us, is contingent upon acts of cognition. On that view, it is easy to imagine alternatives to our mindedness: namely, it is the mindedness of anyone who does not figure in the aggregative 'we'. And it poses no obstacle to supposing that there are such beings even if we are unable to say any more about them.

No such alternatives make sense on the Wittgenstein–Davidson view. Nevertheless, it has been claimed that this view is a form of idealism, since it describes things in terms of *our* language and *our* world. But since it leaves no room for the hypothesis of a differently constituted group of cognizers, it must be a form of transcendental idealism. Bernard Williams, who discusses this possibility, though non-committally, gives two connected reasons for an idealist interpretation of Wittgenstein here.

(a) '[E]verything can be expressed only *via* human interests and concerns.'
(b) Nothing can 'ultimately be explained in any further terms'.[15]

The terminal phenomena – those which do not admit of any further explanation (and thus no further justification) – are *our* interests and concerns; and it is through them that our mindedness is acquired. The view's boundaries are set in terms of what is accessible to us as an imaginable human concern: hence transcendental idealism.

11 THIN VS. THICK HUMAN INTERESTS

Eventually I shall argue that, despite my initial remarks, upon viewing the details of (a) and (b), they lead us neither to idealism nor, in any way that need concern us, to anti-realism. But first I want to show why this way of looking at the issue mislocates it. For, in so far as (a) and (b) are taken as an interpretation of idealism, they are just the other side of the coin in the mistaken characterization of global realism whose faults were exposed in Chapter 1, section 4: namely, the view that realism claims, (C), that our best or ideal theories might turn out to be false. On that view realism is the position that acknowledges the possibility of a gap between the way things are, on the one hand, and the way we believe them to be (explain them, express them, view them and so on), on the other. The interpretation of transcendental idealism rests on that characterization by maintaining that if things are expressible only by way of human interests and concerns, there can be no possibility of a gap between the way things are and the way we view them from the perspective of our interests and concerns.

I am not suggesting that the distinction between views that allow the gap and views that do not is not a useful one. It is the contention that this distinction encapsulates that between realism and anti-realism that I want to resist. Moreover, it may be true that the discovery of the possibility of such a gap is conclusive evidence for metaphysical realism. For if we know that the way things are is independent of the ways in which we can express claims about the world, the former couldn't very well be cognition-dependent for its constitution. Nevertheless, this misconstrues the issue, because the difference between realism and anti-realism emerges initially from the proper way to account for truths (or references) that are in fact expressed by us. Thus, the realist and anti-realist differ primarily not about the extensiveness of the cases – namely, whether they outrun our expressive capacities – but over *each instance* of truth that we express. Since the realist and anti-realist accounts of truth lock horns over each instance of truth (or reference if we include metaphysical realism), (a) and (b), could they be established, would not settle the issue against global (or metaphysical) realism.

However, let us set aside that obstacle. Still, it is unclear that this representation is entitled to be considered idealist. Let us begin to see why with a consideration of Williams' reason (a).

According to (a), references to cognizers, as human or us, are ineliminable. But they are also too thin to support an idealist interpretation. An analogously empty form of idealism might argue as follows: 'In the end, the judgments we make about the world are *ours*, and we cannot get around the fact that we experience things through *our* faculties.' These are truisms; but to derive anything of significance from them we must see what sorts of restrictions they place on our faculties. The only unattainable judgment would be one that was not ours; but the argument does not suggest that any judgment, out of the possible ones not described in terms of our judging them, is unavailable to us; and, of central importance, it does not imply any restrictions on the contents of available judgments. No *type* of information other than that described irrelevantly as 'information we have not happened upon' is denied us by the truism. Similarly, if the Wittgensteinian interpretation could be contrasted with a type of world that might be imagined by anyone not to be ours, or with interests and concerns that were not human, it could indicate the dependence of our cognition on the peculiarities of our situation. But our cognition is limited only by what is inconceivable (and there is no hint that this too might differ for others).

How did we acquire the 'human interests and concerns' upon which the allegedly idealist interpretation rests? Not by repackaging the objects of cognition to make them accessible to a parochial outlook; but instead by taking advantage of the potentialities in our commodious mindedness to expand our interests and concerns to whatever is conceivable. How does this differ from viewing things *sub specie aeterni*? What more needs to be added to this before we have achieved realism? Mightn't we say of this sort of idealism, applying to it a remark Wittgenstein makes in the *Tractatus* about solipsism, 'when its implications are followed out strictly, [it] coincides with pure realism' (TLP, 5.64)?

The point comes into clearer focus when we examine more minutely the limitation vocabulary with which our (alleged) viewpoint is circumscribed. This vocabulary rules out alternatives as either *impossible* or *unthinkable*. But there are noteworthy differences between these ways of expressing the limit. Let us divide the vocabulary into two sub-groups: an anti-realist one canonically represented by 'unthinkable', but also including 'inconceivable', 'nonsensical', 'unintelligible' and 'incomprehensible'; and a realist one canonically represented by 'impossible'. When used in proper context, common modal terms such as 'cannot', 'could not', 'may not' and 'might not' will also go in the realist sub-vocabulary. The realist sub-vocabulary contains the suggestion that the boundaries are supplied by the nature of things. The anti-realist sub-vocabulary, when taken strictly, carries the suggestion that the limitations are located in the cognizer rather than the world cognized. Unfortunately, there appears to be no limitation vocabulary free from one or another to these biases.

For various reasons these sub-vocabularies do not always coincide in judgment. What is impossible may be in some broader sense conceivable or thinkable; and by defending certain truths as synthetic *a priori*, even when not in precisely these terms, philosophers have subscribed to the view that there are propositions whose falsehood is inconceivable or unthinkable, though possible. But given a choice between two sets of expressions which lead to conflicting commitments on the issue of concern, how may we describe the limits on a form of life (mindedness)? Wittgensteinians generally shy away from the realist sub-vocabulary: perhaps, in part, because to say that another mindedness is impossible could be taken as offering *an explanation* of why there isn't one. But the unthinkability vocabulary is no less inappropriate, though its bias is one with which proponents of the view may feel more comfortable. For it seems to locate the limits in our faculty of cognition. Moreover, once this is done it is difficult to resist the temptation to backslide from transcendental into empirical idealism; since if the limits are located in cognizers, isn't it plausible to believe that there might be other sorts of cognizers and thus other sorts of mindedness? What is wanted is a vocabulary to describe the limits on mindedness which is not committed to locating them in one of our two explanatory categories. Since that is not available, before the unthinkability vocabulary can be appropriate to describe the limits, it must be purged of its customary associations. That in turn destroys whatever capital might be made of describing what occurs within the limits possessively: as *human* or *ours*. The basis for anti-realism in (a) evaporates.

12 AN AMICABLE RESOLUTION OF THE DIFFICULTY

But we shouldn't expect the resolution of this puzzle by itself to remove the challenge to global realism. It is still true that the mindedness of this account prohibits any explanation or justification of the whole of it in terms of what is not contained within it. Since realism of any form is perceived as, *inter alia*, providing just such explanations for our speaking in certain ways, it appears that even on the so-called idealist interpretation the scheme of language-games, forms of life and so on is incompatible with realism.

Our only interest here is with *global* realism, and it is difficult to know just how the Wittgensteinian view is imagined to conflict with it. Thus, it is difficult to know what would count as a relevant response. Global realism and the mindedness scheme simply don't seem to lock horns anywhere. For example, consider the following two consequences of this picture on mindedness as it is taken to bear on global realism.

First, the elucidations ruled out by the account of mindedness are supposed to explain *the whole* of our language *qua* collectivity. Even if we ignore the fact that this will include a good deal of behaviour that could not be construed, on the most generous interpretation, as the expression of a proposition, Correspondence could be taken at most as an attempt to explain or justify certain propositions that have a place within this larger form of life. Thus, in order to demonstrate that the account of mindedness is incompatible with global realism, it must be shown how an explanation applicable to certain elements (propositions) within the collectivity violates a restriction placed upon the collectivity. Of course, we have not demonstrated that this is an impossible task. But I believe it clarifies just how unhelpful are the account's strictures against certain kinds of explanation. What further might the Wittgensteinian say about the injunction to show convincingly that it applies to our case?

Second, the relevant mindedness is more than the collection of things we hold true – that is, our beliefs – for its boundaries are not those of our 'world view' in any narrow sense. It is bounded, on the idealist interpretation, by whatever we find intelligible, conceivable, possible. Unless we think of the false propositions in this set as bearing implicit possibility prefixes (an assumption that is quite gratuitous), our mindedness will embrace a very large proportion of falsehood. In that perfectly good sense, the whole of our mindedness will not be explained, much less justified, by global realism. Of course, the true and false will be divided, thus explained, by the global realist solution. But if it is the whole as such which constitutes our mindedness, what is wanted is an explanation of why certain things are conceivable or possible, not why they are true or false. And global realism essays no account of why propositions are conceivable or possible. Thus, on a natural rendering of the view in question, there is no justification for taking the ban in question to exclude global realism.

No doubt, there is the ever-present danger in any of the anti-realist arguments that confusions we have already exposed from other sources will enter. In the case before us, if what is conceivable is so because it is infected by our conception of it, then talk of a mind-independent world determining the truth or falsity of many of our propositions will appear illicit. But this will not be because of the mindedness restriction on explanation, but rather because our conceptual contribution has been read into conceivability. We have dealt with that problem elsewhere (Chapter 3, sections 4–5) and needn't rehearse it here. Suffice it to note that it does not improve the prospects of the mindedness scheme as an anti-realist weapon.

Because proponents of the Wittgensteinian arguments often promote a language-game outlook as the only way to do justice to the messy facts of common practice, it is worth noting that our defence of Correspondence, though conducted at a very abstract level, is not wholly divorced from concerns with garden-variety assertions. Of course, we did claim that Correspondence is basically a theory about what truth consists in, not about which particular potential bearers are in fact true, and we sharply disjoined the role of its constituter from the requirement that it be a useful general test for determining truth. But we also mentioned in Chapter 1, section 5 that if Correspondence emerged from anti-realist objections unscathed, we had no compelling reason to doubt that much of our ordinary chat is true. For the chief reason we had been given for supposing otherwise was the anti-realist charge that unless truth is constructed from elements in our cognitive practices, we can never know whether our utterances are true. The gain of interjecting truth in this is only that Correspondence, unlike certain neo-anti-realist views, is not *eo ipso* a refutation of the form of scepticism that would raise such doubts (though, strictly, the doubts are about knowledge rather than truth). But the form of scepticism hasn't been well defined, it hasn't been shown that it is irrefutable by other means, and the fact that truth is not a construct out of our practices does not preclude *many* truths of interest to us from being adequately (fully?) confirmable by methods within our ken. This is not to deny that we are fallible, but the grounds for mistake need only be the customary boring ones, not the spectacular philosophical ones. Thus, even the most robust commonsense view ubout *truths* can be a natural corollary of our theory of *truth*.

We have not been urging the abjuration of all interest in language-games. Quite the contrary, since the form of our rejoinder was to show that conceiving our practice in terms of language-games did not imply the refutation of global realism, we can say, conversely, that the acceptability of global realism doesn't imply a rejection of language-game philosophy. They are simply not in competition. Thus, the language-game picture may still gain interest from other of its employments that were mentioned in passing. In sum, global realism does not commit us to any stand on the view that our assertive utterances are best viewed, for many purposes, as moves in a language-game; for nothing in the former endangers the notion of a language-game or many of its foremost applications.

IX

SCIENTIFIC ANTI-REALISM: THE KUHNIAN CHALLENGE

1 GLOBALIZING SCIENTIFIC REALISM

The last of our major neo-anti-realist challenges comes from the view that competing scientific theories are incommensurable, combined with the proviso that the evidence for each theory, at the level of observation, is too infected by the theory it serves to say anything independently of it. However, before plunging into Thomas Kuhn's refined version of that view, let us look more broadly at the theory–observation distinction and the relationship between local and global versions of scientific realism and anti-realism.

The theory–observation distinction has fallen on hard times. Originally, it was supposed that we could sharply distinguish theoretical sentences and the distinctively theoretical terms in them from observation sentences, which were taken as strict reports of the evidence, and their distinctive observation terms. The theoretical sentences, it was supposed, would account for (that is, explain and predict) observation reports, and thereby be testable by the truth or falsity of such reports. If they failed, theories weren't always abandoned, but they might be amended, and at a minimum were in crisis. But difficulties with this view abound. There has been trouble in precisely characterizing observation sentences and terms in such a way that they do not contain theoretical elements. It is generally accepted that no theory by itself implies any particular observation; difficulties can always be avoided by adjustments in a multitude of places in the theoretical network, including at the observational level; where drawable, the distinction doesn't seem exhaustive or exclusive, and may shift from context to context; and theories appear as capable of changing the way we describe the phenomena they purport to explain as the latter are in influencing the former. Nevertheless, there are those who would rather cleave to a heavily qualified version of this distinction than give it up altogether. They include those, including some holists, who believe that our theorizing requires an empirical grounding somewhere. Thus, in these early stages I shall assume some such distinction, intuitively drawn and as open to qualification as is compatible with the exposition, in order to see how juggling these categories can affect the differences between realists and anti-realists.

Even if we suppose a relatively stable set of observational facts to be explained by a theory, a widely received view is that theories are always *underdetermined* by the facts. That is, given all the relevant facts, more than one theory can be found to account for them, and there need be no further fact that would, were it discovered, favour only one of them. The theories may even be strictly incompatible, and not merely cross-classifications of the same data (as in Quine's famous example[1] of a lepiform experience prompting an utterance of 'Gavagi', which might be translated into the target language as 'Lo a rabbit!' or as 'Lo an undetached-rabbit-part!'). What conclusions must would-be realists draw from this circumstance?

Because no more than one of a set of incompatible views can be true, if we think of the inconclusive set of data as the sole truth-constituter, we cannot include theories among our truths. But we may still retain global realism as the correct view for what has truth-value: namely, the observational reports. We might adopt the realist outlook that 'the facts of nature outrun our theories as well as all possible observations'.[2] If we also think that the only realistic interpretation of theories is that they are either true or false, this would lead to anti-realism about theories. But though it might be called 'scientific anti-realism', it would be local, not global. On the other hand, we might think that what holds for theories holds for observational reports as well. If we gave up Correspondence as the account of truth along with this, the ensuing scientific anti-realism would be global. Still further, we might allow a different interpretation of what makes our theories realistic. Perhaps it will be a looser relation of 'fitting the facts' that amounts to not conflicting with them (and perhaps accounting for a certain proportion of them). This might satisfy a realist, though he would be prevented from calling such theories true because of the presence of an equally 'fitting' incompatible theory. Finally, a global realist might maintain that it is something over and above a theory's accounting for a set of facts that constitutes its truth (perhaps its framing the mechanisms that account for the phenomena exhibiting those regularities), and he can thereby hold that one of the theories is true, and the others false, although both fit the facts. In sum, once we settle everything about under-determination, everything about global and metaphysical realism remains to be settled.

I take this as an object lesson on the bearing of some central issues in the philosophy of science upon our question. But, although one's views about the status of scientific theories do not commit one to any position with respect to global realism, the issues can become global if one holds not only that theories lack truth-values, but that they also influence the so-called observable facts so profoundly that none of our statements can have *inter-theoretic* truth-value. Once again, one might still desperately cling to the notion that Correspondence is the correct account of truth. But a view that regards all facts as theory-dependent implies the cognition-dependence of the world. And there are powerful motives for seeking another theory to explain ordinary ascriptions of truth in such a world. It is with this notion of a theory-dependent world and the anti-realism it serves that we shall be concerned in the present chapter.

Before proceeding to that work, let us make one further crucial preliminary point. We must carefully distinguish the theory-dependence of facts (/states of affairs/situations/objects) from that of the statements relating them. For it is only with the former, the facts (and so on), that a line of argument of the relevant type clearly tends to support epistemologized truth. For example, suppose someone holds that a sentence could not be used to express a certain proposition unless it was understood (/inter-preted) in light of a certain theory. If, say, the facts were not similarly dependent on the theory, for all that this could still be compatible with Correspondence. The truth-value of the prop-osition expressed, when expressed, might be determinable by a state of the world that was not reliant upon the theory. And it is not even clear that the proposition requires for its truth that the theory, which by interpreting a sentence makes its expression possible, be itself true. (Recall the example in Chapter 5, section 5, of a Newtonian stating that a certain object weighs between 2 and 3 grams.) We must look carefully at any view arguing to epistemologized truth on the sole basis that our words have their meanings determined or influenced by prevailing theories. If the facts stated by the statements made with those words are not equally theory-dependent, no threat to Correspondence has yet been identified.

2 GROUNDS FOR INCOMMENSURABILITY

Thomas Kuhn's influential work, especially in his *magnum opus The Structure of Scientific Revolutions* (hereafter SSR) will serve as our concrete instance of global scientific anti-realism. Kuhn contends that competing scientific theories, the type that succeed one another in the history of science, are *incommensurable*. By this he means that the legitimate success of one theory over another cannot be explained by a set of objective criteria which the winner satisfies exclusively or better. But he does not rely heavily on the underdetermination of theory by evidence. Not only is Kuhn's explanation of incommensurability different from this, but, as we shall see, it changes in different passages. However, in a crucial few pages of SSR[3] he explains the incommensurability of actual incompatible theories in terms of the following factors (and he tends to repeat the explanation elsewhere,[4] though not in so nicely compact a list):

(1) *Lack of common problems* – whereby followers of competing theories cannot agree upon a set of core or even legitimate problems which a theory in the field should address.

(2) *Lack of common meanings* – whereby dominant theories *influence* the meanings of terms (observation terms) used to report crucial factual or observational consequences, thereby subtly changing the meanings of the seemingly constant vocabulary that survives theory change.

(3) *Lack of common perceptions* – whereby paradigm changes cause scientists to *see different things* (not just 'see things differently'), thus making it appropriate in some yet-to-be-explained sense to say that scientists with competing theories live in different worlds.

(Throughout this chapter it will be convenient, albeit corny, to refer to these as the three 'lacunae'.) In other contexts Kuhn emphasizes that, although scientists share a set of vaguely described objective *criteria* – which he prefers to call 'values' because of the highly individualized ways in which they are applied – they leave sufficient latitude for each competing theory to claim it is vindicated by them. Because they do not provide 'an algorithm able to dictate rational, unanimous choice', 'they are not themselves sufficient to determine the decisions of individual scientists'.[5] The ultimate decision then must reside not in the set of objective criteria, values, maxims or norms, but in the uncodifiable, but educated, perceptions of well-trained scientists. The criteria Kuhn mentions, though the list purports to be neither complete nor well articulated, includes items such as accuracy (of consequences deducible from the theory compared with results of existing experiments and observations), simplicity, scope, consistency (internal and with other accepted theories) and fruitfulness.[6] Elsewhere he also mentions a balance of esoteric to everyday subject-matter and the number of different problems solved;[7] but there the issue is not choosing a theory, but determining the progressiveness of past choice. The difficulties with criteria such as those from the first list are, among others, that different scientists may give different relative weights to their satisfaction – so that, say, one scientist may rate the spectacular satisfaction of one criterion as more important than deficiencies in several others – and that different scientists may apply the same vaguely described criterion in different ways (for example, qualitative versus quantitative accuracy of prediction). Because some objectively undecidable cases are compatible with one's choices still being objective, (1)–(3) – especially (2) and (3), which imply the absence of a common language and world for scientists to contend for – seem to be the more profound grounds for incommensurability. No doubt they are more troublesome to global realism, for they form the basis for rejecting any notion of theory-independent reality.

The two sets of considerations may even introduce rather different understandings of incommensurability. Associated with the failure of a list of objective criteria or values would be merely the inconclusiveness of an exclusive objective choice. Associated with the three lacunae would be the partial breakdown of communication between scientists from competing paradigms, and the inevitability of working at cross-purposes. These may bear a revealing comparison to patterns (I) and (II) of veramental relativism, respectively (see Chapter 6, sections 2–3).

We should say something further about Kuhn's list of criteria. According to him they seem to exhaust the 'objective' factors in theory-choice, but not *eo ipso* the rational ones. Although he thereby implies an arguably narrow view of objectivity, he is certainly not claiming that these objective considerations can be ignored. Indeed, though they must be supplemented for a decision in the usual case, if there were a candidate theory that failed them deplorably it would be a non-starter. Just what the list of criteria lack for sufficiency is not made as clear as we might hope. Occasionally Kuhn characterizes what is missing as an algorithm, and he says that 'the algorithms of individuals are all ultimately different by virtue of the subjective considerations with which each must complete the objective criteria before any computations can be done'.[8] And at least once he describes the needed algorithm as something that would produce unanimous, or at least near-unanimous, agreement. He does not highlight, and I do not know if he countenances, the possibility that some of the disputants may simply be objectively mistaken, or have a wrong algorithm (even if there is no *exclusively* correct one), and that this would be discoverable by a detailed examination of the case. He seems more impressed by the ability of each rhetorically to stand his ground as satisfying criteria in his area, and by the fact that certain theories which have turned out, on history's near unanimous judgment, to be correct were upon their introduction less favoured by an application of the criteria to what was then known. (Of course, it is not unheard of for an opinion to have been at one time both unreasonable and objectively correct. But at this stage more important than passing judgment upon Kuhn's views on objectivity is getting straight about what they are.)

251

3 ORIGINS OF THE KUHNIAN ACCOUNT

An overview of Kuhn's position would be useful here. Our particular interest is best served in seeing it through its opposition to what we may call the traditional philosophy of science. We would not be far off the mark in saying that the tradition represents the collected wisdom on the subject from Bacon and Descartes to the present. More significantly, it provided the dominant framework for thinking about science in 1962, when the first edition of SSR appeared. At about that time Kuhn's work supplied the most influential of a spate of attacks on the traditional philosophy. By then the tradition had been refined by the philosophers who have since come to be collected under the aegis of logical positivism. They set the dominant tone in the philosophy of science in the second and third quarters of this century. I shall give a brief portrait, shamefully oversimplified, of a general positivist version of the tradition. Even so sketchy an account will help toward a better understanding of Kuhn. For some of what he maintains is profitably viewed as a reaction to the tradition's contemporary manifestations.

According to the tradition, theories arise from a need to organize common experience. Thus, we may begin with a distinction between observation and theoretical *terms*, which, once worked out, leads to a further distinction between observation and theoretical *statements or sentences*. Roughly, observation statements are supposed to be direct reports of experience. When accurate, the experience reported – perhaps only through controlled experiment – may be used to justify and test theories. Theories are related to observations by way of correspondence rules; but since this invariably falls short of a total reduction of theory to observation, it is said that theories are only partially interpreted (by observation). Better theories replace inferior ones with more exact and all-embracing explanations, predictions or even control, of the observational evidence. Accordingly, the history of science exhibits a linear progress in which succeeding accounts ideally bring us closer to the whole truth about nature. (It need not be assumed that complete or perfectly precise truth is an attainable ideal.)

This view is certainly realist in temper, though varieties can embrace local anti-realisms. For example, attempts may be made to eliminate or fully elucidate theories through reductive analyses to actual and potential observation statements. This occurs in phenomenalism, instrumentalism and operationalism. The picture also admits qualifications of other sorts, of which I shall mention only a prominent few. For one, the inability to discover an unsullied observational vocabulary has led some traditionalists to abandon a *sharp* contrast between theory and observation for a distinction *of degree*. At the level of contact with experience, reports may contain a minimum of theoreticity, but are not wholly free of it. Originally, the observation language was conceived as something 'neutral' between theories and wholly 'fundamental' as a source of data for any theory. This view is not completely scuttled just because of the need to admit that the observation language is infected with theory. For the relatively low level of theoretical commitment in the observation language still allows it to be a useful instrument for theory testing, and the small traces of theory found in observation statements do not disrupt the possibility of virtually full communication between adherents of competing theories. A second qualification: theories may arise in all sorts of accidental circumstances, prompting a distinction between the logic of discovery and that of justification. Inspiration being willy-nilly and not reducible to a recipe, traditionalists demur from offering a logic of discovery. But once in place theories may be tested by their observational consequences: thus, a logic of justification is a reasonable ambition.

This composite view generally promotes the objective evaluation of theories, comparatively and separately, by an appeal to phenomena relevant to them, linear progress toward attaining full truth or more of it, and the emergence of theories out of a pool of publicly accessible experience. Against this Kuhn maintains that (a) the succession of one theory by another is characteristically marked by incommensurability, which involves a serious lack of full communication, that (b) the meanings of the expressions we use to report observations, the observations themselves, and the sorts of puzzles that are important and legitimate for scientists to work on are all 'influenced' by the predominant theories of the day, and that (c) progress, though evolutionary, is a more delicate matter of refinements of puzzle-solving techniques. According to Kuhn we get our common conception of science from periods of normal research, distinguished by the fullness of communication among scientists, cooperation, and the development of finer test equipment and methods of experimentation. This view of science is enforced upon scientists themselves by a dogmatic education. But normal science depends upon sharing common theories and research paradigms, which can remain relatively unarticulated till scientific anomalies place them in trouble (as they always will). If the anomalies grow too basic or prolific, or elude explanation for an extended period, this may induce a crisis, which in turn promotes extraordinary research. Out of this research may emerge a new theory with new paradigms.

A brief word about Kuhn's use of 'paradigm' is also in order. As he concedes, the term was used in a number of senses in SSR.[9] One of these senses is as a term for the set of commitments, vague as they may be, shared by and delineating a single scientific community. It is such shared commitment that permits the cooperative and cumulative enterprise associated in the popular imagination with the core of science, and which Kuhn calls a normal research tradition. He later prefers the term 'disciplinary matrix' for this shared set of commitments.[10] Theories, especially those prominent enough to serve as models for scientific communities (such as Evolution, Copernicanism, Galileo's law of falling bodies) are also called paradigms. But he later says that the preferred use of the term was for striking concrete instances of research or discovery, used in the education of young scientists and whose imitation. defines for the community the nature of research. Such concreta needn't have official formulations, and even when they do their application to the diverse sub-fields covered by them will not be made evident by a formula alone. Here is one place in which primitive similarities precede their formulation.[11] It will make it easier to interleave passages from Kuhn with our exposition if 'paradigm' is occasionally used in more than one of these senses. In each occurrence the context should protect us from confusion.

4 KUHN AND RELATIVISM

Kuhn's critics charge him with relativism. He pleads guilty on one count: namely, with respect to the role of truth in elucidating scientific progress.[12] Although he holds that there is unidirectional, evolutionary inter-theoretic progress in science, it is not because subsequent theories better approximate the truth. We shall return to this view shortly. But first let us note that Kuhn's relativism concerning truth is also more extensive than that admission suggests. In SSR he writes, 'There is, I think, no theory-independent way to construct phrases like "really there"; the notion of a match between the ontology of a theory and its "real" counterpart in nature now seems to me illusive in principle.'[13] And he proclaims elsewhere, 'If I am right, then "truth" may, like "proof", be a term with only intra-theoretic applications.'[14] Though the passage preceding the last remark concerns only the empirical consequences of theories, the claim cited is unconditional, applicable presumably to any truth. *Taken strictly*, it is tantamount to claiming that each legitimate ascription of truth contains a qualification, no doubt normally implicit, of the form 'in such and such theory', and it is a clear specimen of veramental relativism (Chapter 6, section 2). But, when combined with other things Kuhn wishes to claim, we should have grave doubts about its coherence, and perhaps about the seriousness with which Kuhn intended it.

For one thing, it requires that some statements made with sentences of the form 'p is true in theory T_1' be true *sans phrase*. What more legitimate way to describe the success-dimension of claims about the truth of statements made within theories? Perhaps, taking a leaf from the theory of types, it might be rejoined that our second-level statements are only true within a more comprehensive metalanguage in which we are allowed to compare lower-level theories; thus we are still predicating truth within some theory (= language) or other. The rebuttal fails to convince. How can a view of truth committed to treating the concept as it occurs in 'truth-in-theory-T_1' and 'truth-in-theory-T_2' as no more similar than the 'ant' in 'antelope' and 'reliant' be plausible? This treatment of truth may be inspired by Tarski. But it exposes its limitations when we inquire what the various relative truth-predicates have in common.[15] Even so, it is unclear that Kuhn could avail himself of this assistance. For axiomatizable formal languages bear a tenuous relationship to the kinds of theories that interest Kuhn. Indeed, in other contexts he has warned readers against thinking of theories as mere approximations to what logicians call a theory. Thus, the use of this device to show that my second-level predication of truth is theory-relative manages only to bring the term under the umbrella of something called a theory, but does not deliver the sort of explanation Kuhn intends to give of the way in which theories provide an interpretation of truth.

A second point. Kuhn has suggested that we replace truth in descriptions of progress with descriptions such as 'evolution-from-what-we-do-know [to] evolution-toward-what-we-wish-to-know'.[16] This is not the only place at which he prefers descriptions in terms of *knowledge* to that in terms of truth. But how are we to compare knowledge in two adjacent scientific epochs? Doesn't the notion of knowledge require that the thing known be *true*? *True-in-T_1* and *True-in-T_2* are different properties, and it is difficult to see how truth-in-T_2, supposing T_2 is the last theory to have evolved, could be of value to anyone other than a votary of T_2. Why should we consider this, from any point of view other than the provincial one of T_2, as the march of progress rather than merely a change in fashion? Kuhn may have in mind a conception of knowledge that relinquishes the condition that if S knows that p, p must be true. But we may be pardoned a suspicion that any such conception will be unable to preserve the cross-theoretical significance which allows the original one to elucidate progress. Things are not much improved when an explicit appeal to knowledge is suppressed, but it is still relied upon, by comparing successive theories in terms of their puzzle-solutions.

This deployment of knowledge is a tactic about which I had earlier complained (Chapter 4, section 4); that is, the use of reliability-vocabulary customarily truth-linked, but without that link, and, indeed as a substitute for a truth-associated notion. Were we able to dissociate knowledge from truth, we might replace truth with it in our explanations. But the difficulty is in comprehending the new notion in its old role. The perplexity is not merely that, as Goldman has noted, the epistemic notions are 'far more in need of explication than truth'.[17] That is problem enough. But, even more centrally, once the epistemic notion has been openly disconnected from its truth-yielding potential, the difficulty is in grasping why we should continue to invest in a proposition having that epistemic quality the value we had formerly accorded it. If the very notion of truth that knowledge provides is relative to the theory for which it provides it, why should it be of value to anyone not in the throes of that theory?

But the core of Kuhn's case for veramental relativism is still his argument for incommensurability. The one express reason he gives for such relativism is the lack of common meanings between theories. Thus, he says that a sentence such as 'elements combine in constant proportion by weight' expresses different propositions in different chemical theories[18] because there is no neutral language in which it can be framed. We shall examine (2) and its companion lacunae later in this chapter. But for the nonce recall a remark we made at the end of section 1: although a particular theory may be necessary for a sentence to express a certain proposition, that in itself does not show that the proposition expressed in true only *in the particular theory* rather than *sans phrase*. Dalton's chemical theory may allow us to express a proposition, but it is a truth *of* Dalton's theory, not *in* it. Kuhn's comment could lead us to a deeper appreciation of what is needed for the expression of a proposition, but is not thereby a comment on how truth is constituted.

5 THEORIES AND TRUTH-VALUE

Before closing these preliminary remarks we should also note a distinction between the thesis

(A) Theories have truth-value (or possess truth *to a certain degree*);

and the theses

(B) Theories can be tested (compared) on the basis of their truth or their degree of it;
(C) The goal of theorizing is to continue approaching closer to the truth.

The distinction between criteria for truth and an account of what constitutes it, emphasized in Chapter 2, should be sufficient to distinguish (A) from (B). And since we tend to describe any goal we may project for theorizing in terms only of what is available for testing, thus in terms of criteria for better theories, this should also impress on us the distinction between (A) and (C). Nevertheless, Kuhn and others[19] argue directly from the rejection of (B) and (C) to the rejection of (A).

By disavowing Kuhn's inference, I am not claiming that some theories *are* true or even approximate truth. A whole theory may, unlike some of its lawlike generalizations, be too indefinite an agglomeration of tenets, variously formulable, not all perfectly essential and with varying weights, to allow raising a question so definite as 'true or false?' On the other hand, the elusiveness of identity-conditions for theories does not itself imply that statements which may be justly called 'theoretical' have no truth-values. However, it is not my present purpose even to defend that claim. The point is that if theories or theoretical statements were true or false, there still might be excellent reason for denying (B) and (C). A theory's fugitive identity, its truth aside, would be one reason for doing so: for this itself could create greater obstacles to deciding on a theory's truth than our practice of theory choice could bear. Much better to confine ourselves to a list of criteria such as Kuhn's, which, though their attraction may ultimately rest on their truth-yielding capacity, can at least be applied without first raising the separate question whether the theories satisfying them are true.

However, as we recently noted, the core of Kuhn's case against global realism is identical with that of his case for incommensurability: namely, the lacunae earlier cited. We can no longer defer a direct examination of those.

6 THE EVIDENCE FOR THEORETICAL INFLUENCE OF MEANINGS

The lack of common problems, (1), is the least bothersome of the lacunae for global realism. What I have to say about it can await the resolution of the semantic issue. Thus, let us begin with (2), the lack of common meanings. On traditionalist assumptions, terms such as 'mass' and 'motion' characterize phenomena which different theories attempt to account for. But, according to Kuhn, the meanings of such terms, and perhaps of all or most predicates, change subtly from theory to theory. Theories needn't totally determine the meanings of these sorts of terms, but they do influence meanings through their laws, rules and concrete results.

These forces affect not only the applications of predicates, but their meanings as well. Consequently, in moving between theories we are deprived of the full communication and jointly accredited test procedures characteristic of normal research.

What are the arguments for these claims? We may overlook Kuhn's indifference to any distinction between changes in *the concept X* and changes in *the meaning of 'X'*. But, in both cases, he offers readers a variety of instances, with some uncertainty about the grounds for his evaluation of them. For example, 'space', we are told, changes its meaning for an Einsteinian when it is allowed that it can be curved,[20] both 'earth' and 'motion' mean something different for geocentrists and heliocentrists,[21] 'mass' means something different for Newtonians and Relativity theorists because it is conserved for the former, convertible with energy for the latter,[22] and even terms such as 'element', with us since Aristotle, 'gain full significance only when related . . . to other scientific concepts'.[23]

More is needed before we can accede to Kuhn's assessments in individual cases. As the examples indicate, the evidence consists of *differences of application* of the relevant terms. But traditionalists would certainly not deny that changes of theory force significant mutations in the applications (namely, extensions) of crucial expressions. Moreover, the alterations are not always that great during a change of theory, and sometimes occur within groups of scientists who belong to the same normal research tradition, and thus for whom this explanation of communication breakdown should not work. Consequently, if differences in application are to perform the task of (a) explaining changes of meaning, (b) accounting for communication breakdowns of a fundamental kind, and (c) distinguishing between the circumstances of communication in normal and extraordinary (revolutionary) periods, more has to be said. What further arguments can Kuhn muster?

His main argument apparently consists in his detailed study of cases. He refers readers of SSR to his earlier work, *The Copernican Revolution*,[24] to show by a detailed examination of facts how subtle changes in the meaning of 'motion', brought about by the conversion from scholastic Aristotelian theories to Newtonian mechanics, made possible the consolidation of Copernicus's victory. Let's examine some highlights of Kuhn's elaborate narrative.

259

Kuhn emphasizes that there were few converts to Heliocentrism from the time of the publication of Copernicus's theory to that of Newton's *Principia* (1543 to 1687, a 144-year interval). (In support of that view, Wolynski has counted 2,336 works on astronomy published during that time, only 188 of which were Copernican.[25]) Though religious bigotry no doubt had a hand in all this, the chief obstacles to the acceptance of Copernicanism were scientific: the earth's orbital revolution or axial rotation simply could not be fitted into the physical theory of the day. On the basically Aristotelian theory then prevalent, natural motion was always specified in relation to the centre of God's cosmos, roughly the centre of the earth. Objects naturally moved towards, away from or about this locus. The earth's occupying that central position explained why heavy bodies thrown in the air fell back to it. Though the scheme was designed only for terrestrial (sublunary) matter, Copernicus's astronomy was incompatible with it and did not promise an alternative physical scheme with which to replace it. How could the earth move if a large stone which took two seconds to fall from a tall tower fell at the foot of the tower? If the earth's axial rotation was, say, 600 feet per second to the east, shouldn't the stone fall roughly 1,200 feet west of the tower? And why don't objects not fastened to the surface of the earth fly off it, the way they would off a speeding coach? The Copernican theory raised these questions, settled long since by the Aristotelian view, but supplied no answers.

The Copernican revolution was completed only when the Newtonian conceptions of motion and space were firmly in place. But the Newtonian conceptions introduced yet further differences with the Aristotelian ones. The Aristotelian–Ptolemaic universe was finite, Newton's infinite; Aristotle's space was a plenum, Newton's contained vacua; for holders of the Cartesian–Newtonian principle of inertia, uniform rectilinear motion is as unforced as rest; Aristotelian space, teleologically conceived, was alive with subtle influences, Newton's was causally inert. Considerations of this order amounted to a change in the very conception of motion (that is, in the meaning of the term 'motion'), and only with this change in the term did a Copernican orthodoxy become possible.

However, setting aside Kuhn's occasional use of loaded language, I cannot find anything decisive in his eloquent narration of the events leading up to the new science to show that, over and above major shifts in its application, the meaning of 'motion' changed. The reader could dismiss these doubts out of hand if they were merely fastidiousness about a quasi-technical sense of 'meaning'; but in fact they go to the heart of Kuhn's project. For we are seeking a change, by whatever name, so prodigious that scientists advocating competing frameworks must significantly misunderstand their counterparts when they say either that the earth is fixed or that the earth moves. But far from this, what we are given are changes in theory about *why* things move and *when*, or under what circumstances, they move. We are not given evidence to show that the relevantly competing scientists differed over *what* the motion of an object from A to B consisted in, or even that – the cases of a few astronomical bodies aside – they differed in the great mass of their judgments over whether something had moved. Quite the contrary; Kuhn provides evidence that the competing scientists agreed on the basic nature of motion, and knew perfectly well what their counterparts meant. Thus, Ptolemy had no trouble understanding Aristarchus, Heraclides and the rest of the Pythagoreans when he rejected their views. And the relevance of his objections attests to the strength of his understanding if not to that of his physical theories. He denied his opponents the dynamic mechanisms to produce the motion for which they contended, but the proposition we would express with the sentence 'the earth moves' seems to be just the one his opponents affirmed and he denied.

This is not to say that changes in physical theory are never relevant to changes in the meanings of terms already in circulation. But the changes that would bear more directly on what 'motion' meant are ignored by Kuhn, and at any rate they divide scientists that fall on the same side of the Heliocentrism dispute. For example, the division between those who believe that space is absolute and those who think all position is relational would make a difference to an account of what it is for a body to move. But Newton believed the former and Descartes the latter, and both were opponents of Ptolemy. Also the distinction between those who believed in a plenum and those who accepted vacua might seem to make a more central difference about what motion consisted in. But again the Cartesians, agreeing with the geocentrist Aristotle and his medieval admirers, differed from the

Newtonians on just this issue. Even if one resists the suggestion that these differences were of greater significance to the meaning of 'motion' than the revolution in mechanics, they were certainly comparable. How then does the one but not the other explain an inter-theoretic breakdown in communication of the right sort?

Thus far we have assumed that Kuhn accepts the classical semantic distinction between what is true in virtue of a term's meaning and what is contingently true of the class of things so denominated or of its instances. Perhaps it will be contended that the argument would fare better if we adopted Meaning Holism. This would make every difference in the application of 'motion' relevant to a difference in its meaning, and certainly some of the differences (such as the adoption of the law of inertia) effected considerable changes in application.

Just as a matter of interpretation, Kuhn usually accepts the classical semantic distinction, even if he thinks it is a volatile and shifting one.[26] Moreover, some such distinction is occasionally essential to understanding his claims. For example, he believes that a theory, A, *may be* subsumed under a higher-level theory, say B, without changing A's identity.[27] In semantic jargon this amounts to saying that the formulation of A does not change its meaning, although it will have all sorts of new applications – for example, its connections with B and the other theories subsumed under B. But Kuhn is not inhospitable to Holism either. For example, in reply to a challenge to 'specify the "cash difference" between change in meaning and alteration in the application of a term' he writes, 'Need I say that, in the present state of the theory of meaning, there is none.'[28] But although the holistic construal seems out of step with most of what he says, could it be used to support the incommensurability thesis as Kuhn understands it? I think not.

While Kuhn may have little vested in the semantic distinction, he has a significant interest in the distinction between normal research and revolutionary science. The notion of incommensurability gets its bite by contrasting the former case, in which we have a model for objective choice and smooth (if not full) communication, with the case in which those requisites are lacking. If the contrast is to be preserved, what must be shown is that the *extent* of the differences in the instances he calls revolutionary mark them off sharply from the sorts of differences inevitable between two scientists who presumably can resolve their disputes objectively. And though some of the differences cited by Kuhn are indeed large, it has been the burden of my commentary on his narrative to show that the differences between heliocentrists alone, or geocentrists alone, about the nature of motion were comparable in disparity. Moreover, for this sort of Holism in particular it is important to demonstrate that competing theorists profoundly and thoroughly misunderstood one another. However, the large extent to which Ptolemaic and Newtonian criticisms were relevant to and well-taken against their opponents must count as counter-evidence for (this sort of) meaning change. And what is usually neglected in such expositions, though it seems to me perfectly clear upon reflection, is that Ptolemy understood quite well what Aristarchus and others were saying, and that Descartes and Galileo thoroughly understood the astronomical views of their geocentrist opponents. We may also discover, if we look closely, certain respects in which these scientists misunderstood their antagonists. But if we look hard enough, we will undoubtedly find respects in which even epigones misunderstood their master's views. This is a phenomenon likely to arise between any two students of roughly the same subjects. Kuhn has failed to show that the degree of misunderstanding is sufficient to separate members of divergent theoretical matrices from those belonging to the same matrix. And in the process he has overlooked the different respects in which the major theoretical objections like those just mentioned were directly on target. What might the holist, using (2) as his defence say about this?

7 THEORIES AND THEORETICAL TERMS

The distinction between normal research and revolutionary science aside, Meaning Holism has not been refuted, and we have not shown that lacuna (2) isn't a support for it. This being so, there might still be a reason in (2) for claiming that holders of competing theories are fated critically to misunderstand one another. I have nothing decisive to say about this, other than that this knot of claims opens a broad subject which we cannot begin to explore. However, there are some dampening observations about this particular line of argument and the source of its support from which we can profit and which can be summed up relatively briefly.

Certain current versions of Holism suffer from a confusion between different construals of 'theory' and cognate terms. On one reading 'theoretical' can be glossed by 'non-observational'; on the other, it is not easy to find a compact metaphrase, but it is the sense in which a theory is a high achievement and product of scientific activity. Since the type of Holism under consideration must show that *any* term's meaning is influenced by prevailing theory, the need for a cheap supply of theories is crucial. This may encourage the confusion.

The notion of a theoretical (= non-observational) term does not derive primarily from the study of scientific theorizing, but from the observational–theoretical distinction. The former category was the almost exclusive interest of those who used the distinction. It was from observation terms that our sentences, including theoretical ones, acquired their meaning. Thus it was important to those thinkers that the class of observational terms and sentences be precisely delineated. As we mentioned it is now generally agreed that the efforts to make the distinction perfectly sharp failed. This failure is sometimes reported by saying that all terms or sentences have a degree of theoreticity. But what is theoreticity on this distinction? Well, originally it was a miscellany of whatever could not be fitted into the observational. There was little reason to believe that the members of this catch-all class would have much of interest in common. While the distinction was thought viable, it allowed us on some accounts to count terms with strong scientific interest, such as 'motion' and 'planet' as non-theoretical, and less fruitful vocabulary items such as 'frivolous' and 'strenuous' as theoretical. Moreover, theoreticity's mongrel nature ill-suited it for the elucidation of a philosophically central notion such as meaning.

On the other hand, the more substantial notion of a theory is that of a kind of general or basic account that could support a research programme. There is much dispute about what this sort of scientific theory consists in; but it can be taken without question that it *is not* the grab-bag notion of whatever doesn't fit somewhere else.

Of course, the divisions of opinion we catalogue are seldom as neat as this. Some philosophers have developed notions of theory broader than that of scientific theory, but narrower than that of the non-observational. Thus, it has been said that the overall network of an individual's or a community's beliefs is a theory, and even inborn predispositions with which we proceed to gather beliefs are occasionally called theories. But here I am only interested in the distinction between the non-observational and the product of scientific summation.

This ambiguity of 'theory' is not yet a confusion. Confusion results subsequently because, as we mentioned, holists who rely upon the theoretical saturation of observation must find an easy way to show that *all* expressions, and not just a select few, are influenced by theories. But our grasp of scientific theories is very piecemeal, and even for the few in our possession, it does not seem possible to provide at this stage of our knowledge a detailed account of just how they influence the meanings of the great mass of our vocabulary. When embarrassed by details, it is easier to grab the fig-leaf of non-observationality. That is, we can show with minimum effort and by perfectly familiar routines that just about any expression we choose will not be a pristine observation term. Of course, Holism does not have to fall into this confusion. But it does appear that it must remain a very programmatic view without this kind of illicit support; though the nature of the case makes it difficult to gauge just how notably the confusion has contributed to its attraction.

8 QUALIFICATION VS. CAPITULATION

Whichever conception of meaning fits Kuhn best, classical or holist, the support of incommensurability by (2) suffers the painful death of a thousand qualifications. Their cumulative effect is to narrow the gap between the revolutionary and the normal, until we are eventually unable to see how such meaning changes, even in concert with other lacunae, can seriously hinder the fullest rational communication that could be expected between supporters of different paradigms. Because the qualifications never occur in a single list, and some are mined from passages directed at other concerns, the enfeebling of (2) may not be readily apparent. Nevertheless, it is very real, and when the list is compiled the combined qualifications make (2) look like a very weak stanchion on which to rest the case for the incommensurability of competing theories.

A first qualification, mentioned earlier, is that theories only *influence* the meanings of terms that seem to survive theory-change; they do not wholly determine them. Thus, a component of meaning not depending upon the issues dividing quarrelling adherents remains. Kuhn does not make it clear whether he thinks that there is a non-theoretical component of meaning, or whether the remainder is exhausted by the influence of other theories. In either case, that wouldn't increase communication problems of the sort being considered.

A second qualification – effective against any view allowing a difference of application to bear upon meaning – concerns the fact that we can find differences of belief of the kind Kuhn cites in his arguments between virtually any two scientists in the same tradition. (Here the differences presumably do not lead to serious communication problems.) Any two speakers, say, of English are bound to differ in various of their beliefs about tomatoes, the colour blue or the property of being rural. (I recently had one such disagreement with another native speaker about whether a suit was blue or charcoal.) Kuhn even shows why it is almost certain to happen. In his most central sense, paradigms are very partially articulated examples of ways in which to solve problems. They serve as concrete models, not general rules. And the scientific learner must devise her own similarity classes from instances. But, as Kuhn emphasizes, this is like what goes on in the learning of the majority of common nouns, adjectives and verbs. As learners we are presented with instances from which we project what does or does not belong with them. The similarity employed here must be (psychologically) natural, and pre-formulable.[29] This supplies two reasons why scientists in particular and learners in general almost inevitably differ over the extensions of their terms. First, it is unlikely that any two learners are exposed to exactly the same class of examples. Second, there are likely to be differences, if only minor, in the quality-spaces of any two individuals (that is, in the way in which they project a similarity-class from examples). Since these differences occur under any circumstances, we cannot rely upon them to elucidate (2). The situation is critical, since these differences are comparable in nature, if not extent, to the evidence of application Kuhn cites as relevant to meaning change.

A third qualification concerns the fact that members of scientific cultures in conflict do have recourse. They share 'a general neural apparatus, however different in programming, . . . a history (except the immediate past), a language, an everyday world, and most of a scientific one',[30] all of which enables them to translate their differences into the other's language. This will not be a *neutral* language, and Kuhm may argue that something is always lost when a neutral description is not used. We shall examine the importance of a neutral language later. But here I must satisfy myself with the dogmatic reply that *objectivity* isn't always, or even normally, tantamount to *neutrality*. The two are often confused, especially in arenas in which passions are engaged. But some views may be simply objectively better than others. If we can translate the relevant part of another's beliefs into our own language, then, human foibles aside, it is unclear why we cannot render a balanced and objective judgment on the relative merits of the two sets of beliefs.

Another important qualification emerges when we consider the extent to which competing theories share problems. For the other side of (1), lack of common problems, would be the claim that some problems *must be* shared by competing theories. For this, let us come to closer quarters with (1).

9 PROBLEM-SOLVING AND THEORY CHOICE

According to (1) a paradigmatic theory replacing another will not only differ from its predecessors in its solutions, but it will also rewrite the agenda of important and legitimate problems to be solved. A theory dictates what is central to its scientific speciality, and thus which problems the speciality itself is suited to. For example, when Cartesian mechanics replaced the theory of substantial forms, an object's colour and weight were no longer categories of explanation; colour was now explained in partly non-physical terms and by other basic processes, and wasn't itself involved in the explanation of any basic physical processes.

We needn't gainsay (1); but nor need we agree that it inevitably serves a breakdown in communication. However, Kuhn largely

ignores the equally impressive selection of problems which divergent theories must share. A novel theoretical matrix materializes,
according to Kuhn, when an older tradition precipitates a crisis
through its persistent failure to solve certain problems. These
problems become serious anomalies for the older matrix, and a
new paradigm makes dramatic inroads by solving some of these
sticky problems and not failing miserably with all other problem
solutions. No doubt, the newcomer may be unable to solve everything the older paradigm did, and it may resort, as did Cartesian
mechanics in the recent example, to declaring senseless certain
sorts of previously accepted demands for explanation. But it
cannot wholly neglect a field satisfactorily covered by a preceding
paradigm unless it is prepared to show that wide areas of would-
be phenomena are spurious; and this becomes increasingly
unlikely with the greater maturity of the supplanted science. Kuhn
no longer supposes that a crisis is essential for the emergence of
new theories; but he still believes it the usual and most revealing
sort of scenario. However, it demands an assemblage of common
problems, mutually understandable by advocates of the competing
theories. Thus, meaning change cannot hinder the identity of
these problems, regardless of the absence of a neutral vocabulary,
if the case is to be specified as Kuhn requires.

In addition, the problems solved in the upstart theory must
have been taken as sufficiently central or pressing by the old one
for the new one to become attractive just by solving them. This
is not to say that the problems which scientists, in the heat of
researches, find most striking are the ones most important for a
would-be objective account of theory choice. Laudan[31] has
charged Kuhn with confusing these. But they could not be negligible to an understanding of the theory either. And here *the
identity* of the problems, whatever the likely misunderstandings
of the participants, is what counts. In allotting to competing
theories this much commonality we are only providing what is
necessary to see them as *competitors*. If they did not have this
much to quarrel over, we might wonder why the second replaces
the first rather than opening a new scientific speciality alongside
it.

Similar difficulties infect Kuhn's notion of inter-theoretic
progress. Recall that he does not believe 'that there is some one
full, objective, true account of nature and that the proper measure

of scientific achievement is the extent to which it brings us closer to that ultimate goal'.[32] But his view is salvaged from relativism because scientific theories do exhibit progress by means of 'the number of different problems solved'.[33] He cites several other measures of progress, but this one is mentioned several times, and latched on to by commentators, no doubt because it is the one having most to do with *the contents* of successive theories. He reiterates, '[l]ater scientific theories are better than earlier ones for solving puzzles in the often quite different environments to which they are applied. That is not a relativist's position, and it displays the sense in which I am a convinced believer in scientific progress.'[34]

When writing guardedly, as he was *not* doing above, Kuhn distinguishes problems from puzzles. Puzzles are believed to have assured solutions. 'I use the term "puzzle" in order to emphasize that the difficulties which *ordinarily* confront even the very best scientists are, like crossword puzzles or chess puzzles, challenges only to [the scientist's] ingenuity. *He* is in difficulty, not current theory.'[35] Problems needn't come with any assurances, and scientists may eventually see their theories endangered by them.

It is therefore puzzles that make theories comparable. Tallies of number of puzzle solutions will no doubt be rough estimates, the identity criteria for both puzzles and solutions being only very rudimentary. But the formulation of a puzzle must be independent of the theory solving it; for we cannot restrict the referees to holders of the theory in question if the standard is to evade relativism, as Kuhn maintains.

We must clarify what this does and doesn't show. We may distinguish two outlooks for assessing theories: that for theory choice and that for theoretical progress. The situation in which we assess progress is retrospective: we determine on the merits of various fully mature theory matrices whether successors have improved upon their predecessors. But for theory choice the situation confronting scientists in times of extraordinary research is quite different. The novel paradigm's puzzle-solving capacity is still largely unactualized potential. We can only compare the number of puzzle solutions for progress between two *mature* theories. This will not help scientists who must choose between a mature and a promising theory to achieve a mutual understanding or to avert communication mishaps. Thus, numbers of puzzle solutions is not a way around the Kuhnian claim that during theory choice situations miscommunication develops, *save indirectly*. That is, *if*, as Kuhn's ground rules for judging progress indicate, puzzle solutions can be framed without distortion for referees who are not advocates of the theory in question (which is a necessary condition to count them), then the putative successes of a given scientific theory cannot be so intimately tied to the theory's framework as to make misunderstanding by anyone not accepting the theory inevitable. We have no reason to suppose a competing scientist *must* distort her competitor's claims just by not holding the theory for which those claims serve as evidence.

There are several other important morals we may draw from this. For one thing, if we are allowed to compare different theories in this respect without unacceptable levels of distortion, then Kuhn has forfeited one of his strongest grounds for prohibiting objective comparisons in other respects: namely, that rephrasing a theory's tenets other than as they would be phrased in the theory involves unacceptable meaning changes. Kuhn may have different arguments against other objective comparisons in terms, say, of truth or capturing nature. But this is one sort of consideration to which he can no longer appeal. Next, the reformulation of the puzzles obviously needn't take place in a neutral language. There is no requirement that the referee of progress be a theory-free observer of the past scene. Thus, Kuhn's practice belies his injunctions. For elsewhere he demands that any objective comparison of theories have a neutral vocabulary into which each theory's claims can be translated. This is a matter which we shall shortly explore more thoroughly when we examine the last of the lacunae. Finally, we may suspect that the meaning change attendant upon all theory changes is not so great as to produce inevitable distortion. For whether or not we continue to use the same words to report puzzle solutions in a theory we no longer hold, whatever effect the theory had on the meanings of the terms originally will have completed its work. But if, taking that into account, the change is not great enough to prevent us from identifying *that* particular puzzle solution, it is difficult once again to see why the theoretical component of the meanings must lead to incommensurability.

However, whatever the outcome of Kuhn's views concerning (1) and (2), at the end of section 1 we warned against the sort of an argument for epistemologized truth that claimed theory-dependent meanings without also claiming theory-dependent worlds. Thus, the case must ultimately depend upon (3), lack of common perceptions, to supply the variation in an observational world that gives the other lacunae their bite.

10 THEORIES AND OBSERVED WORLDS

On a straightforward reading of (3), the phenomena themselves are a partial function of one's theories, thus cognition-dependent. Under that circumstance, Correspondence would be a poor account of our actual employment of truth and falsity.

Lacuna (3) relies upon the diverse and incompatible ways in which scientists adhering to competing paradigms describe theoretically relevant observations. Though Kuhn begins with *Gestalt* switches, this mode of explanation is eventually abandoned because a change of *Gestalt* requires *a single thing* which is seen in more than one way. Instead, he presents his point through a variety of instances: seeing oxygen is not the same as seeing dephlogisticated air; what Ptolemaic astronomers saw as a planet we do not see when viewing the sun; seeing Proust's chemical compounds, distinguished from physical mixtures, is not the same as seeing Dalton's atomic compounds; and seeing a pendulum (Galileo), or anharmonic oscillation, is not the same as seeing constrained fall (Aristotelians). This leads Kuhn to the verge of saying that scientists with different paradigms 'see different things' and 'inhabit different worlds'. I say 'the verge', because he shies away from stating it outright. I quote a number of passages in which he approaches saying it; but notice the important qualifications which I have italicized in each passage.

Insofar as their only recourse to that world is through what they can see and do, *we may want to say that* after a revolution scientists are responding to a different world.[36]

When [the chemical revolution] was done, even the percentage composition of well-known compounds was different. The data themselves had changed. This is the last of the senses in which *we may want to say that* after a revolution scientists work in different worlds.[37]

271

The very ease and rapidity with which astronomers saw new things when looking at old objects with new instruments *may make us wish to say that*, after Copernicus, astronomers lived in a different world.[38]

At the very least, as a result of discovering oxygen, Lavoisier saw nature differently. And *in the absence of some recourse to that hypothetical fixed nature* that he 'saw differently', *the principle of economy will urge us to say that* after discovering oxygen Lavoisier worked in a different world.[39]

. . . two groups, the members of which have systematically different sensations on receipt of the same stimuli, do *in some sense* live in different worlds.[40]

Though Kuhn distances himself from the unqualified claim, he does not wish to hold that putting it this way is merely a temptation we are free to resist. Indeed, he maintains there is something right, or superior, about this form of expression; and occasionally he suggests it is even imperative to speak of competing scientists as inhabiting different worlds.[41] But elsewhere he suggests just the opposite: '[w]hatever he may see [after a revolution], the scientist . . . is still looking at the same world.'[42]

To instance an extent to which Kuhn *doesn't* want the different worlds idiom taken, at one place he writes:

Practicing in different worlds, the two groups of scientists see different things when they look *from the same point in the same direction*. Again this is not to say that they see anything they please.[43]

But 'same' in this passage couldn't just mean *qualitatively similar* (as when two people may be said to have the same build or hair-style); and on its only natural interpretation, two perceivers cannot occupy the same point and look in the same direction if they are, strictly speaking, in different worlds. In fact, Kuhn continues to write as if such scientists are occupying the same world and that the object of their perception is identical: '[b]oth are looking at the world, and *what* they look at has not changed'.[44] He consistently maintains that even during communication break-downs resulting from shifts in paradigms scientists have a recourse in talking about their crucial experiences, for their perceptions emanate from the same stimuli.[45] But this, he argues, should not lead us to suppose that they see the same things, for we do not perceive stimuli as such. Nor is it even true that our perceptions and perceptual judgments normally involve inferences from or interpretations of stimuli or anything else neutral between divergent ways of reporting. Kuhn describes what we do perceive as *sensations* and *data*; and these are not to be confused with the stimuli which make it possible for us to perceive the data.

Yet even if stimuli are insufficiently robust to insure the identity of what different subjects perceive, their constant role is already too much commonality to allow us to say *literally* that the subjects are in different worlds. That description now seems to be a trope, however illuminating. Strictly, it appears that we just see things differently, not that we see different things.

Kuhn doesn't agree. He insists that we must 'make sense' of different worlds talk because 'what occurs during a scientific revolution is not fully reducible to a reinterpretation of individual and stable data'.[46] In what ways is it not reducible? Ultimately, his reasons for rejecting the suggestion that 'different worlds' talk is a mere metaphor seem to be that there are certain conditions to be met by any perceivers who share a common world of perception. Assuming that the perceivers describe what they see differently, those conditions are:

(I) that there be neutral descriptions which capture the common things they perceive;

(II) that the difference in their perceptual descriptions not have vastly different implications (of a type to be specified).

In each case the condition is not met for adherents of divergent theories. The reason for the failure in (I) is that ordinary observation reports are neither inferences from nor interpretations of more basic data. As for (II), two sorts of phenomena prevent it from being satisfied:

(a) New ways of reporting observations bring a wave of new discoveries. Discoveries supporting a new theory increase exponentially; the rate is extraordinary when compared with levels during stable research periods. The new

discoveries *would not (could not?)* have been made were
it not for the new theory.

(b) The previous data are even measured differently (with
different results) on the same standards (for example,
different values for oxygen weight ratios of copper oxides
on Dalton's and Proust's chemical theories).

We shall examine (II) in section 13; but first let us look at (I) in
a broader context.

11 THE LIMITS OF COGNITIVE SATURATION OF OBSERVATIONS

Lacuna (3) instances a widely held doctrine[47] known among cognitive scientists as New Look Psychology. But I shall refer to the
version relevant to our concerns simply as a top-down theory of
perception, and usually employ sight for a sample sensory
modality. Roughly, the view maintains that perception is dictated
by our general cognitive attitudes (/beliefs/theories). But whatever the detailed truth about perception, the top-down theory
cannot be right.

The central point is that if it were correct, there is no reason
why things shouldn't always appear to us the way we believe (or
know) them to be. That we have a flourishing industry of
magicians shows that this cannot be so. In this vein Zenon Pylyshyn[48] has argued that the output of our sensory transducers is
not (freely) penetrable by cognition. Jerry Fodor illustrates the
point[49] with the familiar Müller-Lyer diagram (see Figure 1), in
which two lines of equal length look unequal because of the

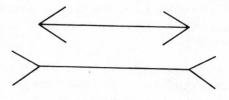

Figure 1

positioning of their angle brackets. The bottom line not only looks longer, but that appearance survives our knowledge that the lines are equal, and even survives our possession of a theory explaining why they look other than they are. A multitude of commonplace examples reinforce the point, such as parallel rails appearing to converge in the distance, the impression of backward motion when the train we are on is seen to be passed by another going in the same direction, the image in a mirror looking as if it were several feet behind it, the surface consisting in a dense array of small red dots on a white background looking (while a few feet away) uniformly pink. If perception were freely accessible to, much less mandatorily determined by, relevant beliefs, why should these recalcitrant appearances survive? I am not suggesting that our inclination for reporting cannot be influenced by our beliefs; but at most this shows that we are suggestible *in reporting* our *considered* view.

There seems to be a straightforward explanation for the failure of top-down theories; but it invites a spate of misunderstandings and thus must be issued with caveats. Put a bit opaquely, the explanation is that when top-down theories dissented from the empiricist interpretation of the observation-theory distinction, they did not realize how bad that interpretation really was, and thus their rejection of it was insufficiently thorough. In fact, the distinction was a mismatch in much the same way that modern educational theory's popular opinion–fact distinction, foisted upon masses of unwitting schoolchildren in 'scientific method' units, is also a mismatch: that is, in both instances something fundamentally psychological or linguistic (a theory, an opinion) is contrasted with something which, on the face of it, is neither (*what* is observed, a fact). Modern empiricists treated observations as if there was no distinction to be made between them and their reports and descriptions. They may be excused because they also believed in a language that captured perception in its purity; and thus the language, even if distinguishable from the perceptual object, was perfectly calibrated to the experience. But the belief in both immaculate perception and its matching vocabulary fell into disfavour; and it was concluded that though there is no better vocabulary for reporting observational evidence than the one we ordinarily use, with perhaps some local refinements, that vocabulary is charged with theoretical commitments. Thus far the critics are, I venture, error-proof. The top-down theorists' original sin seems to have been in not giving up the old empiricist notion that whatever vocabulary accurately reports perception must also perfectly calibrate it, thereby permitting us to import as conclusions about perception (/observation) whatever we could discover about the vocabulary in which it was reported (/ described). Instead, they should have inferred that it was a mistake in the first place to think of any kind of language calibrating perception or observation. Thus, it is a mistake to demand that there be the right kind of language, a neutral description, before we can identify what Galileo and the Aristotelian, or Tycho and Kepler, or Priestley and Lavoisier, or Proust and Dalton, saw.

But now the caveats. I am not claiming that what we see is in any way ineffable. So far as I can determine, we do not see (/sense/experience) sense-data as distinct from a largely public and mind-independent world, and our ordinary ways of describing it are in perfect order. But because observing (even if it can only occur to the observer *under* some description) is not identical with describing, and taking into account the subtle differences, we cannot automatically assume either that every vocabulary distinction marks one between objects of perception, or that every implication of the vocabulary item used to report a perception implies something about what has been perceived. (Concrete examples are given when we discuss perceptual idioms below.) Nor is there a reason to suppose that the best and wholly appropriate way to describe observations must fit perfectly what we take ourselves to have observed. Moreover, I certainly do not hold out any hope for a more accurate or purer way of reporting or describing observations. The difference here emphasized is not between perceptions and certain levels of description, but between perceptions and descriptions as such. Finally, this is not the usual distinction between the inexhaustibility of perception and the gappy nature of description. Rather, what is being stressed tends in the other direction. Distinctions can be made and implications drawn from *any* description or report of a perception that may not mark distinctions between perceptions or implications about the perception itself.

The polar opposite, bottom-up, theory held by Fodor is that perceptual output is 'informationally encapsulated' in a very restrictive way. I have not discussed the degree to which our beliefs might penetrate our perception, other than to argue that it must be limited in some very definite ways. And it is unnecessary to defend the view that perception is an informationally encapsulated module in order to show that (3) must be mistaken. Nevertheless, much of what Fodor says in defence of his own view[50] is useful in showing why information cannot have unlimited access in shaping how things look to us, and we can employ this evidence without requiring that we settle the issue about bottom-up theories. The main point, for the purpose of assessing (I), is that since the issue of what we perceive can be uncoupled from features of the vocabulary with which we report it, it is not plausible to require a 'neutral' or 'fixed and more fundamental' vocabulary[51] for reporting what scientists with different theoretical matrices both see.

We are able to treat this complicated issue only in the most superficial manner. But I hope that enough has been said to show why the radical consequences Kuhn takes to flow from (3) needn't obtain. But, beyond this issue, his crucial notion of a neutral description – and it is not solely his – remains quite baffling. He doesn't tell us what one might be, or even what it must be neutral between. (If, say, between two theories, is it possible for it not to belong to a third theory? Would this be good enough? I have no handle on what could resolve such issues.) In fact, as may be evident from what we just said, the notion of a neutral description seems to be a remnant of the positivist view that there could be a language with no theoretical commitments. Condition (I) is therefore a peculiar requirement to impose for someone who rejects the remainder of the positivist paraphernalia. As Alan Musgrave has perceptively noted, whenever one begins to explain how perceptions and vocabularies might be comparable across theories, 'adherents of incommensurability launch into a diatribe against that positivst daydream'.[52] Given both the provenance of (I) and an assortment of its quite independent deficiencies, I am puzzled why Kuhnians conceive the matter in these terms, much less take (I) to be so vital.

Having raised the issue of perceptual *reports*, let us proceed a step further. To illustrate just how poorly (3) sits with the facts, let us probe a bit more into our practice of reporting observations (/perceptions).

12 'SEEING THINGS' AND 'SEEING THAT'

There are a number of idioms for reporting seeing, but two of the most common should particularly interest us: let us label them the propositional and direct-object idioms. The former can be introduced with the schema 'S sees that p', in which 'p' is a propositional clause taking separate truth-value. 'S sees that p' implies the following set of conditions;

   (i) p is true (or, simply, p);
   (ii) S takes what is seen as being that p',
   (iii) S is correct in so taking what is seen.

In the other idiom, forms of the verb 'to see' are followed by a direct object: a noun or noun clause. We may represent it with the schema 'S see ϕ'. In examining this idiom I de-emphasize first-person reporting because it tends to blur what is the case with what the perceiver is in a position to report about it, and this is an important distinction that other voices of the direct-object idiom makes possible. Thus, this idiom leaves room for mistaken identification. For example, imagine that I am in a helicopter hovering over the shoreline when I utter, 'I see an oil slick'. In fact, it is a beached whale I misidentified, so that 'G.V. sees a beached whale', is true, while 'G.V. sees an oil slick' is false. Not only would it be wrong for you to describe what I had seen in the terms I would be inclined to use; it would be equally mistaken to deny that I see something. This is directly relevant to the case in which one or more scientists may differently identify what in some sense they do see. Philosophers have shown greater concern for cases in which a subject is deluded into believing he sees what is not there at all, as in hallucinations. But while those cases are not of special interest to the Kuhnian problem, misidentifications are pivotal.

The direct-object idiom fails to support conditions comparable to (i)–(iii). Of course, there is no proposition-like perceptual object to be true or taken as such by a perceiver. But that is not the crucial disanalogy here. For even if we could find strictly analogous properties for direct objects, nothing like S's taking what he sees to be ϕ or S's being correct in doing so is a condition for S's seeing ϕ. We could even contrive cases in which S needn't take what he sees to be anything at all, as when he mistakenly believes his visual experience results wholly from a mind-altering substance. Thus, the direct-object idiom provides a vehicle in ordinary perceptual reporting for saying that what a scientist really sees is what another correctly identifies. We have not supplied a case of this actually happening across paradigm differences. But the availability of an idiom for doing this in ordinary reporting may help to show just how fanciful is Kuhn's requirement that we need a neutral or basic description in order to accomplish it. Neither 'a whale' nor 'an oil slick' is the more basic description, nor is another at hand. Why then should we demand one when the perceivers seem to be describing what we are inclined to call a pendulum or a planet?

In this interlude we have unearthed two rather familiar idioms. No doubt both have a place in reporting scientifically relevant observations. But which of them best suits the phenomenon used by Kuhn to support his claim that advocates of different theories don't see the same things?

At first, it might seem that the propositional idiom is preferable. Only on it must we accept that the object is the way in which the perceiver takes it to be. This is essential to Kuhn's case; the resistance to unsympathetic redescription of the objects of one's perception is the backbone of the view that the scientists in question do not share a common perpetual world. But the propositional idiom has a few serious drawbacks as an *exclusive* way of reporting theory relevant observations. For one thing, the propositional idiom requires that what is seen be *true*. But to hold that when an Aristotelian saw what he took to be an instance of constrained fall, *it was true* that that was an instance of constrained fall, is to make a much more ambitious claim than Kuhn has thus far ventured. Indeed, it leads to paradox. For Kuhn wants to say that Galileo's description of what he saw as an instance of the periodic motion of a pendulum is incompatible with the Aristotelian's description. But that that is an instance of a pendulum must also be true if Galileo's propositional report is correct. And this lands us in a classical dilemma: incompatible propositions cannot both be true. Previously Kuhn implied nothing stronger than that Galileo's and the Aristotelian's descriptions were equally (or at least comparably) plausible. But no increment of plausibility adds up to truth, and condition (i) of the propositional idiom demands truth.

279

It may be obvious that this difficulty depends on accepting condition (i); and, since Kuhn maintains that truth has only intra-theoretical applications, it appears that we should not hold it against his view that it fails to satisfy an illegitimate application. I shall ignore, in responding to that charge, that it is lacunae (1)–(3) that must supply the reasons for truth having no more than intra-theoretical application (see section 4). Nevertheless, in dropping (i) we would have forfeited the basis for the alleged incompatibility of the two descriptions, and thereby also our inducement for supposing that the perceivers inhabited different perceptual worlds. This may also be shown by noting that we would have to understand (iii) differently as well. In saying that S is *correct* in taking what is seen as it is described in *p*, we are now saying S is correct within S's theory. If this is not merely to be construed as relativism gained, to borrow Russell's phrase, through the advantages of theft over honest toil, how can that say any more than that S takes himself to be correct? On this interpretation we are not left with a view that each description *is correct* in any way that would *force us* to say that they are describing different things. For that could only be so if the respects in which they were correct would otherwise conflict. By retreating to intra-theoretic truth and correctness we have eliminated the conflict.

Another shortcoming of the propositional idiom for Kuhn's purproses is its clumsiness, when compared with the direct-object idiom, in reporting the selective and refined observations, frequently under controlled conditions, of value to the scientist. Kuhn remarks that 'the operations and measurements that a scientist undertakes in the laboratory are not "the given" of experience but rather "the collected with difficulty" '.[53] This seems just the sort of experience in which one encounters misidentifications that get redescribed by further reflection and experiment. It is not the sort of experience that can only be described propositionally: that is, as the perceiver is inclined.

If, as I have maintained, we do not need neutral descriptions, how may we describe the single thing that Galileo and the Aristotelian supposedly saw? Of course, if our current theories are correct, we can describe it as anharmonic oscillation. But do we need to assume the correctness of our current theories to answer Kuhn's baited question? I think not. We can always say that they both saw what the Aristotelian would describe as constrained fall and what Galileo would describe as a pendulum. We do not require a special description revealed by peeling off all cognitive commitments, or a scientifically final description, for the objects of the two experiences to total one. Neither the deficiencies of a present vocabulary, nor the absence of a final theory, nor the unavoidable insularities of our epistemic situation is relevant to the possibility of identifying what two scientists saw.

This is not to say that in each case in which scientists from competing frameworks describe differently what originates at a common stimulus do they in fact see the same thing. In some cases, the description in terms of a certain principle may prohibit us from finding *anything* with which it could be identical on another theory. Philip Kitcher[54] has suggested that referring terms associated with scientific theories be treated as *context-sensitive*. We needn't enter into the details of Kitcher's account of the way in which reference is fixed to draw a lesson from his general point. However one believes reference gets fixed, there will be some cases in which, say, 'dephlogisticated air' should be taken to refer to oxygen, though perhaps in others – say, when it is the product of passing steam over heated iron – it may refer to something else or, in yet other cases, to nothing. This gives a clue to the possibilities for identifying the relevant observations of alchemists with those of chemists without requiring a mutually accepted vocabulary.

13 INFLUENCES OF THEORY ON DISCOVERY AND MEASUREMENT

That leaves (II) from section 11 as the remaining support for lacuna (3). It was broken up into (a) and (b), which say, respectively, that observations fall into place and new ones are made once a new theory is introduced, and that supposedly stable quantities of phenomena take different values under competing theories. There are instances of both sorts of occurrence. We may be able to explain why each occurs by noting that a change of theory creates different expectations in scientists who adopt the new theory. Although Kuhn freely admits this, the explanation is basically non-Kuhnian because, once fully appreciated, it is no longer imperative to go beyond it to say that the perceivers are in different perceptual worlds. Let us look more closely at each circumstance.

Starting with (a), it seems uncontroversial that a dominant theory directs research into certain channels and selects some phenomena as having greater significance. What wouldn't have been sought without the theory, or overlooked if happened upon, leaps to the eye with it. What a dedicated geocentrist might have dismissed as a defect in the lens of the telescope is the discovery of Jupiter's moons for Galileo. Would the geocentrist have seen the moon? In the spirit of direct-object reporting, yes; but he does not take it for a moon, and thus *does not see that* it is a moon. The devotee of a new theory may recognize things that her traditional colleagues do not, especially if their identification requires greater subtlety than the Galileo–geocentrist experiences. Were it not for Newton's second law of motion, no one would have recognized perturbations in the orbit of Uranus; and thus Leverrier would never have produced the calculations that led a colleague to train his telescope on a certain part of the heavens the scanning of which led to the discovery of Neptune. Such instances make clear the psychological basis of (a).

But if we have accurately reported it, the phenomenon is really a rather commonplace one. I reread a book with a new interest in certain parts of the subject, and I am struck for the first time by material I had read earlier. Or I acquire friends with different interests, and thus come to appreciate a new art form or new hobbies. My attention is redirected, I notice different things and infuse old ones with new significance. But should I say *non-figuratively* of someone who undergoes any of these changes that he now lives in a different world? Even where this judgment is made, it seems more an evaluative commentary on the quality of the changed person's life than an animadversion upon his physical surroundings.

In fact, the inglorious history of Piltdown man marvellously documents this phenomenon, and exposes not only Piltdown but also the limits of what can be shown by the theoretical influence upon observation. Even before the exposure of the hoax Franz Weidenreich noted what every scientist would claim to see plainly in a few years: 'It is the artificial combination of fragments of a modern human braincase with orang-utanlike mandible and teeth.' To this Sir Arthur Keith, a charter member of the pro-Piltdown consensus, replied, 'This is one way of getting rid of facts which do not fit into a preconceived theory; the usual way pursued by men of science is, not to get rid of facts, but frame [a] theory to fit them.' In the instructive essay from which these quotes are taken, Stephen Gould[55] points out that Keith's attempt to claim for himself the cachet of objective scientific method did not itself fit the facts. Not only did his theoretical predispositions lead him to misdescribe the skull, but to mismeasure it as well. Indeed, to give one remarkable illustration of the way in which our theoretical wishes can overwhelm sober judgment, Keith writes in defence of the claim that Piltdown was only a precursor of modern man that '[h]is forehead was like that of an orang, devoid of a supraorbital torus'. But as Gould hastens to add, *Homo sapiens* also lacks a supraorbital torus.[56] How are we to summarize this apparent high-handedness with the empirical evidence? It is certainly an instance of deeply ingrained prejudice. But no worthy realist will deny that this sort of thing occurs. However, we would need to suppose that Keith *couldn't have* been more open-minded, *couldn't have* overcome his loyalties, even if he was a proponent of the genuineness of the fossil, in order to support the claim that he and Weidenreich lived in different perceptual worlds. All I can add is that the plain facts of the case seem to be a formidable obstacle to a conclusion as ambitious as that.

If this shift-of-attention phenomenon is the basis for Kuhn's point (a), and, contrary to my assessment, it warrants the intro-duction of different worlds, then so would its quotidian counter-part of two paragraphs back. Worlds would then proliferate far beyond Kuhn's wildest imagination. But we needn't dwell on such an absurdity. Talk of different worlds still looks like an exaggeration or, more charitably, a matter of emphasizing the overall significance of the change. Its claim to be literal description is unlikely to find much resonance.

But (b) may seem at first a less tractable phenomenon for the realist. How can scientists employing a single standard arrive at incompatible measurements without one being incorrect? Such measurements are careful and precise experiments, not subject to the hasty glimpses that help make possible *Gestalt* shifts. (However, recall Keith's mismeasurement of the Piltdown skull.) These cases lead Kuhn to exclaim that 'the data themselves have changed',[57] an excellent reason, it would seem, for introducing different perceptual worlds.

However, if we pay attention to the following facts, often neglected in these situations, even (b) will appear less unsettling for realism. (i) These results are averages, not single tests. (ii) An entrenched theory determines which tests are discarded as aberrant. For example, consider why lab instructors treat as mistakes undergraduate experiments which do not achieve the textbook result. (iii) The theory is consulted to determine when the test machinery is working properly, and the kinds of adjustments made for accuracy are directed by the theory. (iv) Different theories will lead one to round off in different directions (say, up rather than down) and with different degrees of precision (say, one decimal expansion rather than another).

Kuhn's one detailed example – Dalton's evidence for the law of multiple proportions, which differed from Proust's values for the same relative weights – lends itself to explanation through this set of factors. Dalton's results have been difficult to reproduce.[58] This may be because, given the crudity of his experimental values, he made 'a very generous allowance for experimental error'.[59] In short, we have factor (ii). Also, historians now agree that Dalton discovered his chemical atomic theory before his law of multiple proportions, and thus no doubt used the former to direct his research toward the latter. Nash comments[60] that this may have enabled him to 'round off' his new raw data to conform to his theory. Dalton's critical ratios – 1.7:1 and 3.4:1 – are only a few among those discoverable in his notebooks, and would not leap to the eye of anyone who didn't have a hint of what he was looking for. Thus, his arriving at these figures, in so far as it deviates from the results reported by Proust, also may be explicable by factor (iv). The results were clearly averages rather than single experiments, factor (i), and though I have no historical evidence concerning his treatment of aberrant cases or how he regarded the accuracy of a piece of equipment, the very repetition of the experiment gives latitude for these factors. One of (i)–(iv) might have been sufficient to explain Kuhn's facts without having to advert to different worlds. We have found grounds for three of them, and a basis for suspicion that the fourth was active.

If there were a stable world with constant data that competing theories tried to capture, (a) and (b) are what it seems upon reflection we might expect to occur in it. The various ways in which it is possible to cross-classify the world, discussed in Chapter 3, section 4, should itself warn us against too naïve a view even of a stable world. But that naïve conception is the only realist alternative offered by Kuhn to his own view. How else are we to explain his demand that if there is a stable world it must be neutrally describable and its items should appear just the same to observers regardless of their individual preconceptions and preoccupations? Am I being unfair? Well, he certainly does have a tendency to say things such as '[i]n the absence of a neutral language, the choice of a new theory is a decision to adopt a different native language and to deploy it in a correspondingly different world'.[61] If this does not imply the naïve conception of a world of stable data of which I have just spoken, I am at a loss to know what he is getting at.

We might summarize the point of (a) and (b) by saying that differences of prevailing theory lead to differences of goal and emphasis, and the latter in turn have implications which can amaze the unwary and which certainly have been undervalued by the philosophical tradition. But once this much is conceded, what is added by saying that scientists from competing theories inhabit different worlds? As a restatement of my summary, it is at best very opaque. As an addition to it, it seems superfluous. On the other hand, as a preferred substitute for my summary it seems to do nothing more than obscure the bases for the differences in (a) and (b).

X

SUMMING UP

The task of Part I, in a sentence, was to show that global realism is a credible view, and that, in the form of Correspondence, it may even be an inevitable one. But various significant tendencies in recent philosophy – whether heralded as anti-realism, internal realism, pragmatism, incommensurability or hermeneutics – seem to have converged upon the idea that this couldn't be right because of the cognitive or epistemic commitments of the concept of truth. Hence Part II. The views examined there were chosen to represent this tendency partly because they are typical and prominent sources for it; but also because the kinds of attacks mounted in them are as good as any I could muster. Although it was only their disagreement with global realism that prompted our concern with them, I have tried to avoid the appearance that the aspects from which we dissented exhausted the contributions of the views in Chapters 7, 8 and 9. Nevertheless, in each case we discovered that they had not made out their melancholy conclusions concerning truth.

On the other side of the coin, we have not defended any grand realist architectonic erected on Correspondence's foundation. Perhaps a partial explanation of the failure of neo-anti-realism is that it shared with many of its realist antagonists the assumption that such structures were an indispensable part of realism. Then, with more than a grain of historical justification, it proceeded to confront realism not head on, as it were, but through those vulnerable would-be consequences. However, a main theme of this work (especially Part I) has been that the issue of Correspondence, dedicated to answering the question 'What makes a belief (/statement) true?', can be detached from many of the most conspicuous tenets with which realism is popularly associated. While this may temper realist aspirations, it does not deprive us of significant results about the nature of truth or about our commitment, *via* truth, to a mind-independent reality. And it may help eliminate a source of anti-realist temptation to throw out the baby with the bathwater. But, whatever the reason, the canvassed attacks upon realism haven't overturned the latter's plausible answer to our recent question. Having shown this, further words won't add a whit to our success.

NOTES

CHAPTER ONE: INTRODUCTION – THE TOPIC EXPLAINED

1 McGinn (1979).
2 Devitt (1983), p. 70.
3 Mill (1865), ch. 11.
4 Michael Williams (1986), p. 228.
5 E.g., Dummett (1978), pp. xx–xxi.
6 Putman (1977), p. 485; (1978a), p. 125.
7 Dummett (1973a), p. 465.
8 Outside of formal disciplines the concept is not rigorous. But roughly what it amounts to is that our faculties are not suited to the (direct?) detection of the conditions that make the statement true.
9 Horwich (1982), pp. 186–8.
10 Fine (1984), p. 54.
11 Cf. Michael Williams (1986), p. 225.
12 Berkeley (1710), Part I, section 3: 'The table I write on I say exists, that is, I see and feel it; and if I were out of my study I should say it existed – meaning thereby that if I was in my study I might perceive it, or that some other spirit actually does perceive it.'
13 Rorty (1979), p. 338.
14 Dancy (1985), p. 117.
15 Goldman (1986), p. 69. Cf. Bonjour (1980), p. 54; Dancy (1985), p. 117.
16 Kuhn (1970a), p. 206; Chalmers (1982), pp. 153–7; Arthur Fine (1984), p. 62. (Chalmers, it should be noted, is a self-styled realist, but rejects Correspondence.)
17 Van Frassen (1980), pp. 202–3; Nancy Cartwright (1983), e.g., pp. 2–3.

Notes

CHAPTER TWO: THEORIES OF TRUTH: SOME PRELIMINARIES

1 Davidson (1969), pp. 47–8.
2 Aristotle, *Metaphysics*, 1011b26 ff.
3 Aristotle, *Categories*, 14b20–2. Cf. Russell (1966): 'The question we have to discuss is therefore: What is the difference between a true belief and a false belief? By this I mean, What is the difference which actually *constitutes* the truth or falsehood of a belief?' (p. 149)
4 Russell (1956), p. 182.
5 *Pace* Blackburn (1984), pp. 224 f.
6 E.g., Ayer (1946), p. 87.
7 Quine (1960), p. 246.
8 Strawson (1950), p. 194.
9 Barwise & Perry (1981), p. 669.
10 Sommers (1969), pp. 261–3.
11 For possibilities see Stroud (1984) and Michael Williams (1986), p. 225. Although Stroud rejects each anti-sceptical rebuttal, it is crucial that the ones requiring no justification-condition semantics fare no worse, or less plausibly, than those that do.
12 Dummett (1969), p. 364; (1976), *passim*. Also see Hacker (1972), p. 302; Baker (1974); Wright (1976).
13 Strawson (1954), pp. 268–9.
14 Dummett (1959a), pp. 2–4.
15 Strawson (1950), p. 213; Davidson (1969), pp. 53–4.
16 Frege (1970), p. 64.
17 Ramsey (1931), p. 142. My emphasis.
18 Ramsey (1931), pp. 142, 143.
19 Dummet (1978), p. xxi.
20 For example, Alan White (1970), pp. 92–3; Mackie (1970), p. 329.
21 Tarski (1949), p. 55.
22 Tarski (1956): 'when the function is a sentence . . . the satisfaction of a function by a sequence does not depend on the properties of the terms of the sequence at all' (p. 194).
23 Tarski (1949), pp. 70–1.
24 Tarski (1949), p. 65.
25 Tarski (1956), p. 188.
26 Field (1972), pp. 365–9.
27 Davidson (1969), p. 43. My emphasis.

CHAPTER THREE: SOME FAMILIAR OBJECTIONS TO CORRESPONDENCE – AND ONE NOT SO FAMILIAR

1 Strawson (1950), p. 197.
2 Strawson (1976), p. 273.
3 Alan White (1970), p. 83.

4 Russell (1956), pp. 187–8; Ramsey (1931), pp. 139–42; Ayer (1963), pp. 172–6; Prior (1967).
5 Sellars (1963), p. 209.
6 Putram (1981), chs. 1–3. Subsequent references to Putnam in the text of this chapter are to this work.
7 E.g., Craig (1982), p. 543.
8 Evans (1973), pp. 195–6.
9 See Kripke (1982), ch. 2.
10 Platinga (1982), pp. 60–1.
11 Of course, this is just upward Lowenheim-Skolem; but we must qualify the generalization when an identity-predicate is present, though that shouldn't impair the present point. I owe this reminder, as well as other useful suggestions, to discussions with Bill Wisdom.
12 Borges (1962), p. 9.
13 Descartes (1972), p. 168 (*Meditation* III).
14 Hume (1958), p. 167 (Bk. I, Pt. III, Sec. XIV).
15 Blackburn (1984), p. 234.
16 Wiggins (1980), pp. 218–19.

CHAPTER FOUR: COHERENCE, PRAGMATISM AND REDUNDANCY

1 Ewing (1934), pp. 229–30.
2 Bradley (1914); cf. Joachim (1906), esp. pp. 64–84; Blanshard (1940), ch. XXVI.
3 For accounts of their work, and pertinent references, see Ayer (1959), pp. 20–1; Hempel (1935), esp. pp. 50–1.
4 Hegelian (e.g., absolute or personal) idealists needn't be committed to Coherence. A notable exception is McTaggart (1921), pp. 10 ff., who supports Correspondence.
5 E.g., Rescher (1973), ch. 1.
6 Russell (1966), p. 135.
7 Bradley (1914), pp. 213–15.
8 Dancy (1985), p. 115.
9 Russell (1940), p. 132.
10 James (1975a), p. 42.
11 Dewey (1920), p. 157.
12 Michael Williams (1980), p. 248.
13 Dancy (1985), pp. 116–17.
14 Schiller (1912), p. 60.
15 Peirce (1957), pp. 53–4.
16 James (1975a), p. 97.
17 Dewey (1920), p. 156.
18 Rorty (1979), p. 308.
19 James (1948), p. 95.
20 Morton White (1972), p. 334.

21 From Richard Henson's as-yet-unpublished book of little philosophical verses:

> Try James' brisk and bracing view,
> It picks you up,
> It sees you through,
> And that's exactly why it's true.

22 Rorty (1980), p. 722.
23 *Ibid.*
24 James (1975b), p. 117.
25 Chisholm (1977), p. 98.
26 A degree of logical rigour has been sacrificed for the sake of exposition. First, I assume that '*p*', whatever sentence is its substituend, is identical with '*p* is true' save for the problematic predicate. Also, I generally omit the 'that' before writing '*p* is true'. Next, I have supposed that the language about which we are concerned contains its own truth predicate.
27 In addition to our earlier citations, see, for example, Wittgenstein (1964), p. 50 (Part I, Appendix I, para. 6); Strawson (1954), p. 261; Ayer (1963), p. 164; Prior (1971), pp. 11–12, 18; Baker & Hacker (1985), p. 317.
28 Quinton (1973), pp. 141–2 is an example of one who is not a Redundancy theorist, but who concedes (B). He takes (B) to be trivial, and so not to imply (C).
29 Dummett (1978), p. xx; Ayer (1946), p. 89.
30 For the distinction, see Dummett (1978), pp. xviii-xix.
31 Cf. Alan White (1970), p. 82; Austin (1950), pp. 95–6.

CHAPTER FIVE: CORRESPONDENCE

1 Donnellan (1966), pp. 300–1.
2 Austin (1950).
3 Strawson (1950), (1964), (1965); Warnock (1962), (1964).
4 Mackie (1970).
5 Austin (1950), p. 122.
6 Mackie (1970), p. 326.
7 See, e.g., Ayer (1963), p. 181; Pitcher (1964), pp. 9–12.
8 For a discussion of the issues raised by act-identity see Davis (1979), ch. 2.
9 Strawson (1965), p. 295 [(1970), p. 241.]
10 Strawson (1965, p. 298 [(1970), p. 246]. My emphasis.
11 Austin (1950), pp. 98 f.
12 Grice (1975), pp. 66–7.
13 See Lewis (1979), pp. 351–4.
14 Field (1973), pp. 474 ff.
15 Indeed, for Stalnaker (1987), pp. 163 f., this needn't be a reduction, but the place at which to discover subjunctive facts.

CHAPTER SIX: TRUTH EPISTEMOLOGIZED

1 E.g., Wittgenstein (1970), para. 437.
2 Cf. Dancy (1985), p. 117; Goldman (1986), pp. 116 ff.
3 Hacking (1982), p. 60.
4 Cf. Newton-Smith (1982), p. 111.
5 See Nagel (1986), p. 92.
6 Goodman (1978), p. 17.
7 Davidson (1974).
8 Rorty (1979), p. 374.
9 Mannheim (1936), p. 293.
10 Popper (1957), p. 208.

CHAPTER 7: MEANING, TRUTH AND THE HUMAN CONDITION

1 See Hacker (1972), p. 302.
2 Dummett (1978), p. xxi.
3 This is not meant to deny that I may not be justified in a similar evidential situation if I believe I am being purposely deceived.
4 E.g., Dummett (1969), p. 362; (1976a), p. 116.
5 E.g., Dummett (1979), p. 130; (1978), p. xxii.
6 McGinn (1979), p. 26.
7 E.g., Dummett (1963), p. 146; (1973b), p. 227; (1976a), pp. 110–11; Baker (1974), pp. 173–4; Wright (1976), pp. 225, 234; McDowell (1976), p. 127.
8 Dummett (1978), p. xxxviii.
9 E.g., Wright (1976), pp. 223–4.
10 Wright (1976), p. 224. Cf. Dummett (1969), pp. 362–3. 'The anti-realist's case consisted of an application to statements about the past of the general form of anti-realist argument. We learn the use of the past tense by learning to recognize certain situations as justifying the assertion of certain statements expressed by means of that tense. . . . The only notion of truth for past-tense statements coincides with the justifiability of assertions of such statements, i.e., with the existence of situations which we are capable of recognizing as obtaining and which justify such assertion.' (*Ibid.*, p. 363)
11 Dummett (1976a), p. 93; cf. (1959a), p. 14; (1963), p. 155; (1959b), p. 175; (1973a), p. 466; (1973b), p. 225; (1969), p. 358.
12 Dummett (1978), p. xxx.
13 Baker (1974), p. 165.
14 Locke (1700), Bk. III, ch. 6, section 26.
15 The example is adopted from Kripke (1975), pp. 691–2.
16 Dummett (1963), p. 146.
17 Dummett (1976b), p. 274.
18 Dummett (1978), p. xxix; cf. (1973b), pp. 215–16.
19 Dummett (1978), p. xxvi.

20 Hart (1948–49), p. 175.
21 Dummett (1963), p. 155; cf. (1959a), p. 23.
22 Dummett (1979), p. 129; cf. (1976a), p. 116.
23 Dummett (1978), p. xxxvi–xxxviii.
24 Wright (1979), p. 289.
25 Wright (1979), p. 288.
26 Wright (1979), p. 289.
27 Wright (1981), p. 51, and note.
28 Goldman (1986), p. 69. Cf. Bonjour (1980), p. 54; Dancy (1985), p. 117.
29 Putnam (1978b), p. 103.
30 Strawson (1977), pp. 19–20.
31 Dummett (1959a), p. 3.
32 Dummett (1969), pp. 363 ff.
33 In fact, Dummett's direct response to the case is to rebuke Strawson, who 'unblushingly rejects the whole polemic of Wittgenstein's that has come to be known as "the private language argument" ' (1978), p. xxxii. Dummett then proceeds to discuss a difference case of Strawson's, one not concerning the past. As Mackie remarks (1985), p. 241, blushes might be more becoming to someone who replies so offhandedly to criticism. Even were Wittgenstein's polemic not in pressing need of radical interpretation, would Dummett accept everything there? On what interpretation? For reasons of this kind, I choose to concentrate on reasoning that could be culled from Dummett's original article. In section 8 we consider an anti-realist defence deriving more directly from part of the private language argument.
34 Dummett (1969), p. 369.
35 Cf. Mackie (1985), p. 237.
36 Wright (1979), p. 291.
37 Wright (1976), p. 229.
38 Wittgenstein (1953), I, para. 354.
39 Wittgenstein (1953), I, para. 350.
40 Dummett (1976a), pp. 89–92.
41 Dummett (1976a), p. 100.
42 Stalnaker (1987), pp. 161–5.

CHAPTER 8: LANGUAGE-GAMES AND ANTI-REALISM

1 Anscombe (1981); Black (1986), p. 86.
2 Hintikka & Hintikka (1986), esp. ch. 9.
3 Pears (1987), pp. 7–9.
4 In this chapter it will be convenient to refer to Wittgenstein's works in the main text by work and page or paragraph number. The following abbreviations will be used for Wittgenstein's writings:

Philosophical Investigations = PI
Blue Book = BB

Tractus Logico-Philosophicus = TLP
Remarks on the Foundations of Mathematics = RFM
On Certainty = OC
Zettel = Z
Lectures on Aesthetics = LA

Further information on these works may be found in the Bibliography.

5 Cf. Kenny (1973), pp. 164–5; Baker & Hacker (1985), p. 72.
6 I have been greatly aided by a list of features of what I have called 'artificial' language-games in Baker & Hacker (1985), pp. 54–5, though the list here is substantially different since it is compiled for a different purpose.
7 E.g., Baker & Hacker (1985), pp. 317–18; Hacker (1975), p. 302; Dummett (1978), p. xxxiv.
8 See Baker & Hacker (1985), pp. 55, 102 ff.
9 Shusterman (1986), p. 99.
10 Cf. Black (1986), pp 79–81.
11 Lear (1982), p. 385.
12 Bernard Williams (1974), p. 91.
13 Davidson (1974).
14 Davidson (1974), p. 192.
15 Bernard Williams (1974), p. 85.

CHAPTER 9: SCIENTIFIC ANTI-REALISM: THE KUHNIAN CHALLENGE

1 Quine (1960), ch. 2.
2 Quine (1987), p. 10.
3 Kuhn (1970a), pp. 148–50.
4 E.g., Kuhn (1970b), pp. 266–7.
5 Kuhn (1973), pp. 326, 325.
6 Kuhn (1973), pp. 321 ff; (1970b), p. 261.
7 Kuhn (1970a), p. 206.
8 Kuhn (1973), p. 329. Cf. (1970b), pp. 260–1:

In a debate over choice of theory, neither party has access to an argument which resembles a proof in logic or formal mathematics. In the latter, both premises and rules of inference are stipulated in advance. If there is disagreement about conclusions, the parties to the debate can retrace their steps one by one, checking each against prior stipulation. At the end of that process, one or the other must concede that at an isolable point in the argument he has made a mistake, violated or misapplied a previously accepted rule.

9 See Masterman (1970); Shapere (1964).
10 Kuhn (1974a), p. 297.
11 Kuhn (1970a), pp. 45–6; (1970b), p. 274; (1974a), pp. 305 ff.

12 Kuhn (1970a), p. 205; (1970b), p. 264; (1974b), p. 289.
13 Kuhn (1970a), p. 206.
14 Kuhn (1970b), p. 266.
15 See Blackburn (1984), pp. 266–9.
16 Kuhn (1970a), p. 171.
17 Goldman (1986), p. 147.
18 Kuhn (1970b), p. 265.
19 See, e.g., Chalmers (1982), pp. 155–7.
20 Kuhn (1970a), p. 149.
21 Kuhn (1970a), p. 150.
22 Kuhn (1970a), p. 102.
23 Kuhn (1970a), p. 142.
24 Kuhn (1959), chs. 4–7.
25 Wolynski (1873), p. 13.
26 E.g., Kuhn (1970a), p. 149.
27 Kuhn (1970a), p. 95.
28 Kuhn (1970b), p. 266, note 2.
29 Kuhn (1974a), pp. 309 ff.
30 Kuhn (1970b), p. 276.
31 Laudan (1984), pp. 96–9.
32 Kuhn (1970a), p. 171.
33 Kuhn (1970a), p. 206.
34 *Ibid.*
35 Kuhn (1974b), p. 271, note 6.
36 Kuhn (1970a), p. 111.
37 Kuhn (1970a), p. 115.
38 Kuhn (1970a), p. 117.
39 Kuhn (1970b), p. 118.
40 Kuhn (1970a), p. 193. The emphasis is the author's.
41 Kuhn (1974a), p. 309, note 18; see also (1970b), p. 270.
42 Kuhn (1970a), p. 129.
43 Kuhn (1970a), p. 150. My emphasis.
44 *Ibid.* My emphasis.
45 Kuhn (1970a), p. 201; (1970b), p. 276.
46 Kuhn (1970a), p. 121.
47 Cf. Hanson (1961), ch. 1; Goodman (1978), ch. 6.
48 Pylyshyn (1986), pp. 133 ff.
49 Fodor (1984), pp. 33–4.
50 Fodor (1983), part III.
51 Kuhn (1970a), pp. 126, 128.
52 Musgrave (1980), p. 52, note 9.
53 Kuhn (1970a), p. 126.
54 Kitcher (1978).
55 Gould (1980), p. 98.
56 Gould (1980), p. 100.
57 Kuhn (1970a), p. 135.
58 Partington (1962), p. 791.

59 Nash (1956), p. 105.
60 Nash (1956), pp. 104–5.
61 Kuhn (1970b), p. 277.

BIBLIOGRAPHY OF WORKS CITED

Austin, J. L. (1950), 'Truth', *Supplementary vol*. XXIV. *Proceedings of the Aristotelian Society*. Cited in Austin (1970), pp. 117–33.

—— (1970), *Philosophical Papers*, 2nd edition, J. O. Urmson and G. J. Warnock, (eds), London, Oxford University Press.

Ayer, A. J. (1946), *Language, Truth and Logic*, New York, Dover Publications.

—— (1959), *Logical Positivism*, New York, The Free Press.

—— (1963), *'Truth', the Concept of a Person*, New York, St Martin's Press, pp. 162–87.

Baker, Gordon (1974), 'Criteria: a new foundation for semantics', *Ratio*, vol. 16, pp. 156–89.

—— and Hacker, P. M. S. (1985), *Wittgenstein: Meaning and Understanding*, Chicago, University of Chicago Press.

Barwise, Jon and Perry, John (1981), 'Situations and attitudes', *Journal of Philosophy*, vol. 78, no. 11, pp. 668–90.

Berkeley, George (1710), *A Treatise concerning the Principles of Human Knowledge*, Dublin.

Black, Max (1986), 'Wittgenstein's language-games', *Ludwig Wittgenstein: Critical Assessments*, vol. 2, Stuart Shanker (ed.), London, Croom Helm, pp. 74–88.

Blackburn, Simon (1984), *Spreading the Word*, London, Oxford University Press.

Blanshard, Brand (1940), *The Nature of Thought*, vol. II, New York, The Macmillan Co.

Bonjour, Laurence (1980), 'Externalist theories of empirical knowledge', *Midwest Studies in Philosophy*, vol. V, *Studies in Epistemology*, Peter A. French, Theodore Uehling, Jr. and Howard K. Wettstein (eds), Minneapolis, University of Minnesota Press, pp. 53–73.

Borges, Jorge Luis (1962), 'Tlon, Uqbar, Orbis Tertium', *Labyrinths*, New York, New Directions Publishing Co., pp. 3–18.

Bradley, F. H. (1914), 'On truth and coherence', *Essays on Truth and Reality*, London, Oxford University Press, pp. 202–18.

Cartwright, Nancy (1983), *How the Laws of Physics Lie*, London, Oxford University Press.

Cartwright, Richard (1962), 'Propositions', *Analytical Philosophy*, 1st series, Oxford, Basil Blackwell, pp. 81–103.

Chalmers, A. F. (1982), *What is This Thing Called Science?*, 2nd edition, Milton Keynes, Open University Press.

Chisholm, Roderick (1977), *Theory of Knowledge*, 2nd edition, Englewood Cliffs, N.J., Prentice-Hall.

Craig, Edward (1982), 'Meaning, use and privacy', *Mind*, vol. 91 n.s., pp. 541–64.

Dancy, Jonathan (1985), *An Introduction to Contemporary Epistemology*, Oxford, Basil Blackwell.

Davidson, Donald (1969), 'True to the facts', *Journal of Philosophy*, vol. 66, pp. 748–64. Citations in Davidson (1984), pp. 37–54.

―――― (1974), 'On the very idea of a conceptual scheme', *Proceedings of the American Philosophical Association*, vol. 47. Citations in Davidson (1984), pp. 183–98.

―――― (1984), *Inquiries into Truth and Meaning*, London, Oxford University Press.

Davis, Lawrence (1979), *Theory of Action*, Englewood Cliffs, N.J., Prentice-Hall.

Descartes, René (1972), *The Philosophical Works of Descartes*, vol. I, Elisabeth S. Haldane and G. R. T. Ross (eds), Cambridge, Cambridge University Press.

Dewey, John (1920), *Reconstruction in Philosophy*, New York, Henry Holt & Co.

Devitt, Michael (1983), 'Dummett's anti-realism', *Journal of Philosophical Review*, vol. 80, no. 2, pp. 73–99.

Donnellan, Keith (1966), 'Reference and definite description', *The Philosophical Review*, vol. LXXV, pp. 281–304.

Dummett, Michael (1959a), 'Truth', in Dummett (1978), pp. 1–24.

―――― (1959b), 'Wittgenstein's philosophy of mathematics', in Dummett (1978), pp. 166–85.

―――― (1963), 'Realism', in Dummett (1978), pp. 145–65.

―――― (1969), 'The reality of the past', in Dummett (1978), pp. 358–74.

―――― (1973a), *Frege: Philosophy of Language*, New York, Harper & Row.

―――― (1973b), 'The philosophical basis of intuitionistic logic', in Dummett (1978), pp. 215–47.

―――― (1975a), 'Frege's distinction between sense and reference', in Dummett (1978), pp. 116–44.

―――― (1975b), 'What is a theory of meaning? I', *Mind and Language*, Samuel Guttenplan(ed.), London, Oxford University Press, pp. 97–138.

―――― (1976a), 'What is a theory of meaning? II', *Truth and Meaning*, Gareth Evans and John McDowell (eds), London, Oxford University Press, pp. 67–137.

—— (1976b), 'Is logic empirical?', in Dummett (1978), pp. 269–89.

—— (1978), *Truth and Other Enigmas*, Cambridge, Mass., Harvard University Press.

—— (1979), 'What does the appeal to use do for the theory of meaning?' *Meaning and Use*, A. Margalit (ed.) Dordrecht-Holland, D. Reidel, pp. 123–35.

Evans, Gareth (1973), 'The causal theory of names', *Proceedings of the Aristotelian Society*, Supplementary vol. 47, pp. 187–208.

Ewing, A. C. (1934), *Idealism: a Critical Survey*, London, Methuen & Co. Ltd.

Field, Hartry (1972), 'Tarski's theory of truth', *Journal of Philosophy*, vol. 69, pp. 347–74.

—— (1973), 'Theory change and the indeterminacy of reference', *Journal of Philosophy*, vol. LXX, no. 14, pp. 462–81.

Fine, Arthur (1984), 'And not anti-realism either', *Nous*, vol. 18, pp. 51–65.

Fodor, Jerry A. (1983), *The Modularity of Mind*, Cambridge, Mass., M.I.T. Press.

—— (1984), 'Observation reconsidered', *Philosophy of Science*, vol. 51, pp. 23–43.

Frege, Gottlob (1970), 'On sense and reference', *Translations from the Philosophical Writings of Gottlob Frege*, Peter Geach and Max Black (trans. and eds), London, Oxford University Press, pp. 56–78.

Goldman, Alvin I. (1986), *Epistemology and Cognition*, Cambridge, Mass., Harvard University Press.

Goodman, Nelson (1978), *Ways of Worldmaking*, Indianapolis, Ind., Hackett Publishing Co.

Gould, Stephen Jay (1980), 'Piltdown revisited', *The Panda's Thumb*, Harmondsworth, Penguin Books Ltd, pp. 92–104.

Grice, H. P. (1975), 'Logic and conversation', *The Logic of Grammar*, Donald Davidson and Gilbert Harman (eds), Encino, California, Dickenson Publishing Co., Inc., pp. 64–75.

Hacker, P. M. S. (1972), *Insight and Illusion*, London, Oxford University Press.

—— and Baker, Gordon (1985), *Wittgenstein: Meaning and Understanding*, Chicago, University of Chicago Press.

Hacking, Ian (1982), 'Language, truth and reason', *Rationality and Relativism*, Martin Hollis and Steven Lukes (eds), Cambridge, Mass., M.I.T. Press, pp. 48–66.

Hanson, N. R. (1961), *Patterns of Discovery*, Cambridge, Cambridge University Press.

Hart, H. L. A. (1948–49), 'The ascription of responsibility and rights', *Proceedings of the Aristotelian Society*, n.s. vol. 49, pp. 171–94.

Hempel, Carl (1935), 'On the logical positivists' theory of truth', *Analysis*, vol. 2, no. 4, pp. 49–59.

Hintikka, Jaakko (1986), 'Language-games', *Ludwig Wittgenstein: Critical Assessments*, vol. 2, Stuart Shanker (ed.), London, Croom Helm, pp. 89–105.

Hintikka, Merrill B. & Hintikka, Jaakko (1986), *Investigating Wittgenstein*, Oxford, Basil Blackwell.

Horwich, Paul (1982), 'Three forms of realism', *Synthèse*, vol. 51, pp. 181–201.

Hume, David (1958), *A Treatise of Human Nature*, L. A. Selby-Bigge (ed.), London, Oxford University Press.

James, William (1948), 'The will to believe', *Essays in Pragmatism*, Alburey Castell(ed.), London, Hafner Publishing Co., pp. 88–109.

—— (1975a), *Pragmatism*, Cambridge, Mass., Harvard University Press.

—— (1975b), 'The meaning of the word truth', *The Meaning of Truth*, Cambridge, Mass., Harvard University Press, pp. 117–20.

Joachim, Harold H. (1906), *The nature of truth*, London, Oxford University Press.

Kenny, Anthony (1973), *Wittgenstein*, Cambridge, Mass., Harvard University Press.

Kitcher, Philip (1978), 'Theories, theorists and theoretical change', *The Philosophical Review*, vol. 87, pp. 519–47.

Kripke, Saul (1975), 'An outline of a theory of truth', *Journal of Philosophy*, vol. 72, pp. 690–716.

—— (1982), *Wittgenstein on Rules and Private Language*, Cambridge, Mass., Harvard University Press.

Kuhn, Thomas S. (1959), *The Copernican Revolution*, New York, Vintage Books.

—— (1970a), *The Structure of Scientific Revolutions*, 2nd edition, enlarged, Chicago, University of Chicago Press.

—— (1970b), 'Reflections on my critics', Imre Lakatos and Alan Musgrave (eds), *Criticism and the Growth of Knowledge*, Cambridge, Cambridge University Press, pp. 231–77.

—— (1973), 'Objectivity, value judgment, and theory choice', in Kuhn (1977), pp. 320–39.

—— (1974a), 'Second thoughts on paradigms', in Kuhn (1977), pp. 293–319.

—— (1974b), 'Logic of discovery or psychology of research', in Kuhn (1977), pp. 266–92.

—— (1977), *The Essential Tension*, Chicago, University of Chicago Press.

Laudan, Laurens (1984), *Science and Values*, Berkeley, University of California Press.

Lear, Jonathan (1982), 'Leaving the world alone', *Journal of Philosophy*, vol. 79, pp. 382–403.

Lewis, David (1979), 'Scorekeeping in a language game', *Journal of Philosophical Logic*, vol. 8, pp. 339–59.

Locke, John (1700), *An Essay concerning Humane Understanding*, 4th edition, London, Awnsham and John Churchil.

Mackie, John (1970), 'Simple truth', *Philosophical Quarterly*, vol. 20, pp. 321–33.

—— (1974), *The Cement of the Universe*, London, Oxford University Press.

—— (1976), *Problems from Locke*, London, Oxford University Press.

—— (1985), 'Anti-realism', *Logic and Knowledge*, London, Oxford University Press, pp. 225–45.

Mannheim, Karl (1936), *Idealogy and Utopia*, New York, Harcourt, Brace & Co.

Masterman, Margaret (1970), 'The nature of a paradigm', Imre Lakatos and Alan Musgrave, *Criticism and the Growth of Knowledge*, Lakatos and Musgrave (eds), Cambridge, Cambridge University Press, pp. 59–89.

McDowell, John (1976), 'Turth conditions, bivalence and verificationism', *Truth and Meaning*, Gareth Evans and John McDowell (eds), London, Oxford University Press, pp. 42–66.

McGinn, Colin (1979), 'An *a priori* argument for realism', *Journal of Philosophy*, vol. 76, pp. 113–33.

—— (1980), 'Truth and use', *Reference, Truth and Reality*, Mark Platts (ed.), London, Routledge & Kegan Paul, pp. 19–40.

McTaggart, J. M. E. (1921), *The Nature of Existence*, vol. I, Cambridge, Cambridge University Press.

Mill, John Stuart (1865), *An Examination of Sir William Hamilton's Philosophy*, London.

Musgrave, Alan (1980), 'Kuhn's second thoughts', *Paradigms and Revolutions*, Gary Gutting (ed.), Notre Dame, Ind., London, University of Notre Dame Press, pp. 39–53.

Nagel, Thomas (1986), *The View from Nowhere*, London, Oxford University Press.

Nash, Leonard K. (1956), 'The origin of Dalton's chemical atomic theory', *Isis*, vol. 47, no. 148, pp. 101–16.

Newton-Smith, William (1982), 'Relativism and the possibility of interpretation', *Rationality and Relativism*, Martin Hollis and Steven Lukes (eds), Cambridge, Mass., M.I.T. Press, pp. 106–22.

Partington, J. R. (1962), *A History of Chemistry*, vol. 3, London, Macmillan & Co. Ltd.

Pears, D. F. (1987), 'Wittgenstein on philosophy and science', unpublished manuscript.

Peirce, Charles S. (1957), 'How to make our ideas clear', *Essays in the Philosophy of Science*, Vincent Tomas (ed.), New York, The Liberal Arts Press, pp. 31–56.

Pitcher, George (1964), *Truth*, Englewood Cliffs, N.J., Prentice-Hall, Inc.

Platinga, Alvin (1982), 'How to be an anti-realist', *Proceedings of the American Philosophical Association*, vol. 56, no. 1, pp. 47–70.

Popper, Karl R. (1957), *The Open Society and Its Enemies*, vol. II, London, Routledge & Kegan Paul.

—— (1963), 'Truth, rationality, and the growth of scientific knowledge', *Conjectures and Refutations*, New York, Harper & Row, pp. 215–50.

301

Prior, A. N. (1967), 'The correspondence theory of truth', *The Encyclopedia of Philosophy*, vol. II, Paul Edwards (ed.), pp. 223–32.

—— (1971), *Objects of Thought*, London, Oxford University Press.

Putnam, Hilary (1977), 'Realism and reason', *Proceedings of the American Philosophical Association*, vol. 50, no. 6, pp. 483–98.

—— (1978a), *Meaning and the Moral Sciences*, London, Routledge & Kegan Paul.

—— (1978b), 'Reference and understanding', *Meaning and the Moral Sciences*, London, Routledge & Kegan Paul, pp. 97–117.

—— (1981), *Reason, Truth and History*, Cambridge, Cambridge University Press.

Pylyshyn, Zenon W. (1986), *Computation and Cognition*, Cambridge, Mass., M.I.T. Press.

Quine, Willard Van Orman (1960), *Word and Object*, New York, John Wiley & Sons, Inc.

—— (1987), 'Indeterminacy of translation again', *Journal of Philosophy*, vol. 84, no. 1, pp. 5–10.

Quinton, Anthony, *The Nature of Things*, London, Routledge & Kegan Paul.

Ramsey, F. P. (1931), 'Facts and propositions', *The Foundations of Mathematics*, R. B. Braithwaite (ed.), London, Routledge & Kegan Paul, pp. 138–55.

Rescher, Nicholas (1973), *The Coherence Theory of Truth*, London, Oxford University Press.

Rorty, Richard (1979), *Philosophy and the Mirror of Nature*, Princeton, N.J., Princeton University Press.

—— (1980), 'Pragmatism, relativism and irrationalism', *Proceedings of the American Philosophical Assocation*, vol. 53, no. 6, pp. 719–38.

Russell, Bertrand (1940), *An Inquiry into Meaning and Truth*, Harmondsworth, Penguin Books.

—— (1956), 'The philosophy of logical atomism', *Logic and Knowledge*, Robert C. Marsh (ed.), London, George Allen & Unwin, pp. 175–281.

—— (1966), *Philosophical Essays*, New York, Simon & Schuster.

Schiller, F. C. S. (1912), *Humanism*, London, Macmillan & Co. Ltd.

Sellars, Wilfrid (1963), 'Truth and "correspondence" ', *Science, Perception and Reality*, New York, The Humanities Press, pp. 197–224.

Shapere, Dudley (1964), 'The structure of scientific revolutions', *Philosophical Review*, vol. 73, pp. 383–94.

—— (1981), 'Meaning and scientific change', *Scientific Revolutions*, Ian Hacking (ed.), London, Oxford University Press, pp. 28–59.

Shusterman, Richard (1986), 'Wittgenstein and critical reasoning', *Philosophy and Phenomenological Research*, vol. 47, no. 1, pp. 91–110.

Sommers, Fred (1969), 'On concepts of truth in natural languages', *Review of Metaphysics*, vol. 23, pp. 259–86.

Stalnaker, Robert (1987), *Inquiry*, Cambridge, Mass., M.I.T. Press.

Strawson, P. F. (1950), 'Truth', *Proceedings of the Aristotelian Society*, Supplementary vol. XXIV. Cited in Strawson (1971), pp. 190–213.

—— (1954), 'Truth', *Philosophy and Analysis*, Margaret MacDonald (ed.), Oxford, Basil Blackwell, pp. 260–77.

—— (1964), 'A problem about truth – a reply to Warnock', *Truth*, George Pitcher (ed.), Englewood Cliffs, N.J., Prentice-Hall, Inc. pp. 68–84. Cited in Strawson (1971), pp. 214–33.

—— (1965), 'Truth: a reconsideration of Austin's views', *Philosophical Quarterly*, vol. 15, pp. 289–301. Cited in Strawson (1971), pp. 234–49.

—— (1971), *Logico-Linguistic Papers*, London, Methuen & Co. Ltd.

—— (1976), 'Knowledge and truth', *Indian Philosophical Quarterly–*, vol. 3, pp. 273–82.

—— (1977), 'Scruton and Wright on anti-realism etc.', *Proceedings of the Aristotelian Society*, n.s., vol. 77, pp. 15–23.

Stroud, Barry (1984), *The Significance of Philosophical Scepticism*, London, Oxford University Press.

Tarski, Alfred (1949), 'The semantic conception of truth', *Readings in Philosophical Analysis*, New York, Appleton-Century-Crofts, Inc., pp. 52–84.

—— (1956), 'The concept of truth in formalized lagnuage', *Logic, Semantics, Metamathematics*, J. H. Woodger (trans. and ed.), London, Oxford University Press.

Trigg, Roger (1973), *Reason and Commitment*, Cambridge, Cambridge University Press.

Van Frassen, Bas (1980), *The Scientific Image*, London, Oxford University Press.

Warnock, G. J. (1962), 'Truth and correspondence', *Knowledge and Experience*, C. D. Rollins (ed.), Pittsburgh, Pa., Pittsburgh University Press.

—— (1964), 'A problem about truth', *Truth*, George Pitcher (ed.), Englewood Cliffs, N.J., Prentice-Hall, Inc., pp. 54–67.

White, Alan R. (1970), *Truth*, New York, Doubleday & Co.

White, Morton (1972), *Documents in American Philosophy*, New York, Oxford University Press.

Wiggins, David (1980), 'What would be a substantial theory of truth?', *Philosophical Subjects: Essays Presented to P. F. Strawson*, Zak Ban Straaten (ed.), New York, Oxford University Press, pp. 189–221.

Williams, Bernard (1974), 'Wittgenstein and idealism', *Understanding Wittgenstein*, Godfrey Vesey (ed.), Ithaca, N.Y., Cornell University Press.

Williams, Michael (1980), 'Coherence, justification, and truth', *Review of Metaphysics*, vol. 34, pp. 243–72.

—— (1986), 'Do we (epistemologists) need a theory of truth?', *Philosophical Topics*, vol. 14, pp. 223–42.

Wittgenstein, Ludwig (1938), *Lectures and Conversations on Aesthetics, Psychology and Religious Belief*, Cyril Barrett (ed.), Berkeley, University of California Press.

—— (1953), *Philosophical Investigations*, G. E. M. Anscombe (trans.), New York, The Macmillan Co.

—— (1958), *The Blue and Brown Books*, Oxford, Basil Blackwell.

——— (1961), *Tractatus Logico-Philosophicus*, D. F. Pears and B. F. Guinness, (trans.), London, Routledge & Kegan Paul.

——— (1964), *Remarks on the Foundations of Mathematics*, G. H. von Wright, R. Rhees and G. E. M. Anscombe (eds), G. E. M. Anscombe (trans), Cambridge, Mass., M.I.T. Press.

——— (1967), *On Certainty*, G. E. M. Anscombe and G. H. von Wright (eds), Denis Paul and G. E. M. Anscombe (trans.), New York, Harper & Row.

——— (1970), *Zettel*, G. E. M. Anscombe and G. H. von Wright (eds), G. E. M. Anscombe (trans.), University of California Press.

Wolynski, Arturo (1873), 'Relazioni di Galileo Galilei colla Poloniz', *Archivio Storico Italiano*, 3rd series, vol. XVII (Firenzi).

Woozley, A. D. (1966), *Theory of Knowledge*, New York, Barnes & Noble.

Wright, Crispin (1976), 'Truth conditions and criteria', *Proceedings of the Aristotelian Society*, Supplementary vol. 50, pp. 217–45.

——— (1979), 'Strawson on anti-realism', *Synthèse*, vol. 40, pp. 283–99.

——— (1981), 'Critical study: Dummett and revisionism', *Philosophical Quarterly*, vol. 31, pp. 47–67.

INDEX

305

307